Praise for *Stolen Words*

"Lively.... [*Stolen Words*] remains specific and detailed yet manages to cover so much ground and blow away so much of the fog surrounding plagiarism.... Intriguing."
—Christopher Lehmann-Haupt, *The New York Times*

"Mallon is a writer who possesses grace and wit, a delight in incongruity, and a quickness to love hard, and grow furious.... All these qualities are present in Mallon's book on literary plagiarism, except that the love is pretty much replaced by the fury.... It takes Mallon's fieriness... to get us to pay attention."
—Richard Eder, *Los Angeles Times*

"[Mallon] writes vivaciously.... Along the way, he assembles a beguiling portrait of the plagiarist (at least the habitual one) as an oddly plaintive psychopath.... The subject is dismal, but *Stolen Words* seldom fails to make it lively, engrossing and provocative."
—*The New York Times Book Review*

"Mallon is a witty, scrupulous and devastatingly insightful writer.... Entertaining, informative and thought-provoking, *Stolen Words* will, I predict, soon become a standard text for college English majors—and should be as well in classes in law, government and ethics."
—*The Pittsburgh Press*

"Elegant ... entertaining."
—*Newsday*

"Fascinating ... Mallon's account of the Sokolow scandal is a veritable page-turner."
—*The Philadelphia Inquirer*

"Droll, keen-eyed, polished perusal of the curious crime of plagiarism ... The result is often high literary drama—and the opportunity for a splendid zinger of a book."
—*Kirkus Reviews*

Stolen Words

THOMAS MALLON

Stolen Words

A HARVEST BOOK
HARCOURT, INC.
San Diego   New York   London

Requests for permission to make copies of any part of the work should be
mailed to the following address: Permissions Department, Harcourt, Inc.,
6277 Sea Harbor Drive, Orlando, Florida 32887-6777.

www.harcourt.com

First published by Ticknor & Fields 1989
Published by Penguin Books 1991

The author is grateful for permission to quote from the following songs:
"Maybe Baby" by Norman Petty and Charles Hardin. © 1957 MPL
Communications, Inc., and Wren Music Co. © renewed 1985 MPL
Communications, Inc., and Wren Music Co. International copyright
secured. All rights reserved. Used by permission. "Lobachevsky" by Tom
Lehrer. Copyright 1953 Tom Lehrer. Used by permission. The a uthor
wishes to thank the Pierpont Morgan Library, New York, for permission to
quote materials from the Harper Collection of Autograph Letters and
Manuscripts (Reade, Charles, MA 1950).

Library of Congress Cataloging-in-Publication Data
Mallon, Thomas, 1951–
Stolen words/Thomas Mallon.
p. cm.—(a harvest book)
Originally published: New York : Ticknor & Fields, 1989.
Includes bibliographical references and index.
ISBN 0-15-601136-0
1. Plagiarism. 2. Imitation in literature. 3. Literary ethics. I. Title.
PN167.M28 2001
808—dc21 00-046147

Text set in New Baskerville
Printed in the United States of America
First Harvest edition 2001

A C E G I K L J H F D B

This book is for
NICHOLAS JENKINS, *author*
and GREGORY ULLMAN, *lawyer*

Acknowledgments

I am grateful above all to the Rockefeller Foundation for a generous grant funded through the Poetry Center of New York's 92nd Street Y, where I was a scholar-in-residence during the 1986–87 academic year and where I wrote much of this book. I would like to thank the Poetry Center's two directors, Shelley Mason and Karl Kirchwey; their assistants, Ken Jennison and David Low; and my fellow scholar-in-residence, Professor Anne Carson.

As always, I have received imaginative support and good sense from my editors, Katrina Kenison and Frances Kiernan; my agent, Mary Evans; and my manuscript editor, Laurence Cooper.

At Vassar College I am the constant beneficiary of sound advice and assistance from friends and colleagues: special thanks to Ann Imbrie and Robert DeMaria.

The staffs of the following libraries have all helped me: the Vassar College Library, the Elmer Holmes Bobst Library of New York University, the New York Public Library, the Pierpont Morgan Library and the London Library.

The long, undifferentiated list below contains the names of those who have helped me in a multitude of ways, large and small. They have given me interviews, legal and literary advice, translations, tips and clippings. The particular nature of some of their contributions will be clear in the text of the book itself; other examples of assistance remain unspecified, though indispensable, parts of this book's background. I am grateful to every one of the people listed here: Michael Agnes, Martin Amis, Alwyn Barr, William Billick, Brian Blakeley, Rev. Joseph Brennan, James Brink, Pamela Brink, Gerald Clarke, Jacquelin Collins, Edward Condren, Robert Doggett, Robert Dudnik, Lawrence Foster, Richard A. Gadbois, Jr., Jay Geary, Angeline Goreau, Lawrence Graves, John Gross, Tim Jensen, Colton Johnson, Anita Clay Kornfeld, John Kornfeld, Richard Lanham, Oliver Liang, Mary McCarthy, Andrew Martin, Peter Matson, Penny Merliss, Otto Nelson, Benjamin Newcomb, Stephen Nissenbaum, Laurie Parsons, Betsy Peterson, Christopher Ricks, Phyllis Rose, Edith Skom, Corlies Smith, Jeffrey Smitten, Geoff Stewart, James Stolley, Karen Stolley, Briggs Twyman, Joan Weldon and Barbara Bruce Williams.

And thanks to Bill Bodenschatz.

Contents

Preface to the Original Edition

No, it isn't murder. And as larceny goes it's usually more distasteful than grand. But it *is* a bad thing.

Isn't it?

Somehow we're never quite sure about plagiarism. Last week the *New York Times* puts on its front page a Harvard professor of psychiatry who's resigned because plagiarism has been detected in his writings. Then yesterday's op-ed page carries an article ("Much Ado over a Plagiarist") by the *New Yorker*'s Michael Arlen, who, while of course deploring plagiarism — very few people come out for it — can't help wondering what all the fuss is about: "Each day, citizens bludgeon other citizens with ballpeen hammers, or set fire to seniors, or whatever, and in return often receive the most modest of penalties, or sometimes none at all — and rarely, in any event, have their faces plastered on the front page of The New York Times."

The confusion comes from an aura of naughtiness, a haze that shakes like a giggle: people think of plagiarism as a youthful scrape, something they got caught doing in school. "Why don't you plagiarize it?" is the joke I've heard dozens of times in the last several years from people who learned I was writing this book. Aside from tales told out of school, the subject is barnacled with charming literary anecdotes ("I wish I'd said that, Jimmy"; "Don't worry, Oscar, you will") — again, things naughtily amusing, like vicious long-ago theater reviews or quarrels between neoclassicists. But while I have been entertained by these things — and have, I hope, given this side of the subject its due throughout this book — I was, through my research, eventually, and much more than I expected to be, appalled: by the victims I learned of, by the audacity of their predators, by the excuses made for the latter. The inability of the literary and academic worlds adequately to define, much less reasonably punish, instances of plagiarism was something I observed again and again. Our thinking on the subject, I realized, is primitive, and our fear of dealing fully with plagiarism when it's just been discovered — as opposed to recollected from schooldays or literary history — leads us into bungling and injustice. I was also appalled by the toll a sincerely made but finally false accusation of plagiarism can take on both sides.

The last book of nonfiction I wrote, *A Book of One's Own,* was about diaries, books so conspicuously marked by genuineness that they fairly resound with their authors' own heartbeats. After my years of living with diarists, plagiarists proved to be difficult, topsy-turvy company. How does one write a book about them? What does one even call such a thing? *Not a Book of One's Own?*

For better or worse, I decided to restrict myself to investigating the written word. Questions of plagiarism exist in the visual arts, in music and in all forms of design and manufacture, but the literary dimension seemed sufficiently complicated to make going further afield unwise. I decided early on that an anecdotal history wouldn't work: aside from being repetitive (X stole from Y and P stole from Q and then . . .), such a thing would probably end up emphasizing "the lighter side of plagiarism." Two earlier books — Alexander Lindey's *Plagiarism and Originality* and Maurice Salzman's *Plagiarism: The "Art" of Stealing Literary Material* — are immensely useful to anyone investigating the subject but are in some ways constrained by their own comprehensiveness. In their attempts to present a vast array of cases, the authors are able to treat few of them very fully. I thought, instead, that the extended treatment of a few examples from different milieus, and most of them from our own day, would be most useful.

Chapter 1 attempts a fast overview of how our basic sense of plagiarism came to be born in the seventeenth century, and includes an account of how the offense has shadowed the reputations of Laurence Sterne and Samuel Taylor Coleridge. The bombastic life and work of the Victorian novelist Charles Reade — advocate of international copyright and aggressive plagiarist — form the subject of the second chapter. Chapters 3, 4 and 5 concern the 1980s and move from the world of New York publishing to academia and on to Hollywood, showing first how the young writer Jacob Epstein, whose father was editorial director of Random House and whose mother was co-editor of the *New York Review of Books*, was discovered to have stolen quite a number of witty bits of his first novel from another literary scion, Martin Amis; then how, less conspicuously, a young history professor, much of whose scholarship was discovered to be the result of plagiarism, was allowed to resign quietly from Texas Tech University and find a comfortable niche for his talents; and, finally, how the author of a novel about the California wine country took on CBS-TV and the creators of *Falcon Crest* in a fierce, protracted battle in United States District Court in Los Angeles, each side calling an expert witness from the UCLA English Department to prove its case.

My hope is that some of plagiarism's essential features and ironies emerge from these narratives. Plagiarism's psychology and its haphazard exposure and punishment are the chief concerns of what follows. I have found generalizations on this subject to be more perilously porous than those on most others, but I do think a few large conclusions will prove themselves. The first is that plagiarism is something people may do for a variety of reasons but almost always something they do more than once. The second is that almost all of us — writers, common readers, academics — prefer gossip about plagiarism to real inquiry; in fact, we usually show such distaste for its investigation that the taint of small-mindedness can hang over even the most considered accusations. We are also at least as uncomfortable dealing with charges against the long-dead great as we are with those against the living obscure. And, too, we often, and mistakenly, see plagiarism as a crime of degree, an excess of something legitimate, "imitation" or "research" that has gotten out of hand.

No, it isn't murder. But like murder it intrigues us at a comfortable remove, when we're out of the line of fire and have been excused from the jury. Think how often, after all, a writer's books are called his or her children. To see the writer's words kidnapped, to find them imprisoned, like changelings, on some-one else's equally permanent page, is to become vicariously absorbed by violation. The real mystery of writing, like all forms of creativity, is that we don't know what makes it happen. *Where did he find the words?* we marvel rhetorically over an arresting passage. More rare, and therefore shocking, are those moments when we come upon a paragraph and can say, factually, declaratively, *I know where he got that.*

That's where the trouble, and this book, start.

T. M.

New York City
December 8, 1988

Stolen Words

1

Oft Thought, Ere Expressed: From Classical Imitation to International Copyright

The purpose for which Sterne used the novel was to give free utterance to his own way of looking at life, his own moral and intellectual individuality.

> — C. E. Vaughan, in *The Cambridge History of English Literature*, 1913

All his best passages are plagiarisms.

> — George Gregory, *Letters on Literature, Taste, and Composition*, 1809

CENTURIES never start or end on time, and any serious reader of English literature can tell another that the eighteenth ended in 1798, when Wordsworth and Coleridge detonated the *Lyrical Ballads*, thereby blowing up the orderly colonnade of Augustan oaks and clearing the field for the Romantic era's giddy blooms. With such titanic matters afoot in the groves, it hardly seems as if anyone would still be paying attention to Laurence Sterne, who had been dead for thirty years. But in the spring of 1798, a Mr. "R. F." wrote to the *Gentleman's Magazine* in order to have one more thrust at the late novelist's already wounded reputation: =Laurence Sterne

The plagiarisms of Sterne have of late engrossed the attention and research of the Learned World; and, by the labour of Dr. [John] Ferriar and others, that fascinating writer has been stript of many of his borrowed plumes. His far-famed originality and wit have shrunk from the test of enquiry; and the sorry reputation of a servile imitator is almost all that remains of that once cele-brated author.

Alas, poor Yorick!* What a deft skewering of the creator of *Tristram Shandy* and *Sentimental Journey* the passage above appears to be. Actually, it's alas, poor Mr. R. F., because he plagiarized his own accusation. Four years earlier one "Eboracensis" had written the *Gentleman's* to complain about the same — quote — borrowed plumes — unquote. Perhaps Eboracensis and Mr. R. F. were the same ungentlemanly gentleman, in which case the fel-low was plagiarizing from himself, a lesser offense to be sure — and one that this book will take up in due course — but as more people than can be conveniently footnoted have noted, residents of glass houses should assault with caution.† Whether the two accusers were identical or not, the point remains: attacking Sterne's plundering was already, by 1798, old hat.

And yet, the debate over just what Sterne did, and whether it was literary jape or moral wrong, has never really been settled — partly because each age has different artistic axes to grind and partly because even though something clearly happened in the seventeenth century, something that made the border between necessary imitation and reprehensible replication a much more closely patrolled and perilous ground, the offense has never lent itself to absolute definition and consensus. If being charged with plagiarism could be compared to running a red light, the de-fenses have, for centuries now, been on the order not of "I didn't run it" and "It hadn't turned red" but of "What exactly do you mean by a light?" and "Define 'run.'" And so before we can discuss what, if anything, Sterne was guilty of, we have to go back and consider a few historical basics.

*

Hamlet, V, i, 190–191.
†The "borrowed plumes," in fact, long predate both Eboracensis and Mr. R. F. You can find them in "The Jay and the Peacock" in Aesop's *Fables*.

Some of the trouble comes from the way in which our enduring, Aristotelian notions of what literature *is* involve the <u>admirable business of imitation</u>.

[handwritten margin note: one reason why plagiarism is hard to define]

> Imitation is natural to man from childhood; he differs from the other animals in that he is the most imitative: the first things he learns come to him through imitation. Then, too, all men take pleasure in imitative representations. Actual experience gives proof of this. . . . If a man does not know the original, the imitation as such gives him no pleasure; his pleasure is then derived from its workmanship, its color, or some similar reason.

<u>We take pleasure in imitations of life</u>, and our imitative capacities make us want to imitate not only life but life's imitations, too.

Saul Bellow has defined a writer as "a reader moved to emulation." In her diary in 1926, Virginia Woolf wrote: "Reading Yeats turns my sentences one way: reading Sterne turns them another." To some extent every writer's desk top is like a Ouija board, his pen pushed across it by whatever literary ghost he's just entertained. Why should it be otherwise? (And why pick on Sterne, if one of the great modern innovators finds him more influential than influenced?) There was a time when the guiding spirits of the literary dead were deliberately conjured, a time before ancestor worship gave way to that form of youth-enthrallment known as originality. And it was no short period of time, either; it amounts to most of literary history.

<u>The great critical cry of classical literature</u> was not an Emersonian call to "trust thyself" but <u>a Horatian exhortation to follow others</u>. What the *Art of Poetry* says about the creation of dramatic characters is typical. "Either follow tradition," writes Horace, "or else in what you invent be consistent. . . . In publicly known matters, you will be able to achieve originality if you do not translate word for word, nor jump into a narrow imitative groove, from which both fear and the rules followed in the given work prevent your escape." Don't translate *word for word,* but don't cut from whole cloth either — not when creating "publicly known" writings, which were far from the only kind produced by writers whose calling was many centuries away from becoming a profession.

<u>One thing is clear: plagiarism didn't become a truly sore point</u>

with writers until they thought of writing as their trade. Jokes about out-and-out literary theft go back all the way to Aristophanes and *The Frogs*, but what we call plagiarism was more a matter for laughter than litigation. The Romans rewrote the Greeks. Virgil is, in a broadly imitative way, Homer, and for that matter, typologists can find most of the Old Testament in the New. Saint Jerome, in the fourth century, translated and wrote commentaries on the earlier philosopher Origen, developing such an "addiction" to him — to use his biographer's terms — that he had difficulty telling where he and his "drug" diverged. The medieval monks rewrote, quite literally, such manuscripts as they could find.

Chaucer found stories in Boccaccio, and the real sources of both *The Canterbury Tales* and *The Decameron* were stories that came and went on air, transmitted orally by their tellers. It was printing, of course, that changed everything, putting troubadours out of business and numbering the days when one might circulate a few private, prettily calligraphed copies of one's sonnets or epic. The Writer, a new professional, was invented by a machine. Suddenly his capital and identity were at stake. An author-reader relationship that was financial and anonymous replaced something orally and visually cozy — hearing a poem, going to a play, having something highly recognizable passed around — and printing enormously increased the opportunities for misrepresentation. (For one thing, to steal someone's identity on widely circulated paper is inevitably worse than oral misrepresentation. After all, nobody believes that slander is a crime — it's just another word for conversation — but everyone can understand why libel is serious. It's a *permanent* lie.)

Throughout the sixteenth century classical notions of the necessity of imitation largely held, but there was a discernibly rising premium on uniqueness. In a world whose long-run destiny was to be ever less hierarchical, patrons were disappearing. Elizabethan London was filling up with wits who thought of themselves as writers. Adaptation of historical chronicles and Italian romances, and collaboration with one's contemporaries, might be theatrical norms, but in the new "fellowship of authors" there was also a good deal of feuding and possessiveness. Things were now competitive and personal, and when writers thought they'd been plundered they fought back. Probably the most famous line Robert Greene ever wrote was his denunciation of a thieving Shakespeare as having a "tygre's heart wrapped in a player's hide."

Greene wasn't the only angry writer. The forgotten Thomas Churchyard (1520?–1604) was described by Disraeli in *Calamities of Authors* as "one of those unfortunate men, who have written poetry all their days, and lived a long life, to complete the misfortune." Actually, Churchyard had had a hard life as a professional soldier before turning professional poet, and the anxieties of making a literary living seem to have pushed him over the edge on the subject of what belonged to him. Harold Ogden White describes his neurotic territoriality:

> For nearly twenty years . . . Churchyard continued to insist that the classical theory of imitation universally practised by his contemporaries was dishonest, continued vehemently and repetitiously to deny that he ever followed it, continued to accuse his rivals of stealing from him and of denying him the authorship of his own works. He alone of all English writers before 1600 takes this position.

Crazy, perhaps. But the mania would not have been intelligible even to Churchyard himself if the slow undercurrents of a cultural sea change had not begun to move. A modern world was printing and distributing itself into existence. Literary "careers" would be "made," and writerly goods would get sold, not because they were skillful variants of earlier ones but because they were *original*. What Thomas Churchyard had seen, in his far-fetched accusations, was a piece of the future, the time when being in print would not be the vulgarization of authorship so much as its essence. Eventually a bourgeois world would create its own new genre, the novel, and authors would be brand names, the "new Scott" asked for like this year's carriage model.

As the sixteenth century became the seventeenth, and Elizabeth I prepared to die without issue, politically thoughtful people were preoccupied, more than anything else, with questions of succession and legitimacy. Righteous confusion over these matters would lead to decapitation, restoration and revolution over the next hundred or so years. Among thoughtful literary people, similar confusion over standards of legitimacy would bring about much fractiousness and accusation in the decades following 1600.

In classical times a "plagiary" had been one who kidnapped a child or slave. And though Martial used it to designate a literary thief, Ben Jonson was, according to the *Oxford English Dictionary*, the first to use it in that sense in English: "Why? the ditt' is all borrowed; 'tis Horaces: hang him plagiary." Writers and readers and playgoers didn't always quite know when to use it, but there was now a name for what more and more was being seen as a crime, and there was a new fear in the honest writer's heart.

About twenty-five years ago Robert Merton, that literate sociologist, wrote a charming book called *On the Shoulders of Giants*, in which he attempted to trace the ultimate origin of an aphorism often credited to Sir Isaac Newton: "If I have seen farther, it is by standing on the shoulders of giants." Merton wound up finding forms of the saying practically everywhere, and when dealing with the seventeenth century felt compelled to note how "it is quite in keeping with the practice of the time to charge, and be charged with, plagiarism. Can you think of any one of consequence in that energetic age who escaped unscathed, either as victim or alleged perpetrator of literary or scientific theft, and typically, as both filcher and filchee? I cannot." On the lists of plaintiffs and defendants he puts, among others, Bunyan, Descartes, Leibniz, Wallis, Wren, Hooke, Holder, Newton, Halley, and Pascal. Suspicion ran so high that Robert Boyle, Merton tells us, decided to protect himself with a resolution "to write in single sheets, and other loose papers, that the ignorance of the coherence might keep men from thinking them worth stealing."

When Robert Burton published *The Anatomy of Melancholy* in 1621, he took the persona of "Democritus Junior" and, in a preface, confessed his miscellaneous methods to the reader: "As apothecaries we make new mixtures every day, pour out of one vessel into another; and as those old Romans robbed all the cities of the world to set out their bad-sited Rome, we skim off the cream of other men's wits, pick the choice flowers of their tilled gardens to set out our own sterile plots."

If the present reader can wait 140 years, or several pages, he will find this passage being made notorious by somebody else, but it's important to look at it now because, as somebody engaged in writing a book that was truly an *omnium gatherum* of learning, and writing it in a period uneasy about how to deal with something it was only just deciding was a crime, Burton, in his quotation-happy way, was seeking to set a standard: acquire, adapt and acknowledge. Take a deep breath and go through this well-edited chunk of Holbrook Jackson's modern edition of the *Anatomy:*

> As a good housewife out of divers fleeces weaves one piece of cloth, a bee gathers wax and honey out of many flowers, and makes a new bundle of all, *Floriferis ut apes in saltibus omnia libant* [as bees in flowery glades sip from each cup], I have laboriously collected this cento out of divers writers, and that *sine injuria,* I have wronged no authors, but given every man his own; . . . I cite and quote mine authors (which, howsoever some illiterate scribblers account pedantical, as a cloak of ignorance, and opposite to their affected fine style, I must and will use . . .). The matter is theirs most part, and yet mine, *apparet unde sumptum sit* [it is plain whence it was taken] (which Seneca approves), *aliud tamen quam unde sumptum sit apparet* [yet it becomes something different in its new setting], which native doth with the aliment of our bodies incorporate, digest, assimilate, I do *concoquere quod hausi* [assimilate what I have swallowed], dispose of what I take.

Shortly after this passage Burton uses a variation of the aphorism Merton went searching for ("A dwarf standing on the shoulders of a giant may see farther than a giant himself"), attributing it to Didacus Stella, who, Merton points out, is not really its father. But the point is that Burton attributes it.

The extent of one's responsibilities, though, was still cloudy, and in *The Compleat Angler* (1653) Izaak Walton could be both veracious and vague. According to the modern scholar John R. Cooper (who admits he's summarizing Marcus Goldman), Walton tended "to give credit to his sources when possible and, when not, to indicate the debt by referring to his anonymous source as 'a friend,' 'a Gentleman of tryed honestie,' or simply 'one.' When Walton introduced the comparison of foolish fish with wicked men by saying, 'as one has wittily observed,' it is likely that he himself had forgotten who his source was."

But the word was getting around that words could be owned

by their first writers. Dryden was attacked as a plagiarist by the Duchess of Newcastle and others. He defended himself as a watchmaker who applies his skill to the crafting (or adaptation) of others' raw materials. Gerard Langbaine produced a nasty little bibliography in 1687 called *Momus Triumphans, or the Plagiaries of the English Stage*. Milton, who classically urged writers to beautify what they borrowed, was charged with theft in his own time and later: William Lauder, a latter-day partisan of Charles I, sought revenge against Milton's defense of regicide by publishing a pamphlet claiming that parts of *Paradise Lost* were plagiarized; the "evidence" he claimed to have unearthed consisted of lines from the epic that he translated into Latin and interpolated into the works of contemporary poets who wrote in that supposedly dead language — poets he then claimed had been Milton's "sources."

So, if there was still confusion, there was increasing preoccupation. Plagiaristic practices, as H. M. Paull says in *Literary Ethics: A Study in the Growth of the Literary Conscience*, "now needed an apology.... Direct plagiarism was becoming discredited.... [The] subject was in the air."

Its sour waftings were, of course, eagerly sniffed by Alexander Pope, the touchiest man in English literary history. What is probably the most famous dictum in the *Essay on Criticism* concerns, in its way, originality:

> True Wit is Nature to Advantage drest,
> What oft was Thought, but ne'er so well Exprest,
> Something, whose Truth convinc'd at Sight we find,
> That gives us back the Image of our Mind.

The point is that while the reader has had the thought or feeling, only the writer has quite been able to put it into words. True wit, then, is the unique expression of something common. It is *the configuration of the words themselves* that counts.

With this standard we are reaching modern aesthetic and ethical ground. Just a century after the Jacobeans came up with their word for the phenomenon, ambivalence about its nature has given way to scornful opprobrium. There is still enough happy adhesion to the ancients for Goldsmith to feel obliged to declare how it "is one of the chief privileges ... of genius, to fly

from the herd of imitators by some happy singularity" — but to
be called a word-for-word plagiarist is to be accused of the capital
literary crime. Not surprisingly, the term is one of the most
potent and frequently tossed darts in Pope's spiteful quiver.
Book II of *The Dunciad* singles out one false wit in these four
lines:

> Never was dash'd out, at one lucky hit,
> A Fool, so just a copy of a Wit;
> So like, that criticks said and courtiers swore,
> A wit it was, and call'd the phantom, More.

The hapless James Moore Smythe, on whom these couplets were
dropped, lives on, like so many of Pope's victims, only as a footnote to the literary serial murder that is *The Dunciad*. In his brief
life (1702–1734) he strove too visibly for social and literary status
and earned Pope's scorn on a number of epigrammatic occasions.
In *The Grub-Street Journal,* Pope was the anonymous donor of
these lines, from "On J.M.S. Gent.":

> A gold watch found on Cinder Whore,
> Or a good verse on J——my M——e,
> Proves but what either shou'd conceal,
> Not that they're rich, but that they steal.

And when Moore was defensive about such charges, that too was
cause for epigram:

> To prove himself no Plagiary, Moore,
> Has writ such stuff, as none e'er writ before.
> Thy prudence, Moore, is like that Irish Wit,
> Who shew's his breech, to prove 'twas not besh — .

Augustan fastidiousness about acknowledgment was strong
enough to have its effect on even the angry, calamitous life of
the poet and dramatist Richard Savage, whom one would have
thought too busy to notice it, spending time, as he did, cooking
up false stories of high birth; fighting his supposed mother (in a
poem called "The Bastard"); betraying his friends; borrowing
money from them; being sentenced to death for killing someone

in a bar fight; getting reprieved; sleeping in the streets. In his *Life of Savage,* Dr. Johnson tells us that the poet "could not bear to conceive himself in a state of dependence" — understandable enough in someone surviving on handouts. Perhaps less predictable would be what Johnson tells us about

> the delicacy with which he was always careful to separate his own merit from every other man's, and to reject that praise to which he had no claim. He did not forget, in mentioning his performances, to mark every line that had been suggested or amended; and was so accurate, as to relate that he owed three words in *The Wanderer* to the advice of his friends.

This compulsive crediting may have been the psychological flip side of his resentment over other kinds of dependence, but — and this is true for Thomas Churchyard, too — defense mechanisms, like cars, can be started only when the cultural climate is warm enough for them. The eighteenth century was hot for attribution.

By the middle of it there was such hair-trigger vigilance on the subject that Johnson had to come in, in a Johnsonian way, to calm things down. In *Rambler* 143, in 1751, he tells potential accusers to proceed cautiously with any charges, since even false ones "may be sometimes urged with probability." There is, after all, only so much new under the sun, and it is not unreasonable to think that, say, both Horace and Tully can arrive independently at the notion of poetry's being the most lasting way of recording men's actions. There are of course occasions when the charge of plagiarism will be justified; when, for example, "there is a concurrence of more resemblances than can be imagined to have happened by chance; as where the same ideas are conjoined without any natural series or necessary coherence, or where not only the thought but the words are copied." In other words, not the matter but the manner: the generally agreed-upon grounds for indictment from Johnson's time on. This *Rambler* essay ends with the best metaphor ever minted to describe acceptable imitation: "An inferior genius may without any imputation of servility pursue the path of the antients, provided he declines to tread in their footsteps."

Two years later, in 1753, Johnson once again took up the

subject, this time in *Adventurer* 95. He places plagiarism near the middle of iniquity's spectrum: "one of the most reproachful, though, perhaps, not the most atrocious of literary crimes." Finally, in 1755, Johnson offered his official definition of the noun's two forms, between the entries for "placket" (a petticoat) and "plague," in his *Dictionary of the English Language:*

> Plagiarism. n.f. [from plagiary.] Theft; literary adoption of the thoughts or works of another.
>
> With great impropriety, as well as *plagiarism*, they have most injuriously been transferred into proverbial maxims. *Swi.*

> PLÁ GIARY. n.f. [from plagium, Lat.]

> 1. <u>A thief in literature; one who steals the thoughts or writings of another.</u>
>
>   The ensuing discourse, lest I chance to be traduced for a *plagiary* by him who has played the thief, was one of those that, by a worthy hand, were stolen from me. *South.*
>
>   Without invention, a painter is but a copier, and a poet but a *plagiary* of others; both are allowed sometimes to copy and translate. Dryden's Dufresnoy.

> 2. The Crime of literary theft. Not used. *Plagiary* had not its nativity with printing, but began when the paucity of books scarce wanted that invention. *Brown.*

If the quotation from Brown was picked to illustrate the crime's long history, the one from South seems to have been chosen to signify all the new territorial shouting going on.

Johnson saw dictionaries themselves as one literary genre in which accusations of theft would have to be pretty much beside the point. "All definitions of the same thing," he wrote in *Rambler* 143, "must be nearly the same." In fact, the history of lexicography, down through our own time, is full of sly poaching and shrill alarum. The historian of dictionaries Sidney I. Landau declares that Robert Cawdrey's *Table Alphabeticall* (1604), though often considered the first English dictionary, is "wholly unoriginal," depending as it does on Edmund Coote's *The English Schoole-Master* (1596) and Thomas Thomas's *Dictionarium Linguae Latinae et Anglicanae* (1588) — itself an abridgment of Thomas Cooper's *Thesaurus Linguae Romanae et Britannicae* (1565). Landau shows a Johnsonian calm about all this, since a "really new dictionary would be a dreadful piece of work."

R. W. Burchfield, editor of *A Supplement to the Oxford English Dictionary*, takes a somewhat dimmer view of modern maraudings. He allows that clearly acknowledged indebtedness by one dictionary to another is a fine thing, but asserts that all too often the makers of latter-day lexicons approach their predecessors in the manner of second-story men. For example, *Webster's Third New International* (1961) — that permissively unprescriptive dictionary listing most of the four-letter words that would set the tone for the decade that followed its appearance — was actually, and unadmittingly, dependent on the venerable *OED*.*

But we are drifting away from the eighteenth century. It's time to return to it for a consideration of Laurence Sterne, whose troubles over plagiarism are so varied and complicated that they are probably useless as a test case — even as they set a student of plagiarism to considering, if only briefly, nearly every facet of the subject that will be encountered in the course of this book.

Samuel Johnson met Sterne only once, and he came away with a bad impression of both his manners and grammar. Sterne's biographer, Wilbur Cross, quotes an account of the meeting:

> "In a company where I lately was," the lexicographer is reported to have said to a group of friends, "Tristram Shandy introduced himself; and Tristram Shandy had scarcely sat down, when he informed us that he had been writing a Dedication to Lord Spencer; and *sponte suâ* he pulled it out of his pocket; and *sponte suâ*, for nobody desired him, he began to read it; and before he had read half a dozen lines, *sponte meâ*, sir, I told him it was not English, sir."

---

*"*Webster's Third* set the year 1755 as its backward terminal limit. In general terms — Shakespeare and the Authorised Version of the Bible apart — their exclusion zone included the whole of the period before 1755. But their quotation files are extraordinarily rich from the period since 1900, and progressively thinner as one works backwards from 1900 to 1755. In other words, for classes of words that flourished and possibly died in the period 1755 to 1900 they had very little confirmatory or disconfirmatory evidence of their own, and had to resort to the great historical dictionaries, the *OED* itself and the historical dictionaries of special periods and special regions."

As was pointed out at the beginning of this chapter, it is not his own English but rather his appropriation of others' that has caused Sterne such trouble with careful readers. And what's especially odd is that most of the charges made involve a book that no one would dispute is, in its overall design and presentation, among the most original in the language.

If you remember nothing else of *Tristram Shandy*, you can probably recall that retired military man Uncle Toby, who was literally too gentle to hurt a fly and whose last campaign was the courtship of Widow Wadman. In volume VIII, chapter 27, Toby explosively confides his passion to his faithful Corporal Trim. Now, just as life doesn't bother to make all of our days equally eventful, *Tristram Shandy* pays little mind to uniformity of chapter length; so what's quoted below is *all* of volume VIII, chapter 27:

> The world is ashamed of being virtuous — My uncle Toby knew little of the world; and therefore when he felt he was in love with widow Wadman, he had no conception that the thing was any more to be made a mystery of, than if Mrs. Wadman had given him a cut with a gap'd knife across his finger: Had it been otherwise — yet as he ever looked upon Trim as a humble friend; and saw fresh reasons every day of his life, to treat him as such — it would have made no variation in the manner in which he informed him of the affair.
>
> "I am in love, corporal!" quoth my uncle Toby.

I had the good luck to be taught *Tristram Shandy* by Uncle Toby himself, or the closest thing the wicked world could provide in the tumultuous spring of 1970. I was a freshman at Brown, and in that season of Cambodian incursion and campus insurrection, I sat in Wilbour Hall taking English 48 from Professor Robert W. "Pat" Kenny, a hale and hearty gentleman with a full head of white hair and a trim mustache. An old son of Brown (class of 1925), he had held about every post the college could offer, with time out to be a war hero in the Pacific and a brigadier general in the reserves.

That spring he was a wintry lion, in semiretirement, the sort of old character who loved his syllabus and no doubt longed for the more tractable students of the past. It was a period when the exegetical vogue at Brown was turning semiotic, but Professor Kenny's approach remained anecdotal. He told us stories about

Boswell and Smollett; swore that he'd sooner let his granddaughter swim in the Rhode Island state shark hatchery than ask Alexander Pope to settle a quarrel (the origin of *The Rape of the Lock*);
and passed to us such bits of critical history as the fact that in his
undergraduate days Pembrokers (students at Brown's women's
college) were not permitted to read the lubricious *Tristram Shandy*
but had instead to spend that week back on their own campus
("the wenchery") reading *Evelina*.

Of all the books Professor Kenny taught, none provoked more
wonder and merriment in him than *Tristram Shandy*. In fact, the
greatest piece of pedagogy I have ever witnessed came on the
morning he found himself unable to continue with whatever he
was saying about Sterne. He was laughing too hard. His face was
pink, and his buttons were actually ready to burst. When he
recovered enough breath to address the students of English 48,
what he said was as natural as Uncle Toby's declaration to Corporal Trim: "I love this book!"

Sterne was also in love with what he'd written. In the late 1750s
he was an obscure country parson in Sutton-in-the-Forest, a man
in his mid-forties with poor health, a bad marriage, a susceptibility to drinking binges and a hankering after fame. Making his
great novel was the solution. As the *Dictionary of National Biography* tells us: "He turned for solace to literary work, and by way
of relieving the melancholy wrote the opening books of 'Tristram
Shandy.' He laboured with a rare zest. Although he corrected
his manuscript liberally, he had completed fourteen chapters in
six weeks. . . . The employment dissipated most of his cares. He
was so delighted with his facility that he jestingly promised to
write two volumes every year for the rest of his days."

If not for these bursts of activity, he would have lived out his
days as a philandering rural parson, preaching and raking until
his consumptive lungs gave out. But with the publication of
successive volumes of *Tristram Shandy*, he found himself, to his
delight, a chic and cherished author. "With the exception of
Volume IX," writes Arthur Cash, Wilbur Cross's successor in
Sterne biography, "Sterne could manage to keep a clientele of
4000 readers without being the favourite of the entire reading
public. . . . He would continue for the rest of his life a pet of the
fashionable world."

Tristram Shandy managed to send up the English novel almost before it had been fully invented. It is full of narrative tricks and spasms (strings of asterisks, blank pages) that seem more post-modern than neoclassical, and the humorous and pathetic adventures of Walter and Tristram Shandy, of Corporal Trim and Uncle Toby, also seem to anticipate modern psychological notions in any number of ways. But in the 1760s, as he was leading the literary parade, Sterne was also managing to pick the pockets of many bygone writers bringing up the rear.

On the make in more ways than one, this scribbling divine in fact failed to charm a good many of his contemporaries, who were eager to attribute his success to a synthetic imagination possessed of no literary conscience. In his lifetime and just after it there were plenty of complaints about unacknowledged indebtedness: Johnson's friend Mrs. Thrale, for instance, felt sure Sterne got the idea for *Tristram Shandy* from *The Life and Memoirs of Corporal Bates,* a book published in 1756 and which she found in a bookshop in Derby eighteen years later. But it wasn't until the 1790s that real bills of particulars were drawn up against him. Both of them — a gentle one in 1791 and a much more severe one in 1798 — came from the unlikely pen of Dr. John Ferriar, who may first have decided to get hold of *Tristram Shandy* when he heard about the prolonged attention paid to obstetrics in the novel's first volumes. In reporting the results of his investigations, Ferriar seems anxious to avoid appearing a version of Sterne's Dr. Slop, declaring his good will and meticulousness in the Advertisement to *Illustrations of Sterne* (1798):

> Tho' all the pieces of this miscellany may be considered as the fruit of "idle hours not idly spent," in the intervals of an active Profession, I hope it will be found that they have been composed with a degree of attention, proportioned to my respect for the opinion of the public; and that I have not been rendered presumptuous, or careless, by the indulgence which I have experienced on former occasions.

In declaring that "from Rabelais, Sterne seems to have caught the design of writing a general satire on the abuse of speculative opinions," Ferriar is charging no more than many of Sterne's most respectful commentators will willingly concede — after all,

[margin annotation: Sterne / Sterne's Plagarism]

in Johnsonian terms, that's a matter of the path, not the foot-steps. But Ferriar goes on to show that Sterne also adopted some specific "lively extravagancies" from the French writer, as well as some choice conversational matter. From there Ferriar goes on to perform what one might call a "micro" analysis of all the materials that sustain the sparkling economy of *Tristram Shandy;* the writings of D'Aubigné, Beroalde, Tabarin and Bruscambille are discovered in Sterne's warehouse, creating what comes to appear a more and more dubious balance of payments between specialized imports and original manufactures.

Actually, as Ferriar shows, the supplies for Sterne's enterprise came in the greatest abundance not from across the Channel but from an old library in Oxfordshire. Burton's already mentioned *Anatomy of Melancholy,* that huge brooding miscellany of the seventeenth century, may first have been put in Sterne's hand by his licentious friend John Hall-Stevenson, but however it got there it wound up well thumbed. Ferriar's suspicions of Sterne vis-à-vis the *Anatomy* got their start from a sense of anachronism: "I had often wondered at the pains bestowed by Sterne in ridiculing opinions not fashionable in his time, and had thought it singular, that he should produce the portrait of his sophist, Mr. Shandy, with all the stains and mouldiness of the last century about him." Not only, says Ferriar, is the "heroic strain" near the start of volume V of *Tristram Shandy* ("Who made Man, with powers which dart him from earth to heaven in a moment — that great, that most excellent, and most noble creature of the world — the *miracle* of nature, as Zoroaster in his book . . . called him") plagiarized from the *Anatomy's* first paragraph ("Man, the most excellent and noble creature of the world, 'the principal and mighty work of God, wonder of Nature,' as Zoroaster calls him"), but so also are Sterne's comments on plagiarism itself plagiarized from Burton.

From volume V of *Tristram Shandy:*

> Shall we for ever make new books, as apothecaries make new mixtures, by pouring only out of one vessel into another? Are we for ever to be twisting and untwisting the same rope?

From, as you will recall, the preface to *The Anatomy of Melancholy:*

> As apothecaries, we make new mixtures every day, pour out of
> one vessel into another. . . . We weave the same web still, twist the
> same rope again and again.

There are two ways of looking at this. You can see it as a
whimsical literary in-joke, something that *invites* detection and
laughter by its sheer blatancy; or you can see it as a colossal, gold-
medal case of belletristic chutzpah. Most modern critics see it as
the first, as part of a book that manipulates and plays with and
slices and dices hundreds of such quotations for its own ludicrous
purposes. It is this viewpoint that allows Arthur Cash to remark,
without alarm: "Although no commonplace books belonging to
him have been found, it seems highly likely that he had such
books and drew upon them from time to time as he worked on
Tristram Shandy. Otherwise, he could hardly have written, say,
the chapter on sleep . . . which strings together passages or images from Cervantes, Montaigne, Shakespeare, the Bible and
perhaps Sir Philip Sidney."

Most Sterne scholars believe the problem with Dr. Ferriar is
that he just didn't get it. He's a literalist in the funhouse, somebody who came upon the distorting mirrors and felt defrauded
instead of entertained. Furthermore, according to Professor
W. B. C. Watkins, when it comes to the plagiarized passage about
plagiarism, Dr. Ferriar is practically the joke's punchline:

> Dr. Ferriar, with an understatement which is patently a lifting of
> eyebrows, finds it "singular that all this declamation should be
> taken, word for word, from Burton's introduction." Burton would
> have relished perfectly the audacity, the irony with many impli-
> cations, the joke that is more than a joke; indeed, inadvertently,
> Dr. Ferriar has given to that passage its proper richness of context.

Is that all Ferriar amounts to? A chump? Sterne's straight man?
Actually, it would be foolish to think so. For one thing, he was
lacking in neither literary sophistication nor a sense of humor.
He typically mixes praise with censure, and shows himself aware
of the writerly playfulness in *Tristram Shandy;* it's just that the
lack of acknowledgment can't help troubling him ("This is well
rallied . . . but Sterne should have considered how much he
owed to poor old Burton"). In any case, what is one to make of
borrowings where, unlike the one about plagiarism, there is no

question of any clever misuse whose detection will give knowing pleasure to the erudite reader? When Mr. Shandy consoles himself over the death of his brother Bobby, he says: " 'T is an inevitable chance — the first statute in Magna Charta — it is an everlasting act of Parliament, my dear brother — all must die." A hundred years previous, Burton had written: " 'Tis an inevitable chance, the first statute in Magna Charta, an everlasting act of Parliament, all must die." Now, what exactly is the joke here? What is the tricky bit of adaptation or updating designed to make us see Sterne's witty manipulation? The truth is that there isn't any. Readers aren't going to think that Sterne has done something clever with Burton; they're going to think he's said something clever himself. If Sterne's purpose was sometimes parody, it seems just as clear that it was sometimes mooching.

against Sterne

Ferriar's first investigation, its results delivered in 1791, showed his awareness of just how tired the eighteenth century had made itself with the pedantic hunting down of influence and plagiarism: "It has been fashionable of late, to decry the analysis of objects of admiration, and those who wish to trace the mysteries of wit and literary pleasure, are held to be profane dissectors, who mangle the carcase of learning, out of spleen and idle curiosity." Even his sterner 1798 study still has an apologetic sound at times; he proceeds with more sorrow, it seems, than glee. And he is naturally enough careful to acknowledge any indebtedness of his own ("It was observed to me by Mr. Isaac Read, that Sterne had made use of the notes to Blount's Translation of *Philostratus*"). The final paragraph, reaching loftier rhetorical heights than those to which the doctor usually aspires, allows that there may have been some good to come out of all Sterne did with and to his literary predecessors, even as it rebukes him in gentle, poetic terms:

> The use which Sterne made of Burton and Hall, and his great familiarity with their works, had considerable influence on his style; it was rendered, by assimilation with their's [*sic*], more easy, more natural, and more expressive. Every writer of taste and feeling must indeed be invigorated, by drinking at the "pure well of English undefiled"; but like the Fountain of Youth, celebrated in the old romances, its waters generally elude the utmost efforts of those who strive to appropriate them.

Still, Ferriar remains a wet blanket to modern scholars. H. J. Jackson has a neat academic thesis to explain things: "Sterne deliberately seeded the later volumes of *Tristram Shandy* with quotations taken (not without acknowledgment) from Burton's work, and he appears to have meant them to function as allusions, adding an ironic dimension to the novel." But, more or less in contradiction of his parenthesis, Jackson adds: "He must have been aware that few of his contemporaries knew the *Anatomy* well enough to identify the allusions without more authorial guidance than he gave. For almost all readers of Sterne's day, the borrowed phrases and sentences were indistinguishable from the original materials in the text of the novel." Faced with these two irreconcilables — an author who is bent on irony; the same author who knows it will certainly be lost on his audience — Jackson does what most critics do in the absence of any proof. He speculates; i.e., comes up with something; i.e., makes something up: "Sterne was evidently content to keep the complex allusiveness of his book as a private joke for as long as he lived, making it one more game in which the Jester triumphed over most of his Jestees." Oh, *now* we get it: delayed-action, posthumous irony.

Common Reader, show me an author content to wait for this kind of appreciation and I'll show you someone with a stronger belief in the afterlife than that held by martyrs and children.

With unintended humor, Jackson states: "The *Anatomy* has been known since Ferriar's time as a source of learned quotations for Walter Shandy." Yes, indeed: since Ferriar's time, but not since Sterne's! Jackson again: "Sterne's readers do not expect to find quotations from Burton in *Tristram Shandy*, and when they do, they are surprised." They surely must be, since, as Jackson says, most of them would never have heard of Burton anyway. Like Professor Watkins, Jackson sees Sterne as Costello waiting for Abbott — the straight man, Dr. Ferriar, who will complete the act: "In an indirect way, Ferriar was instrumental in bringing about the conditions right for the reading of *Tristram Shandy*, since he was responsible for putting copies of Burton's *Anatomy* into every well-equipped library."

Now, Common Readers, how many of you have read Sterne and Burton side by side? How many of you have refused to proceed to the next line in *Tristram Shandy* before detouring, via each footnote (supplied by later editors), to Burton? I suspect very few of you; just as I suspect many of you have nodded in unironic appreciation of wisdom you thought not Burton's but Sterne's; just as, again I suspect, Sterne wanted you to. If Sterne needed a Ferriar, he could have invented him during his lifetime. He had, after all, no qualms about self-promotion when he wrote David Garrick a letter praising *Tristram Shandy* and had someone else sign her name to it. Why not just put someone up to writing the sort of exposé Ferriar did, thereby assuring the ironic "completion" of the book and Sterne's being able to enjoy the ensuing spectacle of appreciation while still alive? Why take the chance that an actual Ferriar might not come along?

The reason is that Sterne had none of this on his mind. He was too busy enjoying the praise of originality being accorded his book. There is no record of his saying to any adoring Londoner of the 1760s, "Just wait. You ain't seen nothin' yet." As Merton, who calls Tristram his "master," points out in *On the Shoulders of Giants,* the *Anatomy,* first published in 1621, was reprinted in 1624, 1628, 1632, 1638, 1651/2, 1660 and 1676. True enough — but not again, as even Jackson would admit, until 1800. And surely Sterne did not expect most of his faddish readers to have an eighty-year-old book in the house.

None of Sterne's work was to escape charges of plagiarism — charges made more aggressively than most of Ferriar's — even if their substance was only that Sterne had stolen from himself. (Thackeray would claim that the dead donkey in *Sentimental Journey* had first been put to work three years before in the seventh and eighth volumes of *Tristram Shandy*.) Parson Sterne's sermons would be dismissed as poor patchwork affairs. True, most preachers preach from a borrowed text to begin with, and studies of eighteenth-century homilies show that Sterne was hardly alone in loving the words of his colleagues as his own. (Arthur Cash sees only a "venial sin" here.) Still, Sterne seems to have been such a relaxed lily in his field, so certain the library would provide, that scholars have had to find special excuses for him. In *The Life and Times of Laurence Sterne,* Wilbur Cross explains why the country parson couldn't be a man for all seasons: "For forming his style as a preacher he studied the sermons of Hall, Berkeley, Young, Tillotson, and other moralists and divines, from whom he drew liberally, sometimes merely paraphrasing the original when the harvest season, it may be, gave him scant time for independent composition."

What's left? Well, there are his letters. Professor W. B. C. Watkins — who, it should be noted, felt that plagiarism "with [Sterne] is no more important than with Shakespeare — or, rather, is important only insofar as changes and adaptations illuminate his method" — had to admit that Sterne did copy some of the love letters he wrote to his mistress, Mrs. Eliza Draper, from ones he had written, years before, to his wife. Ye gods, was there no page whose print did not turn once again liquid at the approach of his ravenous, vacuuming quill? Or, to ask the long rhetorical question that Joyce asked of Shem, the shamming Penman, in *Finnegans Wake:* "Who can say how many pseudostylic shamiana, how few or how many of the most venerated public impostures, how very many piously forged palimpsests slipped in the first place by this morbid process from his pelagiarist pen?"

What novelists are really supposed to plagiarize, of course, is reality, and like most others Sterne probably had some real-life models for his characters. Nothing could be more reductive than to think of *Tristram Shandy* as a roman à clef, but Cash notes: "It would have been common talk that Sterne had modelled his Dr Slop upon Dr John Burton [!] of York, and his lawyer, Didius, upon Dr Francis Topham, the prominent ecclesiastical lawyer and Master of the Faculties." It's just as common for the novelist, particularly the young one, to create his characters out of himself. What's odd, and what may have been true in Sterne's middle-aged case, is taking the opportunity to make oneself out of one's characters — to live up to them, grow into them — since readers will want to assume they antedated their author. Professor J. M. Stedmond writes that "it was with the success of *Shandy* that Sterne suddenly seemed to 'find himself.' From the time that the first volumes of his book took London by storm, Sterne seemed to recognize the role he had henceforth to play."

In fact, in *The Frenzy of Renown: Fame and Its History,* Leo *by Sterne*

Braudy describes Sterne as "the first English author who can be called a celebrity." It was a kind of celebrity he was not permitted to enjoy for very long. As the 1760s drew themselves out Sterne was more and more estranged from his wife and more and more worn out by his lungs. He had enough doubts about what he'd achieved in the sometimes lascivious *Tristram Shandy* to write *A Sentimental Journey* partly as an act of prim penitence. (He did, however, in this same period, manage his affair with Mrs. Draper.) Legends of his dying friendless, and even of having his cuff links stolen by those attending him in his lodgings, are no more than that, according to Professor Cash; but posterity's eagerness to believe them for so long was part of the punishment that many exacted from the time of his death, not only on his reputation but on his very corpse.

On March 22, 1768, Sterne was buried in the Paddington burial ground used by St. George's Church in Hanover Square, London. Unfortunately, this graveyard also received the handiwork of the hangman in nearby Tyburn. Until the Anatomy Act of 1832 regularized the donation of bodies to science, medical researchers had to avail themselves of the services of grave robbers ("resurrection men") like the father of Dickens's Jerry Cruncher, and the friendless remains of the recently executed, lying in this out-of-the-way spot, were choice pickings. Alas, it seems pretty clear that the mortal container of Sterne's freebooting imagination was itself borrowed in the interest of scientific progress. "In March 1769," writes David Thomson, "the *Public Advertiser* reported the rumour of Sterne's appearance on a university dissecting table." It was later reported that a spectator to the operation recognized the author of *Tristram Shandy* when a cloth was pulled back from the head.

Of course, all writers of consequence wind up on university dissecting tables, but it is expected that postmodern postmortems will be carried out in the library, on what scholars call literary remains. That the corporeal ones of a chronic pilferer should be stolen in the way Sterne's apparently were might have seemed gruesomely apt to his posthumous detractors. Some doubt the truth of the grave-robbing legend, but Arthur Cash, now Sterne's definitive biographer, seems reasonably convinced. In 1969 the old Paddington burial ground, having been sold to an apartment house developer, was searched at the request of Kenneth Monkman, secretary of the Laurence Sterne Trust. One of the skulls that was dug up had a sawn-off crown — a sign of autopsy — and it matched the copy of the Nollekens bust of Sterne in Monkman's house. Two hundred and one years after first being buried, Sterne was reinterred, this time in the Coxwold parish where he had been a parson.

Professor Cash makes large, and apt, claims for Sterne's overall originality and at least potential influence: "Most students of Sterne believe, as do I, that the narrative devices which James and Bergson inspired, notably in the novels of Marcel Proust, André Gide and Virginia Woolf, can be found in *Tristram Shandy*." Or, one might put it as Hazlitt did: "Gross plagiarism may consist with great originality. Sterne was a notorious plagiarist but a true genius."

Plagiarism is almost invariably a paradoxical compulsion. For one thing, the practiced thief takes care to leave self-destructive clues. Cash points to the passage in volume IV of *Tristram Shandy* in which Sterne "mocks, in the figure of Homenas, the clergyman who plagiarizes ineptly" — just one example that seems to have been "written by a man who took some pride in plagiarizing skilfully, but who knew he should not be doing it at all." (Adultery is a kind of sexual plagiarism, and Cash notes Sterne's similar way of flaunting his guilty affections for Eliza Draper: "To make a public show of affections was part and parcel of sentimental love for Sterne. Probably it reassured him that there was nothing shameful in what he was doing.")

The plagiarist also turns paradoxical in being unusually territorial about his own work. Sterne said he wrote "not to be *fed* but to be *famous*." As a schoolboy he felt compelled to write his name on the just-painted classroom ceiling, earning a beating from the usher but praise from the master. "My master," Sterne himself recalled, "was very much hurt at this, and said before me that never should that name be effaced, for I was a boy of genius, and he was sure I would come to preferment." Decades later Sterne would personally sign all four thousand or so bound copies of volume V of *Tristram Shandy* (the portion containing the greatest number of plagiarisms from Burton) as a preventive against forgery: he was warned about an imitation "in the Size and Manner of Tristram Shandy" that had just appeared. Sterne had learned not to give away any of the capital that could buy him the fame he so desired. Years before *Tristram Shandy*, he wrote a Latin sermon for his linguistically inept friend John Fountayne so that Fountayne could get his Doctor of Divinity from Cambridge. Sterne would eventually quarrel with Fountayne and end up wondering, "He got Honour by it. What Got I?" From then on he held tightly to his own creations. As with many plagiarists, the strength of his hold may have caused his arms to cramp. And one way of relieving the strain was to widen his embrace, around others' possessions.

Originality — not just innocence of plagiarism but the making of something really and truly new — set itself down as a cardinal literary virtue sometime in the middle of the eighteenth century and has never since gotten up. As Walter Jackson Bate puts it in *The Burden of the Past and the English Poet:* "The conscience had taken another Trojan horse into the walls. . . . By the 1750s some of the least original minds of the time were beginning to prate constantly of 'originality.' " This new shibboleth, along with the notion of "sincerity" (the literary work as heartfelt self-expression, not witty construct), became what Bate calls "the fearful legacy to the great Romantics."

When the demand for novelty meets the sensitive writer's normal worship of the great literary past, how does he feel? Nervous and depressed. And in order to overcome what Harold Bloom calls "the anxiety of influence," the poet performs the neat trick of deliberately misreading his precursors in order to "clear imaginative space" for himself. But from Romantic times onward, writers and readers, still craving something original, have had a feeling of hopelessness about achieving it, a sense that we can't make it like they used to, because even if we could, we wouldn't like it — it wouldn't be "original." "The death of poetry will not be hastened by any reader's broodings," Bloom notes, "yet it seems just to assume that poetry in our tradition, when it dies, will be self-slain, murdered by its own past strength."

Unlike the poet, we are not "of imagination all compact," but of our reading all composed. In an essay called "Out of a Book," the novelist Elizabeth Bowen wondered if there was in fact any such thing as creative writing: "The imagination, which may appear to bear such individual fruit, is rooted in a compost of forgotten books. . . . Almost no experience, however much simplified by the distance of time, is to be vouched for as being wholly my own — *did* I live through that, or was I told that it happened, or did I read it? When I write, I am re-creating what was created for me."

By the late eighteenth century Thomas Chatterton, the "marvelous boy," made himself marvelously original not by overcoming or misreading the past but by pretending to be part of it. He composed some fourteenth-century-like verses and then asserted that he was only their discoverer, that they'd actually been written by a monk named Rowley. Which is to say he avoided any possibility of plagiarism by committing forgery. His exposure led to suicide, which, in turn, led to immortality.

In our own time, when prolific writers become institutions, they may feel the need to flee the burden of their own pasts, to test whether readers still like them for their work or just their name. Several years ago it was revealed that Joyce Carol Oates had sold a book (*Lives of the Twins*) to Simon & Schuster under the pseudonym of Rosamond Smith. "I wanted to escape from my own identity," she said. She had hoped for a "fresh reading" by people in the publishing industry to whom she'd long been a kind of household product.

In most respects we are still living in the Romantic era — its literary, psychological and political ideals remain largely our own — and from its beginning there has been a general consensus that one way for the modern artist to overcome anxiety about the past is to loot boldly, in broad daylight. The point, however, is always that the writer need not blush about stealing if he makes what he takes completely his, if he alchemizes it into something that is, finally, thoroughly new. In short, one has an intensification of the classical notion of imitation: don't just pay homage to the past; ravish it. When Oscar Wilde, replying to criticism that an early sonnet of his seemed awfully Miltonic, said, "What the critic calls an echo is really an achievement. I set myself to write sonnets like Milton's which should be as good as Milton's," he was actually showing the restraint of the Renaissance craftsman. It is one of the few times he uttered a reactionary aesthetic. More modern, or at least more typical of our extended Romantic era, is T. S. Eliot's famous pronouncement in an essay on the Jacobean dramatist Philip Massinger.

> One of the surest of tests is the way in which a poet borrows. Immature poets imitate; mature poets steal; bad poets deface what they take, and good poets make it into something better, or at least something different. The good poet welds his theft into a whole of feeling which is unique, utterly different from that from which it was torn; the bad poet throws it into something which has no cohesion.

Criticizing Massinger for a halfhearted appropriation from Shakespeare, Eliot boldly scolds: "This is, on Massinger's part, an echo, rather than an imitation or a plagiarism — the basest, because least conscious form of borrowing."

One would be tempted to dismiss paradoxes like these as more clever than true if one didn't find similar sentiments being so often expressed by creators in so many different arts. Virgil Thomson's disciple Ned Rorem has said, "One imitates what one loves. You steal what you admire, then feel so guilty about it you try to disguise it." Less penitent is Martha Graham, who in one of her notebooks declares: "I am a thief — and I am not ashamed. I steal from the best wherever it happens to me." Even Harold Bloom, in *The Anxiety of Influence*, seems to be reworking Eliot's semicoloned sentence on the subject of reworking: "Weaker talents idealize; figures of capable imagination appropriate for themselves."

What's understood, though, is that what's harvested is ploughed back, used to seed the next step in the cycle of creation. It is not put unchanged onto the dinner table by someone who pretends he's been cooking all day. That is what Sterne did with some portions of *Tristram Shandy*, and it is indisputably what was done near the beginning of the past-burdened, influence-anxious Romantic era, by the tormented soul who was that era's greatest literary critic.

Samuel Taylor Coleridge probably knew Burton's *Anatomy* as well as Laurence Sterne did — his notebooks are full of quotations from it — and he made Sterne himself the subject of some extraordinary reflections in a lecture called "On the Distinctions of the Witty, the Droll, the Odd, and the Humorous," positing that some of Sterne's licentious wit depended on a war within himself —

> on a certain oscillation in the individual's own mind between the remaining good and the encroaching evil of his nature — a sort of dallying with the devil — a fluxionary act of combining courage and cowardice, as when a man snuffs a candle with his fingers for the first time, or better still, perhaps, like that trembling daring with which a child touches a hot tea urn, because it has been forbidden; so that the mind has in its own white and black angel the same or similar amusement, as may be supposed to take place between an old debauchee and a prude.

As with most philosophers and psychologists, Coleridge's insights extended more deeply into minds other than his own, and he would likely have denied that what he was really giving in the passage above was not so much an account of what Sterne's brain went through when musing upon female anatomy as of what his own underwent in the presence of German metaphysics.

Was genius ever so troubled, from compulsion within, by circumstance without? He wrote an ode not to a nightingale or upon a beautiful vase but to dejection. He invented the mariner with the albatross around his neck; he himself had a monkey on his back. The most famous drug addict in English literature, Coleridge had problems not just with opium but with love (married to one Sara, enamored of another), health (*his* dissection in 1834 revealed a progressive disease of the heart and lungs that had probably long afflicted him), and work. He had trouble starting some projects, difficulty completing others. He had to fritter away large parts of his genius on reviewing, translating and lecturing. When the muse was upon him, he never knew how long it would stay. "Kubla Khan" came to him in a dream, but he never finished it: the "person from Porlock" came calling and woke him up.

Successive looks into the diary of Dorothy Wordsworth, sister of his collaborator and rival, William, are instructively dispiriting. September 1, 1800: "Coleridge obliged to go to bed after tea." January 29, 1802: "A heart-rending letter from Coleridge — we were sad as we could be." On April 20, 1802, after reading Coleridge's "Dejection" verses: "I was affected with them, and was on the whole, not being well, in miserable spirits."

Writing itself was a kind of trauma, from his earliest practice of it. In *Biographia Literaria* he tells of his instruction by the taskmaster James Bowyer, Head Master of the Grammar School, Christ's Hospital, "a man, whose severities, even now, not seldom furnish the dreams, by which the blind fancy would fain interpret to the mind the painful sensations of distempered sleep; but neither lessen nor dim the deep sense of my moral and intellectual obligations." A paragraph after this acknowledgment of debt, Coleridge makes a memorable remark about influences by and on writers: "From causes, which this is not the place to investigate, no models of past times, however perfect, can have the same vivid effect on the youthful mind, as the productions of contemporary genius."

Bowyer's strict instruction made it possible for Coleridge, in the early 1790s, to attend Jesus College, Cambridge, as a sizar (the exact undergraduate place and status of Laurence Sterne a couple of generations before). But his education was really rounded off just before the turn of the century, at the University of Göttingen, where he bought great quantities of contemporary German books on metaphysics.

Coleridge's thefts from Schelling, Schlegel and other Continental philosophers and critics provide a student of plagiarism with the first fully modern panoply of an offender's compulsions, rationalizations and excuses. They are all there — and we will see them all played out at even greater length in later chapters: the genuine talent that makes the need to steal seem, at least to his own readers, unthinkable; the loud abhorrence of others' transgressions and the spirited denial of his own; the textual incrimination so obvious that one can only wonder if getting caught wasn't part of what he had in mind for himself. But Coleridge's legacy is not only the psychological profile of the plagiarist; it is also the history of indulgent response and uphill rebuttal that has been posterity's typical reaction to plagiarism by the great and, for that matter, the not so great.* In the same

---

*The best short history of Coleridge's plagiarism and literary history's continuing response to it — indeed, the best article on the entire subject of plagiarism, its psychology and sanction — is Peter Shaw's "Plagiary," *American Scholar*, summer 1982, 325–337.

lecture quoted above, Coleridge declared: "Perhaps the most important of our intellectual operations are those of detecting the difference in similar, and the identity in dissimilar, things." Yes, perhaps. But another important intellectual operation is calling a spade a spade, and for more than a century and a half Coleridge has had a host of celebrants who have been unable to do just that.

Coleridge is said to have composed his poetry while walking over rough ground or breaking through woodland. If he tore down real branches while getting ready to write, he added inky ones to the margins of nearly everything he read. "His unpublished marginalia alone would fill several stout volumes," John Lewis Haney wrote. "Assured of his unique Protean place among the world's outstanding poets, critics, and thinkers, Samuel Taylor Coleridge revealed himself most intimately and completely as an annotator of hundreds of books written by other men." A hundred years after his death, scholars had turned up more than six hundred books he had marked. There is an almost predatory intimacy here between author and reader, an odd parasitism in the way reading leads immediately to writing.

The critic Paul Hamilton has recently speculated on why Coleridge's compendious notebooks were the perfect medium for him, one in which the distinction between what was just read and just written begins to blur:

> The notebooks represent an ideal literary form, read by a perfectly sympathetic reader, in which Coleridge's "whole mind," the exchange between inner and outer, private and public, can be recorded without loss. But they only achieve this by refusing to take the decisions which would render a public work coherent and free from contradiction. Their public remains private — the figure of Coleridge himself, cut off from his audience, his own reader.

Like many other plagiarists, Coleridge was both prolific and blocked. Notebooks were the place where things read could be safely hoarded and played with and mixed with his own thoughts. If anyone questioned a confection that was later openly displayed for sale — that is, published — there would always be available the defense that notebook-keeping is such a casual and private affair that confusion — sloppiness — will cause the oc-

casional, innocent problem. Indeed, as this book goes on it will
become apparent that plagiarists take refuge in their notebooks
with roughly the same frequency that scoundrels wrap themselves in the flag.

What is it that Coleridge took? Large pieces of the lectures he
gave between 1811 and 1818, and, more notoriously, sizable
patches of the *Biographia Literaria*. A talented undergraduate can
find them. Go to the *Bulletin of the University of Wisconsin* for June
1907 and find Anna Augusta Helmholtz's masterly bachelor's
thesis reproduced in full. All the incriminating parallel columns
are there. Sober and systematic, she rather sorrowfully lays it
out. A sample of commentary from section 5, "The Lectures of
1818": "The lecture entitled *The Greek Drama, On the Characteristics of Shakespeare's Dramas,* and others dealing with general prin-
ciples of criticism contain hardly a sentence which cannot be
referred back to [Schlegel], not only in idea, but also in phrase."
Other scholars would add Kant, Mendelssohn, and Maass to the
long list of Coleridge's quarries.

C's plagiarism

Norman Fruman, whose 1971 study, *Coleridge: The Damaged
Archangel,* is the most wounding and sustained assault ever made
on that writer's reputation, has to acknowledge that his attack
may have come too late to undo Coleridge's renown: "In every
instance, with the exception of Schlegel, coincidence of ideas was
not discovered till after his death, and in some instances not until
recent years. As a result, many influential formulations have
become attached, perhaps irrevocably, to his name." In our own
time, "popularizers" like Gail Sheehy and John Gardner have
had to defend themselves against charges that they made money
and reputations from jazzing up professorial ideas about psychology and literature with something less than full disclosure
of indebtedness. Each of these cases (involving Sheehy's best-
selling *Passages* and Gardner's book on Chaucer) did some justifiable damage to the writer's reputation, but the attempt to
discern the point at which popularization becomes theft was
something that could at least be debated. Questions about popularization hardly arise over what Coleridge was doing — even
though he said of his relationship to Schelling that it would "be
happiness and honour enough, should I succeed in rendering

the system itself intelligible to my countrymen" — since the ideas he stole were rendered to his English public in words and forms largely and esoterically identical to their German originals.

Thomas De Quincey accused Coleridge of plagiarism shortly after the latter's death in 1834. This was ironic for two reasons. One is De Quincey's stated aversion to plagiarism-hunting, a low critical occupation that he had scorned seven years before in a letter to the editor of the *Edinburgh Saturday Night Post:*

> It is undeniable, that thousands of feeble writers are constantly at work, who subsist by Plagiarism, more or less covert. It is equally undeniable . . . that thousands of feeble critics (such as Todd on Spenser, Dean Milles on Chatterton, &c. &c.) subsist by detecting plagiarisms as imitations, real or supposed.

The second is that De Quincey himself was a plagiarist. "The amount of material he himself lifted or summarized may be conservatively estimated as at least twentyfold that of Coleridge," writes Walter Jackson Bate. Indeed, one can barely conduct a study of plagiarism amid the deafening sound of literary pots roaring at literary kettles.

Six years after De Quincey's accusations, the questioning of Coleridge was carried on more honorably, and coincidentally, by Professor James F. Ferrier (with an *e*), in *Blackwood's Edinburgh Magazine.* But even in Coleridge's lifetime there had been whispers of scholarly impropriety, strong enough to make Coleridge remark upon the "genial coincidence" between his ideas and Schelling's — inevitable between two philosophers who had both studied the same German masters — and to insert, in the very *Biographia Literaria* he was partially plagiarizing, a preemptive defense against accusations:

> Be not charged on me . . . an ungenerous concealment or intentional plagiarism. I have not indeed . . . been hitherto able to procure more than two of his books. . . . I regard truth as a divine ventriloquist. I care not from whose mouth the sounds are supposed to proceed, if only the words are audible and intelligible.

The fact is that in his relationship with divinity Coleridge had a number of German middlemen to pull his strings.

He convinced himself of his own innocence partly by convincing himself of others' guilt — guilt against *him*. He even borrows those promiscuous borrowed plumes, one more time, in order to do it:

> I have laid too many eggs in the hot sands of this wilderness the world, with ostrich carelessness and ostrich oblivion. The greater part indeed have been trod under foot, and are forgotten; but yet no small number have crept forth into life, some to furnish feathers for the caps of others, and still more to plume the shafts in the quivers of my enemies, of them that unprovoked have lain in wait against my soul.

Fruman spends seven pages describing all the charges that Coleridge leveled at other writers, and reaches a mathematical deduction: "It is doubtful whether any other writer in the history of letters has accused so many writers of plagiarism, and so many so falsely." In the *Biographia* Coleridge stresses not only the duty but the pleasure of attribution, though, as Fruman points out, these "statements concerning intellectual integrity frequently occur in the vicinity of unacknowledged borrowings."

Coleridge has had a century and a half of defenders. At the turn of the century, the noted editor John T. Shawcross saw the plagiarism of Schelling as positively felicitous: "The large verbal borrowings . . . in the course of the 'deduction of the imagination' suggest that when he began to write he had accepted Schelling's account of the faculty, or at least found his own conclusions happily expressed therein." Sir Arthur Quiller-Couch blamed not opium but Coleridge's preoccupation with metaphysics for drying up his poetic faculty; after his absorption of the subject in Germany, "he had gone too far . . . and knew too much."

In Cynthia Ozick's novel *The Messiah of Stockholm*, the narrator declares: "A narrow moralist might speak of theft, but what was it if not the halo of the universal that the whole planet strains toward? . . . How ludicrous the leap from 'purely original' to 'Stop, thief!' — everything turns on whose ox is gored: there you are." The desire to keep our literary gods from being indicted is intense and persistent. Everyone enjoys a good scandal in the present; anybody can work up relish for the raw wound. What we seem far less able to endure is that plaster cast falling from the library shelf: its shattering somehow bothers us more than the live body going off the cliff. Scholars will tie themselves up in knots exonerating Coleridge. In one book Thomas McFarland sees his thefts as being not plagiarism but "a mode of composition — composition by mosaic organization." In a later book McFarland decides that literary form is really following psychological function: "It was, I believe, this need to allay the castration anxiety in his own ego by identification with the strength of an accepting brother that provided much of the basis for Coleridge's compulsion to plagiarize."

It was Fruman who made the cleanest sweep of apologists from the temple, showing how Coleridge deliberately "falsified the chronology of his knowledge of Schlegel's work" and came up with the "divine ventriloquist" defense in "a brilliant improvisation designed to meet a delicate situation." While writing the *Biographia* he was out of money and addicted to opium, and Molly Lefebure, writing in the 1970s, finds the "jabberwocky" of self-exculpation in the book to read like the "self-excuses of an articulate junkie," one who, at least in the period around 1815, had "a desperate need to produce a body of work which would earn him quick money, yet which would be of sufficiently high intellectual calibre to fend off criticism that opium had destroyed his former powers." The morphine, she argues, may have left him unable to see plagiarism with the same moral severity others did, or it may have allowed him to hallucinate his own excuses into the realm of plausibility.

The tricks he played on himself were clever and considerable. Shawcross may have stumbled on one, with whatever misplaced admiration he announced the discovery: "He was conscious that the same impulse lay at the root of his poetic and speculative creation, the impulse to give again that which he had felt and known." Coleridge also, like a Soviet encyclopedia, tended to take prior credit for the inventions of others: the idea for *Childe Harold* came to him before Byron got it; Faust paid an infernal call on his imagination before knocking on Goethe's. Or so he claimed.

Yet another common characteristic of the plagiarist — one that will come up a number of times in subsequent chapters and which Coleridge, when not strung out on opium, possessed himself — is the lack of any real need to steal.* In lines more amus-

*This is one of the traits stressed in Peter Shaw's *American Scholar* article.

ingly phrased than he probably knows, Walter Jackson Bate writes that the largely purloined "Chapter XII is far from necessary to the *Biographia*. It is in fact something of an excrescence, and it is rather dull reading, far from Schelling at his best." But at some level Coleridge knew what *he* was doing, and there was a need. Molly Lefebure quotes letters from 1811 in which Coleridge, beset by the need for money and morphine, confesses an inability "to compose anything new." Second best is all he can manage: "To transcribe is the utmost of my power." He regrets his truancy from poetry and his recent history as "a Delver in the unwholesome quick-silver mines of abstruse Metaphysics." It is this phrase upon which Lefebure put a sharp, but not too fine or preposterous, point:

> "A delver in the unwholesome quick-silver mines" speaks tragic volumes. "Quick-silver" is a particularly subtle and revealing term. It denotes, simultaneously, a short-cut to both intellectual material and financial reward. It indicates also that the substance delved for was not genuine ore, but a poisonous substitute. "Delver," as it is used here, is surely also a derogatory word — "a delver," as opposed to a thinker; a manual labourer who retrieves and brings to the surface that which is already in existence, available material ready to hand, yielding to simple muscular exertion.

If this is the "desire to be caught" that Peter Shaw finds driving the plagiarist, one must also back up a step or two to note that Coleridge was already caught, by debt and drugs; he may have been plagiarizing in part to support his habits of mind, and in more practical part to support a habit. Bate reminds us of how Coleridge disclaimed responsibility for "Kubla Khan" by saying it came to him in a dream; similarly, says Bate, opium may have made him feel he could at some point make up for whatever hastiness was hurting the lectures and the *Biographia*.

There is something refreshingly straightforward about those cases of plagiarism that are at least owned up to. When the critic and fiction writer Penelope Gilliatt was caught having appropriated material for her *New Yorker* profile of Graham Greene from another writer's piece on him in the *Nation,* her editor, William Shawn, explained that she had been in "poor health."

Coleridge's case suggests that he may have been addicted not just to opium but to plagiarism itself, flirting with the equivalent of an overdose in the risks of exposure he ran. Robert Graves compared literary thieves to jackdaws who feather their nests in "a haphazard and irresponsible way," but he speculated that all forms of theft were self-defeating: "No one with sensibility enough to realize that he is a thief will be permanently content in the ownership of stolen goods." Bate says that a "happier plagiarist" would have left less obvious clues, and the "death wish" that is discussed by Peter Shaw was spotted long before in Coleridge by Cyril Connolly — not in his plagiarisms but in what he failed to write at all. Connolly called him the "patron saint of those artists . . . who are prevented not so much by vanity and sloth from committing themselves to masterpieces as from a deep horror of the enjoyment and relief." He quotes from a dream recorded in Coleridge's notebooks — "I was followed up and down by a frightful pale woman who, I thought, wanted to kiss me, and had the property of giving a shameful Disease by breathing on the face" — diagnosing it as "a guilt dream; it is Coleridge who half-heartedly pursues his Muse, fearful of contaminating her with the sickness of being himself."

It may be this self-disgust that makes Coleridge, like many other plagiarists, feel compelled to give away the game before he's finished playing it. What is incontrovertible is that he did it, repeatedly and with assiduousness. "The guilt-laden Coleridge," Bate says, "keeps throwing out hints." Would any plagiarist be so *stupid*? The answer to this frequently asked question is yes, so long as one realizes that stupidity isn't really the issue: guilt and compulsion are the forces at work.

But exculpation will out. A decade after Fruman's book, Coleridge was once again being more or less excused in the ways familiarly practiced by apologists for plagiarists. In 1982 Richard Holmes saw the "divine ventriloquist" passage as something marked by "candour and considerable generosity." In their introduction to a new edition of the *Biographia Literaria* Bate and his Harvard protégé James Engell brought up what they delicately called the "problem" of Coleridge's unattributed takings. In their bibliography of "the long history of the discussion of Coleridge's 'plagiarisms,'" Fruman hardly figures with much prominence, but it is worth noting that Ferrier is called "vindictive" and that Sara Coleridge, who after her father's death handwringingly edited his work, is praised for conscientiousness: "The editors of the present edition have great admiration for her courage in trying to meet this problem. She is on occasion forgivably a little vague judged by modern standards of editing."*

One gets the feeling that Bate and Engell, despite some use of parallel columns in their text, would rather not raise the matter at all ("there was no alternative except to pursue this subject"); once on to it, they seem to find some relief in the double-blind defense of sloppy notetaking and hasty composition, the standard plea for mercy.

> Coleridge's use of German books and his own marginalia in them was often so fluid and intertwined — a sentence here, then two or three sentences elsewhere — that our experience repeatedly confirmed what McFarland calls the "mosaic" form of composition in Coleridge. There would be a passage from, say, Maass or Schelling, and then — before going on — he would leap ahead, or he would follow up sources they used, or he would suddenly intermix still other sources or his own marginal notes.

And, questions of method aside, the potentially offending matter is whittled down: "A maximum of a quarter of the total material in the philosophical chapters is used without citing its source; if we put aside the category of summary, then just over one-fifth of the pages covered by these chapters is either translated or paraphrased."

The fact that Coleridge was a thief is found to be neither disgusting nor diminishing but — three times, on three different pages — "fascinating," just as the "divine ventriloquism" passage is part of an "extraordinary paragraph" showing how "the matter is important and troubling to Coleridge." Bate and Engell claim to "present the facts, without the rhetoric of either defence or accusation," but their whole tone is one of advocacy on behalf of a client, tsk-tsking in its sense of the plaintiff's pettiness. Coleridge's learning is made more remarkable than his light-fingeredness, and the creativity of his method is stressed: "We are

---

*Sterne's daughter Lydia was far less Cordelian in her posthumous attentions to her father's letters. She was willing both to forge and bowdlerize in her efforts to realize a profit from her edition.

not dealing — or at least not dealing primarily — with orderly blocks of verbatim translation, but something more like a chemical compound." Bate and Engell give Coleridge credit for citing, as if it were a strenuous feat, the *titles* of "*every work* of Schelling with which there are stong verbal similarities or outright questions of plagiarism for the *Biographia*."

Coleridge's psychology is indeed fascinating, but perhaps not so much as our unwillingness to bring the police into the pantheon. Or as Fruman, the most aggressive detective, put it: "That most scholars still maintain that Coleridge had no deliberate wish to deny his intellectual obligations to Schelling is surely one of the marvels of literary history."

Addicted not to opium but to orchids and beer, the rotund Nero Wolfe (advertised as the "world's most brilliant detective" on the paperback versions of the mysteries he solves) lives a fictional life as regulated as Coleridge's was disorderly. From his West 35th Street townhouse he cogitates about crime between lengthy cultivations of his plants and appetite, delegating the messier aspects of detection to a staff of faithful retainers. In the spring of 1959 he is approached by the Joint Committee on Plagiarism of the National Association of Authors and Dramatists and the Book Publishers of America. Mr. Philip Harvey, a novelist, explains to him that although writers and publishers are frequently adversaries, the "interests of slave and master often jibe." Both of them can get into trouble for trafficking in stolen goods, and surely it's not good for anyone if authors are blackmailed out of their royalties by false charges of plagiarism. What Wolfe is assigned to figure out is the identity of the person behind a string of phony claims against moderately successful authors. Several of them in *Plot It Yourself* have gotten letters charging that their works were based on manuscripts the claimant sent them a long time ago with a request for criticism and advice. The kicker is that the blackmailer manages to plant a back-dated manuscript, similar to the one the author published, on the author's premises, thereby establishing the author's "guilt."

Before Wolfe can solve things a number of people are amusingly killed; so much for the ennobling effects of association with the written word. But throughout the mayhem his most important forensic evidence is "internal" to the manuscript, not the corpse: "diction, syntax, paragraphing." Especially the last: "A clever man might successfully disguise every element of his style but one — the paragraphing." A dubious, if entertaining, notion. Still, it helps Wolfe discover who wrote what and be rid of a case so frustrating to him that, as a kind of mortification, he gives up beer until he solves it.

The psychology of the perpetrator — Amy Wynn, mild-mannered author of *Knock at My Door* — proves curiously Coleridgean once she's exposed. She is desperate to have Wolfe excoriate her for errors in front of all the other principals: "You can't say I didn't make any mistakes. You ought to say I didn't do anything right. Did I?" Wolfe ends up complimenting her for performing "prodigies of sagacity and finesse without knowing it. Not surely by inadvertence; it must be that your singular faculties operate below the level of consciousness — or above it." And yet she's really guilty not of plagiarism but of "plagiarism upside down" — its unfair imputation.

Plagiarism, like certain species of sexual activity, is a blackmailer's dream. In *Plot It Yourself*, Wolfe's trusted gumshoe Archie Goodwin interviews a literary agent and gathers "from his tone that anyone who made a plagiarism claim was a louse." Indeed, the potential for false accusation is unpleasant enough to turn as strong a stomach as Nero Wolfe's.

Wolfe's creator, Rex Stout, was for a long time president of the Authors' League. The writer Robert Goldsborough continues, with the permission of Stout's estate, to produce novels constructed around the large and profitable literary remains of Nero Wolfe. The up-and-up arrangement was consistent with decades of Stout's activity on behalf of expanded copyright protections for authors that began with his listening to Booth Tarkington and Mark Twain complain about the situation in 1909, and continued through his appearances before congressional committees in support of the revised copyright law President Ford signed in 1976.

The history of copyrigh٠ actually has more to do with piracy than plagiarism. Laws are far more useful in protecting authors against wholesale printings of their books by publishers with no rights to them than they are in stopping the dead-of-night authorial theft of a passage here and a paragraph there. Still, plagiarism and copyright are linked, not only in the minds of readers and authors but in history as well, since it was during the same century when the cry against plagiarism became quite loud that the first English copyright statutes were enacted. Some of the same economic factors (authors living by pens instead of patrons) and aesthetic ones (the new premium on originality) led to the concept of literary property as being both imaginative and financial capital.

The Statute of Anne, which took effect in 1710, was probably more in the interest of booksellers than individual authors, but it established registered writing as something that couldn't be printed by anyone with a press: the booksellers (who were also the publishers) could no longer print one another's wares at will. Enormous questions were left unanswered by the act, and none of them was more troublesome than whether protection should be extended in perpetuity. The case of *Donaldson v. Becket* (1774), in which a Scottish lawyer named James Boswell supported the winning side, deemed that there was no perpetual copyright, but during the nineteenth century the twenty-one years of protection offered by the Statute of Anne was lengthened to forty-two. (Macaulay argued against perpetuity; Carlyle thundered in support of sixty years.) Any unpublished work remains protected by common law for as long as it remains unpublished; once it sees print the law must offer, and limit, the terms of protection, and only after a specific application for such protection is made.

The copyright wars of the nineteenth century evolved from civil into international ones. American piracy of British work was particularly notorious. Everyone has heard the stories of American readers flocking to the piers to get the latest installment of Dickens and learn whether the uncopyrighted Little Nell still lived. On his American tour in 1842, Dickens himself begged his audience "leave to whisper in [its] ear two words, International Copyright," trying not to appear self-interested as he made his reasonable pitch:

> I hope the time is not far distant when [your writers], in America,
> will receive of right some substantial profit and return in England
> from their labours; and when we, in England, shall receive some

substantial profit and return from ours. Pray do not misunder-
stand me. Securing for myself from day to day means of an hon-
ourable subsistence, I would rather have the affectionate regard
of my fellow men, than I would have heaps and mines of gold.

It would not be until 1891 that America offered the sort of
protection Dickens was seeking, and in many ways she remained
an international oddity for over a hundred years; only in 1988
did the Senate vote to allow American participation in the Berne
Convention on international copyright that was drawn up in
1886.

In his book *From Copyright to Copperfield*, Alexander Welsh
writes about how Dickens became, in his imagination, "a knight
errant battling for Europe." As the nineteenth century reached
its midpoint, he was not the only crusader on the field. By 1852
the French had granted protection to all written works wherever
they had been written, and it struck the esteemed British writer
Charles Reade that his countrymen were disgracefully retro-
grade in the way *they* continued to pirate works made in France,
especially plays. He now had a great cause to fight for: getting
England to live up to the ethics of her traditional enemy across
the Channel. Welsh shows Dickens as so worried by the possibility
of being seen as selfish that he was ready "to realize subjectively"
the character who would become a dictionary synonym for hy-
pocrisy: Pecksniff. Charles Reade felt no such worries, even
though the charge he might have feared being leveled against
himself was considerably more severe than financial self-interest.
Reade, the greatest champion of international copyright among
English writers of his day, was also one of Victorian England's
most belligerent plagiarists.

2

A Good Reade:
Malfeasance and *Mlle. de Malepeire*

A thief is a man; and a man's life is like those geographical fragments children learn "the contiguous countries" by. The pieces are a puzzle; but put them together carefully, and lo! they are a map.

— Charles Reade, Introductory to
The Autobiography of a Thief

THE RESTORED downtown of Portland, Oregon, is an increasingly lovely place these days, but the city still gets more than its share of rainy afternoons. One imagines that where its handsome library, the Multnomah County Public, is concerned, this is good for business. Someone caught without an umbrella will come in to browse, get to feeling dreamy in the stacks and take down from the shelf a copy of, say, Coleridge's poems, with an eye toward rereading "Kubla Khan." A little later, noticing through a window that the showers have stopped and the sun is trying to break through, he may decide to charge out the book at the circulation desk and continue his travels through Xanadu while seated on one of the commemorative stone benches lining the south side of the library on Southwest Taylor Street. He'll select the bench inscribed for the Victorian novelist Charles Reade, trying to remember, as he wipes it dry, if it was Reade who wrote *The Water Babies* . . . oh, no, that was Charles Kingsley.

As the sky turns unexpectedly sunny, he will realize that this is the wrong afternoon after all for "Kubla Khan" and will get up to walk back toward Main Street. Passing the bench next to Reade's, one named for George Borrow (now what did *he* write?), the word-minded refugee from the rain will smile: READE next to BORROW. Some sort of subliminal advertising for the library by whoever, long ago, designated the benches?

Perhaps. But if the patron has made a mental note to remedy his ignorance of Charles Reade, he'll find out, not long after he begins investigating his career, that there is another good, though unintended, reason for Reade's civic monument to sit beside Borrow's: Charles Reade's attitude toward literary borrowing was an awfully complicated and paradoxical one. Like the thundering evangelist who dallies with the devil, he managed in one pugilistic lifetime to be both a loud champion of international copyright and a shameless smuggler of work penned on the other side of the English Channel.

Before going any further with his story, I should make plain that this chapter got its start when one summer morning I discovered William S. Walsh's *Handy-Book of Literary Curiosities* (1892), not in the Multnomah County Public Library but at the Mid-Manhattan, at the corner of Fifth Avenue and 40th Street in New York City. On page 894, Walsh writes: "The compiler of an adequate 'Curiosities of Plagiarism' would have to devote a special chapter to the Protean adventures of a novelette ["Mlle. de Malepierre"] by Mme. Charles Reybaud." It seems, says Walsh, that a story called "The Picture in My Uncle's Dining-Room," published by Charles Reade in 1883, was not exactly his own. For someone beginning a book on this subject, here was a gift horse smiling so widely that there was no question of not looking into its mouth.*

Charles Reade was born in Oxfordshire, the eleventh child of a modestly fixed country squire, on June 8, 1814. As the latter-day

---

*As it happens, Mr. Walsh made a few mistakes in rendering even these few bits of fact. Reade's story was called, simply, "The Picture," and came out not in 1883 but 1884; and Malepierre was really spelled, in the original, Malepeire. But, given the chock-a-block nature of the gold mine that is the *Handy-Book*, they are surely understandable. Whatever its flaws, the entry is more than enough to get one going — to the 823 (Dewey Decimal) shelves of the library.

editor of his plays, Michael Hammet (apparently forgetting about Reade's beloved sister, Julia), explains: "To be born a tenth son was to be born without capital, for there were elder sons aplenty to live from his father's estate. Moreover, it was to be born into a large world, his eldest brothers so remote that he never met them."* Reade would eventually have to make his own way, and although his heart would set upon writing novels and plays, his career as an author would get off to a very late start — would be a second one, really — during and after a long one in academics.

Reade took a third in "greats" at Magdalen College, Oxford, in 1835, and became a probationary fellow the same year. Though quite without academic temperament and ambition, he would serve Magdalen over the years as junior dean of arts, bursar and vice president. And while he studied law and was called to the bar, he never really practiced it, distracted as he was by dreams of literary success and such quixotic ventures as selling imported violins and operating a herring fishery in Scotland. His fellowship required him to be celibate (a condition he would decry in *The Cloister and the Hearth* — the novel our Portland browser was confusing with *The Water Babies*), but he would in time set up house in London with Mrs. Laura Seymour, the actress.

Success in the theater was his first literary goal, and in 1851, the year Reade turned thirty-seven, his first play, *The Ladies' Battle,* was produced at London's Olympia Theatre. It was "his" play only insofar as he adapted it from the French of Augustin Eugène Scribe and Ernest Legouvé.† The importation and Anglicizing of "well-made plays" from France kept British theatrical managers rich, and native British drama in the doldrums, for much of the nineteenth century. Why should the managers pay for home-grown creativity when there were all these popular Parisian farces and melodramas to bring over for free? Just change "Fifi" and "Jean" to "Effie" and "Jack."

A loophole in an 1851 copyright agreement between England and France allowed for such piracy, and securing overdue protection for French dramatists became a crusade for Charles

---

*The Biographical Notes to Hammet's edition of the plays are plagiarized item for item from the Summary of Events appended to Malcolm Elwin's biography of Reade.

†See page 125 for Legouvé's own thoughts on literary borrowing.

Reade, an apparently magnanimous polemical sideline he pursued even as he was having his own overdue literary launching via dramatic adaptation and collaboration. Shortly after *The Ladies' Battle* opened, he began work on *Masks and Faces* with the author Tom Taylor.

But Reade wanted fame as the original and sole author of plays and books. In 1852 he finished writing *Gold,* a melodrama of greed in the Australian mining camps, full of exotically realistic stage detail. "I want to show people that, though I adapt French pieces, I can invent too, if I choose to take the trouble. And it is a trouble to me, I confess." *Gold,* which had some success on the stage, would reappear as a novel in 1856 under Reade's new title for it: *It Is Never Too Late to Mend.* It was as a novelist, in fact, that Reade was destined to secure real fame, the kind that makes for inscribed municipal benches in places like Portland. A natural-born fighter on any front he could find, Reade would become famous with novels protesting one corrupt institution after another (brutal prisons, venal mental asylums, hypocritical churches), books that sometimes make Dickens, whom Reade worshiped, seem a social quietist.

During his lifetime Reade attracted admirers and enemies equally fervent; since his death, biographers and critics have had feelings just as strong and polar. Malcolm Elwin's 1931 study admired Reade's titanic energies:

> Who can refrain from marvelling at the amazing determination of the man? Solitary, wayward, naturally of a friendly and affectionate nature yet without the comfort of encouragement of any sympathy, who can wonder that he developed a splenetic egotism and became renowned for eccentricity? During the third and most of the fourth decade of his life, when most men are sowing wild oats or laying the tangible foundations of a career, the fire of a secret ambition was smouldering in Reade's heart.

Thirty years later, Professor Wayne Burns, in a book called *Charles Reade: A Study in Victorian Authorship,* made no attempt to conceal his distaste for his subject; indeed, he expressed it with a contemptuous vigor he probably acquired from immersion in the works of Charles Reade himself:

> The personal philosophy which he brought to fiction was made up of scraps from the ragbag of Evangelicism, Toryism, and Ben-

thamism, patched up by the Baconian method to clothe the emotional nakedness of a proud, lonely, and thwarted egotist — a Benthamitic rebel who was yet a son of Mrs. Reade and Tory-Evangelical Ipsden. . . . Self-delusion cannot be carried much further without becoming psychopathic.

Making up for his late start took nerve, stamina and, above all, a system. If Reade was to make his name in the great Victorian age of realistic fiction, he would have to make sure he let slip no bits of life that could be smelted into literature. It was in order to capture everything he could of that most industrious of eras that he set up a series of notebooks, huge heavy volumes into which he poured and pasted clippings, ideas, reviews, rebuttals, memoranda and *facts*. To Reade it was all ore that he could eventually alchemize into plays and novels. Like Coleridge, a compulsive annotator of all he read, Reade went so far as to index these immense gatherings of potentially useful knowledge. From the "List of Subjects Entered as headings in my various guard books and solid digests," the ones beginning with the letter *F* give the reader a sense not only of Reade's energy but of the peculiar proclivities of his inquiring mind:

> F.   Fabulae verae/ Faces/ Facts/ Fagging/ Famous Frauds/ Fallacies/ Fashionable Revelations/ FOEDA OLIGARCHIA or the deeds and words of the Trades Unions/ Fathers/ Female Writers/ Fiction, unprofessional/ Figures/ Finance/ Fires/ Ladies on fire, Dancers on fire, Houses, Prisons, Ships, Railways, etc./ Flint Jack/ Floods/ Foemina Vera, or Woman as she is Foemina Ficta, or Woman as she is drawn by writers/ Forgery/ Foul Play/ Fortune, its vicissitudes/ Foundling Hospital/ Funerals/ Fures generosi.

In 1934 Professor Emerson Grant Sutcliffe, the notebooks' chief scholar, asserted Reade's "position as the earliest deliberately and thoroughly documentary novelist." No less a historian of English fiction than Ernest A. Baker declared, in volume VII of *The History of the English Novel*, that "Charles Reade's note-books are as famous as Zola's." Any inquiry into any part of Reade's busy writing life will eventually bring one to them.

He had enough genius, passion, generosity and unpleasantness to have provided Dickens with a dozen or more characters, all of them versions of Reade himself. In his bombastic satisfaction with his own success, he resembles no one so much as Mr. Bounderby in *Hard Times,* and in his loud preaching of the gospel of facts, he becomes an authorial incarnation of the same novel's Thomas Gradgrind (Facts — "The One Thing Needful"). The preface to *A Simpleton* has Reade blustering: "All fiction, worth a button, is founded on facts. . . . I rarely write a novel without milking about two hundred heterogeneous cows into my pail."

Most novelists perform the same chore less loudly on a smaller herd. In the preface to *Slow Learner,* a volume of his early stories, Thomas Pynchon discusses his use of Baedeker's 1899 guide to Egypt in his own 1959 story "Under the Rose": "Could Willy Sutton rob a safe? Loot the Baedeker I did, all the details of a time and place I had never been to, right down to the names of the diplomatic corps. Who'd make up a name like Khevenhüller-Metsch? Lest others become as enchanted as I was and have continued to be with this technique, let me point out that it is a lousy way to go about writing a story." Which is to say that research is never a substitute for what Pynchon calls "some grounding in human reality." He declares literary theft a "fascinating topic. . . . As in the penal code, there are degrees. These range from plagiarism down to only being derivative, but all are forms of wrong procedure."

Surely not. Where would Shakespeare have been without Holinshed and Plutarch? The truth is that we expect our writers, especially our "historical" novelists and playwrights, to do a little boning up. We then expect them to make sense and life of their researches in words of their own. Sometimes they will and sometimes they won't. When we see how closely Shakespeare followed the way Enobarbus's description of Cleopatra's barge is rendered in North's translation of Plutarch, we're merely intrigued or amused. Take a writer not quite so beyond criticism, and we tend, upon spotting historical lumps in the narrative gravy, to object. In reviewing Gore Vidal's *Lincoln,* Joyce Carol Oates thought the novel would be

> controversial, since it so closely follows historical studies . . . and imposes no unusual novelistic structure or language on its material. (The surprisingly brief scene in which Booth kills Lincoln, for instance, is very similar to the page or two devoted to the episode in Stephen B. Oates's new "Abraham Lincoln: The Man

Behind the Myths," in itself a summary and compilation of research done by Louis J. Weichmann, George S. Bryan, Thomas
Reed Turner and other professional historians.)

In the *Simpleton* preface Reade acknowledged his own debt to
Boyle's South African travel book and recommended the original
to his own readers: "Mr. Boyle has a painter's eye and a writer's
pen, and if the African scenes in 'A Simpleton' please my readers,
I hope they will go to the fountain-head where they will find
many more." This seems generous enough until one remembers
that Reade is only taking up the matter at all because it "has lately
been objected to me, in studiously courteous terms of course,
that I borrow from other books, and am a Plagiarist." As always,
he is glad for the chance to throw some punches, taking this
opportunity to defend his fact-based fiction with the assertion
that "it does not matter one straw whether the facts are taken
from personal experience, hearsay, or printed books; only those
books must not be works of fiction."

One must wonder, however: when one is milking two hundred
cows per book, can one really homogenize every pailful of research with one's own creamy, original fictive prose? And if one
is so accustomed to setting one's milk stool where one wants, how
long will it be before one sets it beneath one of those forbidden
"works of fiction" — and before one makes off with not just the
milk but a whole slaughtered carcass?

In Reade's story "The Autobiography of a Thief," the character Thomas Robinson tells the reader, "It was never my way to
remain at the bottom of any business that I found worth study-
ing." As Reade continued his assault on the theater, he fattened
the notebooks and opened a second front, on the novel. *Christie
Johnstone*, which, like *Gold*, first saw life as a play, became his first
full-length work of fiction to be published, in 1853. From this
Scottish romance with social overtones, Reade went on to produce such rounds of reforming fisticuffs as *It Is Never Too Late to
Mend, Hard Cash, Foul Play, Griffith Gaunt, Put Yourself in His Place,
A Terrible Temptation* and *A Woman-Hater*. As the Edwardian critic
William Dawson noted, Reade's background as a dramatist probably hurt his fulfillment as a novelist: "He works too palpably
towards a crisis; he is always ringing the curtain down upon a
tableau."

Conspicuously different from the social-minded shelf of fiction he produced was his lengthy historical novel, *The Cloister and the Hearth* (1861), a huge medieval romance based on the life of Erasmus's father, much admired by Oscar Wilde and celebrated in a passage from "The Decay of Lying" that took an aesthete's dim view of the rest of Reade's work:

> He wrote one beautiful book, *The Cloister and the Hearth* . . . and wasted the rest of his life in a foolish attempt to be modern, to draw public attention to the state of our convict prisons, and the management of our private lunatic asylums. . . . Charles Reade, an artist, a scholar, a man with a true sense of beauty, raging and roaring over the abuses of contemporary life like a common pamphleteer or a sensational journalist, is really a sight for the angels to weep over.

Disagreeing with Wilde, George Orwell could, a half century later, find Reade's much-researched fiction to be full of "the charm of useless knowledge . . . vast stocks of disconnected information" no longer relevant, if they ever were, to those sorts of atrociousness they sought to alleviate. But like other critics old and new, Orwell credits Reade with "a lively narrative gift."

His storytelling energies were such, in fact, that he could easily have told many other authors' tales faster than they could tell them themselves. Whether he was always, as Orwell called him, "a wonderful contriver of plots," is a question open to some debate.

In 1854, while Reade was still finding his feet as a novelist, Mme. Charles Reybaud was already possessed of the security that comes with being an old hand. The fifty-two-year-old author had for a long time occupied an honorable niche in French political and literary life. Her twenty-second work of fiction, the one that would generally be considered her masterpiece, a little novel of the *ancien régime* called *Mlle. de Malepeire,* was being serialized in the prestigious *Revue des Deux Mondes.* The daughter of a liberal doctor, Fanny-Henriette Arnaud was born in Aix in 1802. Her youthful friends included the future French premier Adolphe Thiers.* She married Joseph-Charles Reybaud, editor in chief

*See footnote on page 99.

of *Constitutionnel;* his brother Louis Reybaud was a key player in the 1848 revolution, a liberal journalist, a political economist and a satirical novelist on top of all that.

Most of Mme. Reybaud's many novels were eponymous romances (*Fabiana, Thérésa, Géraldine, Les Deux Marguerites*) drawing on her own knowledge of convent life and Provençal manners and on tales she had heard of the prerevolutionary world that exploded in the decade before she was born. She is thought to have acquired the knack for novel-writing fortuitously: a friend of hers went to live in Spain, so she decided to study the language and then to translate Spanish romances. This assiduous, if indirect, way of learning her craft eventually gave steady rewards. From the time she was in her mid-twenties hardly a year went by without a reliable new Reybaud finding its way into the *librairies* and *bibliothèques.* Her work inspired protective, even cooing, criticism at home and abroad.

It is difficult to find a nasty word about her in mid-nineteenth-century literary reviews. Emile Montégut, in *Revue des Deux Mondes,* found her to be *"cette femme spirituelle et sensée,"* whose gifts for storytelling seemed to come from the oral tradition and whose sympathy for the displaced aristocrats was remarkable, considering the reformists she ran and wrote with. In some respects, however, not so remarkable: as Montégut rightly pointed out, her narratives are tales of love, unconcerned with philosophical systems and social problems; her gift for storytelling and her talent for accumulating evocative detail were natural endowments oblivious of the socially useful fiction coming to dominate the century. Reade's notebooks, filled with clipped abuses and waiting causes, would have been a mystery to her.

Her work offered consolation to a knowledgeable anonymous critic writing in the *Dublin University Magazine,* someone who looked at the recent greatness of French literature (Hugo, Dumas, Balzac, Mérimée, Sand) and found it giving in to early death and discouragement. At least one dependably "graceful" ornament remained, however — Mme. Charles Reybaud, whose stories were admirably free from "that licence and indelicacy which stain the pages of many French romance-writers of the present day." Not just pure, either; powerful and plausible, too. "One of her characteristics," the Dublin critic went on, "is the peculiar art with which she handles improbable incidents, so as to make the reader temporarily forget their improbability."

Indeed, *Mlle. de Malepeire* has the elegant feel of a long fairy tale: the acceptably wild reversal of an already unlikely event; the emotional careenings between extreme horror and perfect peace. It begins with a narrator recollecting his arrival thirty years before (in 1822, when he was seventeen) at the Provençal house of his kindly old uncle, Dom Gérusac. His settling in is accomplished with the assistance of an old servant named Marian, whose wizened face and "sour temper" are underlined just enough to make the careful reader wonder if the emphasis is given just to highlight the household atmosphere or to drop a clue. (And why doesn't she want to answer the nephew's questions about the old château destroyed in the long-ago Revolution? Hmmmmm.)

The emotionally susceptible narrator actually pays most of his attention to a pastel "rather faded by time" over his uncle's mantel mirror, an oval-shaped representation of "a woman of the most dazzling beauty, in all the splendor of her youth; her dress was something in the style of a shepherdess of Watteau." Dom Gérusac had purchased the portrait — for its frame — in the shop of an old Jew. The young nephew's fascination with the pastel face is soon further stimulated by the arrival of the Marquis de Champaubert, an old friend of the uncle's, both of them aristocratic survivors of some nasty knocks during the Revolution. The marquis begins a long tale, and here the book starts to resemble one of Conrad's Marlowe novels, the tirelessly syntactical narrative filter holding forth all evening and forcing the bulk of the volume into quotation marks. His story concerns the woman in the pastel, whom he says he recognizes as Mlle. Marie de Malepeire.

In the summer of 1789 she is living in the big local château with her parents, the counterrevolutionary baron and the ennui-ridden, piquet-playing baroness. The marquis has arrived chez Malepeire to play the role of suitor in a more or less arranged marriage, and the mademoiselle's coldness only seems to inflame his immediately felt ardor: "I must have appeared a perfect blockhead all that evening, when I felt for the first time that I was desperately in love." It is he who makes the pastel of the *"belle indifférente."*

The mademoiselle is entirely unsmitten, preferring as she does the subversive sentiments of Rousseau's *Nouvelle Héloïse* and the noble-savage attentions of the local wrestling champion, François Pinatel, to whom she awards an embroidered victory scarf on the day of the village games — the same day, in fact, that her unwanted engagement is announced in church. Things happen fast in these parts; on that very evening the peasants march on the château with torches. The baron, baroness and marquis go into the mademoiselle's bedroom to warn her of the approaching rabble. Alas, they find her there in the arms of Pinatel. The baron fires his gun and a bullet grazes the wrestler's hair; he flees; the mademoiselle soon follows. As the poor devastated marquis says, after out-Werthering Werther in expressions of loss, "What a night!"

Here the marquis's story leaves off. All he has left to note is that, afterward, he joined his exiled uncle in Turin, went on to England in 1792 and now serves as an ambassador in the Restoration government of Louis XVIII. The painful memory of the lost mademoiselle has kept him from ever marrying. The young narrator (Dom Gérusac's nephew, one will remember) hears the story in a wide-eyed way that marks him as the emotional heir to the once-young marquis: "My heart was inflated with a jealous indignation. I did not take my eyes off the portrait."

So what ever happened to Mlle. Marie de Malepeire? Fortunately, even three decades later things still happen with opportune quickness in this portion of upper Provence. The next visitor to Dom Gérusac's parlor is an unexpected one, the longtime curate of Malepeire, the Abbé Lambert, driven indoors by stormy weather. In response to questions by the marquis, this new narrative filter talks about his first days in the area. It soon turns out that he knows what happened to the mademoiselle. " 'You know her? You know where she ended her miserable life?' interrupted the Marquis in an agitated manner."

The curate tells the tale of the class-crossed young Pinatels following their elopement. They went to live with the wrestler's widowed mother, who disapproved of the idea of such a marriage and scorned her new daughter-in-law's lack of domestic skills: " 'It is enough to make anyone laugh to see a person of your age who does not even know how to boil the pot over the fire.' " We are now approaching "the sinister days of the Revolution." The mademoiselle is miserable, sullen and lonely; her parents are dead (the château has been pillaged); and Pinatel himself has turned out to be more like Stanley Kowalski than Man Friday ("with a coarse laugh . . . he passed his hand across his stomach"). He is a lazy drunk who gambles away the money his thrifty peasant mother gives him. Inevitably, he strikes his aristocratic wife, and reverting to blue-blood type, she cuts his throat, thereby getting herself arrested and imprisoned. The curate says he never knew until tonight that Dom Gérusac's pastel was of the wretched woman he once tried to comfort.

Back in the present, everyone's tender sensibilities are inflamed. The aging marquis wants to track the mademoiselle down and make sure she is comfortable in what must be her final days. The primary narrator — Dom Gérusac's young nephew — is "still desperately in love" with the "beautiful and lost creature" and can only admire the pluck with which she dispatched her revolting *amant de la boue*.

At this point Marian, Dom Gérusac's old crone of a servant, decides to start dying, and quicker than one can say *coup de théâtre*, we learn that she, of course, is Marie de Malepeire Pinatel. The nephew-narrator: " 'Ah! Marian! 'twas she!' cried I, with horror. The Abbé Lambert and my uncle leaned against the table, with their hands joined; I thought they prayed." Fifteen years later, having been made Dom Gérusac's heir, he claims the picture: "The mice had nibbled the canvas somewhat; and the little finger, which had so shocked my good uncle, had disappeared. I had the pretty pastel renewed, and to-day it figures honorably in my collection of portraits."

When M. Montégut, writing of Mme. Reybaud in the *Revue des Deux Mondes* several years after *Mlle. de Malepeire* ran there, says that she doesn't exaggerate the speech and psyches of her characters ("*Ses héros traversent des aventures exceptionnelles, mais ils parlent et pensent comme tout le monde*"), he is telling an appreciative whopper. And one can hardly agree with his effusive declaration that this novel breaks new emotional ground, that it is so psychologically original as to constitute "*un chapitre inédit du grand livre qui est toujours en cours de publication*." More than anything else,

Mlle. de Malepeire is a terrifically good story. In fact, considered
as anything else, it's pretty risible, but on a pure storytelling basis
one is willing to credit Montégut's designation of it as the author's
chef d'oeuvre. It has drama to spare, enough to make one wonder
if Mme. Reybaud wasn't a little hasty in abandoning the play-
writing ambitions Montégut tells us she had. He says it's a good
thing she never really tried, because Frenchmen from south of
Paris never make it in the theater. Well, *chacun à sa théorie*. Maybe
it is a good thing she didn't risk her efforts there — one thinks
of the head-butting natural-born novelists like Henry James and,
for a while, Charles Reade inflicted on themselves by trying to
succeed at the box office.

Mme. Reybaud was probably able to settle without too much
disappointment for the less clamorous distinction accorded the
popular novelist. Montégut assures us that, like most of her
heroes and heroines, she was *"modeste, patiente, sachant prendre la
vie comme elle se presente."* She would probably have declined the
honor paid her by the English-ruled Irish critic, who specifically
excluded her from an irony he noted in the new copyright law
of 1851 as it applied to her homeland's creative production:

> French literature has rarely been in so depressed a state as at the
> present moment. We speak with reference to its merits, not to its
> commercial prosperity, which has probably received a fillip from
> the recent copyright treaty with this country. But it may almost
> be said that France has obtained protection when she had no
> longer anything to protect.

Merci beaucoup, one imagines Madame replying, her convent-
trained eyes modestly downcast, at being let off the hook of this
Irish barb, and thinking that, really, there wasn't much in this
clever tale she'd produced that any of the day's reform-minded,
blue-book-reading English novelists would consider good pickings.

And certainly not someone just hitting a loud fictional stride.
But years pass; powers fail; temptations arise; compulsions grow.
The young nephew of *Mlle. de Malepeire* waited fifteen years
before deciding to claim his picture, and Charles Reade would
wait nearly twice as long before dusting off Mme. Reybaud's
novelette with his own pen. M. Montégut tells us that she had

the equanimity to take *"le vent comme il souffle,"* but she would never in any case feel the ill wind of Reade's plunder. By the time he got to her she would be gone and largely forgotten by English readers. The time of her demise, 1871, near the end of the Franco-Prussian War, may have accelerated her disappearance from British memories, according to a writer for the *Temple Bar* in 1894:

> The present writer, whilst travelling in France during the "Débâcle," saw her death in a French newspaper. In a railway station crowded with flocks and with herds that were being packed to Paris for the siege, we read: "Madame Charles Reybaud est morte" — this was all.

Throughout his rise as both novelist and playwright, Reade, during the 1850s, went about making himself famous in a third identity: defender of authors and champion of international copyright reform. In 1860 he published *The Eighth Commandment*, a many-decibeled presentation of Charles Reade's crusade and Charles Reade's virtues.* The International Copyright Act of 1851 was a great thing, he declares, an overdue "advance of a Briton's literary property towards the security and sanctity that hedge his house, hovel, haystack, and dunghill." But it left one "Satanic" proviso permitting the continued theft of French plays for production in English theaters. Before losing himself in polemical frenzy, Reade, the trained lawyer, offers a lucid explanation of the loophole:

> The proviso runs thus: *It is understood that the protection stipulated by the present article is not intended to prohibit fair imitations, or adaptations of dramatic works to the stage in England and France respectively, but is only meant to prevent piratical translations.*
>
>   "Adaptation" is an English word, and represents an English practice of two hundred years. "Appropriation," in the French version of the statute, is an attempt to translate this word, and an unsuccessful one. So is "imitations faites de bonne foi" an attempt to render that other piece of "thieves' Latin" into honest French: but the attempt has failed, and the law stands worded somewhat differently in the two languages. So that a dramatic inventor might

---

*The American publishers of *The Eighth Commandment* were Ticknor & Fields, who, unabashed by irony, bring you the volume you hold in your hands.

win in France a suit versus imitatorem that he would lose in England, and the contradictory verdicts rest on the same sentence of the same statute.

Before 1851, the traffic in stolen goods was in several genres and two directions. The French stole English novels, and the English, including Reade, stole French plays. Admitting his own "part under this unjust equity," Reade lists five French works he tinkered with and translated in years prior to the treaty, among them "Village Tale," an adaptation of George Sand's "Claudie." But now that fair is fair, he is willing to pay for French plays, even as his British colleagues in the theater just crow about the free ride they can take on the badly put proviso.

Reade could be persuasive about most things to which he put his pen, and *The Eighth Commandment* is no exception, aside from those long stretches of ranting where the rhetoric is so weird that it must be judged as not just infelicitous but psychologically suspect, too. Recalling his campaign to close the loophole, he roars: "In a nation of twenty millions I was alone. I felt like a solitary camel, thirsting in Zahara for a drop of water; there are times when one drop of sympathy is as precious, and comes not to the parched heart."

Why was Reade so lusty in his assertion of the foreign playwright's entitlement? His answer would have been his own largeness of (albeit parched) heart, and he may have been half right. As Michael Hammet, the modern editor of his plays, puts it: "It was not to his advantage to attempt to preserve the rights of French authors, except to the extent that it would reinforce a general principle from the adoption of which he might benefit in the long run. In fact it was a matter of legal principle to him, and perhaps more than a legal principle, a trait of character." But what trait? Rectitude? Perhaps. But perhaps something else — a compulsion he tried to muffle under the loud beatings of that sleeve-worn heart.*

In *The Eighth Commandment* Reade asks: "Out of every twenty adapters how many are ever heard of in letters except when they bray in a Frenchman's skin? Three? Certainly not: two at the

---

*Norman Fruman on Coleridge: "Statements concerning intellectual integrity frequently occur in the vicinity of unacknowledged borrowings."

very outside." It sounds as if the right answer is one, and there is scarcely room for doubt about who it is he has in mind. He had genius, he was sure; and with genius goes license, the license to do things you wouldn't let others do, because you know they would do them badly, or for the wrong reason. But you yourself are another matter, someone whose finer motives you're convinced of; you've heard yourself speak of them, after all; speak of them often and well. It's other people who are, clearly, the problem.

The eighth commandment in Protestant England is, of course, "Thou shalt not steal." But in a Catholic country, say France, the Decalogue is differently enumerated, and number eight, just before injunctions against coveting your neighbor's wife and goods, is "Thou shalt not bear false witness against thy neighbor." Which is to say, you shouldn't lie about others. The tablets seem to let it go without saying that you oughtn't lie to yourself — especially about things you keep accusing the neighbors of.

Late in the 1860s Reade was charged by journalists with copying portions of his novel *Foul Play* (which concerns forgery) from a French play entitled *Le Portefeuille Rouge*. To exculpate himself from the accusations carried in parallel columns, he blamed his critics for perpetrating a "Sham Sample Swindle," and insisted that he "never saw *Le Portefeuille Rouge* until after the [accusing] article in the *Mask* appeared." Perhaps the surest proof that he was telling the truth in this instance lies in his exoneration by Professor Burns, the latter-day scholar with the warts-and-not-much-else approach to his subject. His disappointment evident, Burns sighs: "For once, it would seem Reade was guiltless."

But in his prime there were always enough other accusations of light-fingeredness to make Reade — the author's friend, the champion of copyright — a bizarrely ironic character. The year 1872 brought two of them. On March 7, Reade sent to Trollope, who had gone to Australia, the news that he, Reade, had taken it upon himself to dramatize Trollope's just-published novel, *Ralph the Heir,* and would be generously giving the bard of Barchester co-authorship credit:

> Dear Trollope, I have been so delighted with "Ralph the Heir"
> that I have dramatized the story, — in three Acts. Though the
> law, as I know to my cost, gives any one the right to dramatize a

novelist's story, I would not have taken this liberty without consulting you if you had been accessible. Having done it, I now propose to give the inventor that just honour, which has too often been denied him in theatrical announcements.

Trollope was less than pleased. A decade later, in his *Autobiography*, he was still shaking his head: "There is no writer of the present day who has so much puzzled me by his eccentricities, impracticabilities, and capabilities as Charles Reade. I look upon him as endowed almost with genius, but as one who has not been gifted by nature with ordinary powers of reasoning." Trollope believed Reade really did mean to be honest, and he recommended *The Eighth Commandment* to his own readers as a noble and underread volume. And yet, he found Reade somehow to miss the point of his own "strange" reformist novels: "He has always left . . . on my mind so strong a conviction that he has not really understood his subject."

At the end of that same year, 1872, Reade published his novel *The Wandering Heir* and soon found himself attacked by anonymous letter writers (who proved to be Mr. and Mrs. Mortimer Collins, the novelist and his wife) for using therein several hundred words of Swift's *Journal of a Modern Lady* without attribution. Reade counterpunched with familiar fury, and his argument found favor with his sympathetic modern biographer, Elwin, who saw the unattributed passage as a legitimate daub upon the seventeenth-century background Reade needed to paint behind a particular scene. "Collins's view was that of the small-minded craftsman," argued Elwin; "Reade's of the genuine artist." Reade himself argued that he provided the setting for Swift's jewel — an assertion in which, Trollope noted, "there was some little wit, and would have been much excellent truth, had he given the words as belonging to Swift and not to himself."

Always quick to extenuate himself when the charges were specific and incontrovertible, Reade was just as likely to fulminate against others for injuries he fancied them making against his own originality. When George Eliot published *Romola* a few years after Reade's *Cloister and the Hearth,* she was rather pointlessly attacked by some critics for jumping aboard Reade's medieval bandwagon. Reade joined in and harrumphed about "Georgy Porgy's" predations. In a later essay called "The Wasp Credited with the Honeycomb," Eliot showed, on the subject of literary piracy, her usual good sense. She knew when it was proper to be appalled, but also that "it must be admitted that hardly any accusation is more difficult to prove, and more liable to be false." Reade, in contrast, was almost never capable of anything but barking loudly on the wrong side of the issue.

Both Eliot and Reade engaged in lengthy research for their medieval triple-deckers. An entire book, *The Making of "The Cloister and the Hearth,"* by Professor Albert Morton Turner, has been devoted to Reade's novel. Turner, who sees Reade's many borrowings of historical material as marvels of assimilation, quotes, from one of the notebooks, Reade's imperative jotting to himself:

> Having wasted too many years to be learned I must use cunning.
> Think of some way to make young active fellows run and collect
> materials for me. Think of a Machinery. . . . German hacks good
> for this. University hacks ditto. Pay them well and keep them
> dark.

Don't tell them what enterprise they're assisting, lest they steal the idea for themselves? Don't let anyone else know you're employing researchers, lest they begin to question the originality of your work? Either could fall within the normal range of Reade's abnormal psychology.

At the time of Mme. Reybaud's death in 1871, Reade himself was at a short-held apogee. In 1869 he and his actress companion, Mrs. Seymour, had moved into 2 Albert Terrace in Knightsbridge. By 1872, the year he finished *A Simpleton* and had his fights with Trollope and over Swift, the fifty-eight-year-old author could put down, in one of the notebooks, a famously belligerent claim of self-satisfaction:

> With the proceeds of a pen that never wrote a line till I was thirty-
> five years of age I have got me three freeholds in the Brompton
> Road, a leasehold in Albert Terrace, a house full of rich furniture
> and pictures, and a few thousands floating, and so I can snap my
> fingers at a public I despise, and at a press I know and loathe.

Three years after this he could triumphantly point to Parliament's repeal of the "Satanic" proviso he had shrieked against in

The Eighth Commandment. With drama now subject to the same protections as other genres, Reade foresaw theater managers being made to pay for native invention instead of stealing French success. The repeal had "laid the first stone of a great British drama, as time will show." In a series of letters headed "The Rights and Wrongs of Authors," originally published in the *Pall Mall Gazette,* he celebrated the loophole's closing and urged America to join her European neighbors on the moral high ground of authorial protection. Disputing Macaulay's famous definition of copyright ("a tax on readers to give a bounty to authors"), he made a case in his customary ink-and-brimstone fashion, insisting that the writer's job is a physically hazardous one, "through its effects on the blood-vessels of the brain, which are a part, not of the mind but of the body. The said vessels get worn by an author's productive labour, and give way. This, even in our short experience, has killed Dickens, Thackeray, and perhaps Lytton. The short life of authors in general is established by statistics." And, as always, it is the French who can teach the English-speaking nations a thing or two about respect for writers.

That the French sometimes do justice to something first is a thing for readers of *this* book to keep in mind — as is, perhaps, the fact that in 1878 Reade published a series of letters recommending the natural virtues of ambidexterity. Charles Reade's life was surrounded by some of the loudest paradoxes ever to be sounded near an author. It is safe to say that he heard none of them. Indeed, he was (to borrow a phrase from Tom Wolfe) "irony-proof," screening out any information that might impede his machete-wielding charge toward success and fame. Still, even Reade had to peak, and not much after "The Rights and Wrongs of Authors" had appeared, his quick decline commenced. He had one crusading novel left in him, *A Woman-Hater* (1877), a tract on behalf of the right of British women to practice medicine. Reade's feminism, like all his other reformist tendencies, was tied up in contradictions. In *White Lies* (1858), he wrote of women:

> They can bubble letters in ten minutes that you could no more
> deliver to order in ten days than a river can play like a fountain.
> They can sparkle gems of stories; they can flash little diamonds

of poems. The entire sex has never produced one opera nor one
epic that mankind could tolerate: and why? these come by long,
high-strung labor.

The death in 1879 of Reade's own female companion, Mrs.
Seymour, made his decline more or less headlong. His health,
invention and energies failed. He ran, unimaginably, out of big
projects. In the four and a half years he had left to him, short
stories were usually the writing order of the day. Tired, ill and,
as always, oblivious, it was time to put all his own unperceived
ironies to work: for the champion of copyright to engage in a
wholesale plagiarism; to get the stolen goods from France; to
make it a woman whose full-length labor he would turn into a
little "gem"; and to fence the swag in America, whose lack of
respect for international copyright, he cried in "The Rights and
Wrongs of Authors," was keeping its national imagination in
bondage.

And so: one day in the third week of February 1884, one J.B.S.
opened up his (her?) copy of *Harper's* — the March issue fresh
from the press — and began reading the first installment of a
new story called "The Picture," by Charles Reade. J.B.S. read
reluctantly, because he or she was no fan of the egotistical author.
"I am now seventy," the story began, "and learning something
every day — especially my ignorance. But fifty-two years ago I
knew everything, or nearly — I had finished my education. I
knew a little Greek and Latin, a very little vernacular, a little
mathematics, and a little war: could march a thousand men into
a field, and even out of it again — on paper. So I left Paris, and
went home to rest on my oars." Well, Reade always did have a
punchy tone, even when he was speaking through a character's
voice; he could bully you into turning the page. He might be full
of himself, brimming over with righteousness and panaceas, but
there was no denying the man's competence in telling a story. So
J.B.S. decided to read on.

No penny dropped in his or her brain as J.B.S. read the first
paragraph. In fact, it probably wasn't until about ten paragraphs
had gone by that the pennies started dropping in a noisy water-
fall of incrimination. This recollection of being a young man
visiting one's uncle; this business of becoming so interested in a

portrait the uncle claims only to have bought for its frame; this "hollow-eyed" and "wrinkled" old servant named Catherine. At least *this* time named Catherine. Wasn't, J.B.S. had to wonder, there something familiar about this?

Later in this first installment, the uncle's old friend the ambassador arrives and begins to tell the story of the woman (" 'She was my betrothed!' ") in the picture: the story of his arranged marriage to the indifferent "Mlle. Irène de Groucy," a freethinking consumer of "pernicious" literature ("I found her reading the 'Nouvelle Héloïse,' in her boudoir"); the story of how he painted her picture; of how the banns of their marriage were announced shortly before she awarded a trophy to the local wrestling giant; of how the peasants marched against the château; and how the wrestler was found in the mademoiselle's bedroom:

> Mademoiselle de Groucy, quick as he was slow, darted before him with extended arms to protect him, but the next moment cried, "Fly, fly, for your life!" The moment she made way for him to fly the marquis levelled his musket, and fired at his head with as little hesitation as he would at a wild boar.

At this arresting moment the first installment of "The Picture" came to an end, and J.B.S. was faced with the decision of whether to keep reading (the item below Reade's story was an editor's note expressing disgust over Alfred Tennyson's willingness to be elevated to the peerage) or get up out of the armchair and begin acting on his or her suspicions.

Either way, J.B.S. could not have waited long, because by February 20 he or she was dispatching a letter from Philadelphia to Boston's snappy-styled *Literary World*, reporting on a discovery, probably made by going through some old boxes in the basement or by making a quick trip to the excellent Athenaeum of Philadelphia on South Sixth Street:

> *To the Editor of the Literary World:*
> Of course you have read Mr. Charles Reade's "Picture" in the March number of *Harper's*. Had it a familiar sound to you? It had to me, and I soon found why. Look at "What the Papers Revealed," in the *St. James Magazine* for August, 1867, and I think you will agree with me in calling this a case of plagiarism. The *St. James*

story is not signed, but it can hardly have been Mr. Reade's. *He* was never in the habit of hiding his light nor his name under a bushel.

Before class

> Yours truly,
> J.B.S.

Philadelphia, February 20, 1884.

The sex of J.B.S. is not known to us, but let us dispose of these awkwardly doubled possessive pronouns by making an educated guess, based only on late-nineteenth-century market research, that J.B.S., with her detectable predisposition against Charles Reade, was a woman. The *Literary World,* after all, had run an item about Reade as recently as February 9, in its "News & Notes" section, concerning the publication of a portion of Reade's *Perilous Secret* in *Harper's Bazar.* "Why the Harpers [brothers] should have changed their plans so as to print Mr. Reade's story in the *Bazar* instead of the *Weekly* — in a paper written for women — we do not comprehend. Reade has never been a favorite with the ladies, a fact which will be borne out by the experience of any book-clerk or library attendant, if circumstantial evidence is wanted."

Now let's consider the circumstantial evidence — not of female antipathy to Reade but of the story dug up by J.B.S. A bound volume of *St. James's Magazine* can be brought up from the stacks of the New York Public Library within minutes; it's in quite good condition, too, though "What the Papers Revealed" isn't so likely to survive into the twenty-second century as J.B.S.'s letter, not unless *St. James's* is eventually put, like the Boston *Literary World,* onto microfilm. But let's return to the problem at hand. No wonder J.B.S. made the accusation she did. All the basic elements of Reade's story are there. Chief among them is the aristocratic girl whose "icy reserve" melts only during her espousal of the egalitarian ideals she's picked up from her reading, and not for the attentions of her well-born suitor, who has come for an arranged marriage but who is instantly "enslaved" by the beauty of the indifferent young woman. Yes, she spurns him for the rustic champion of the village games, who is soon after found in her bedroom. Banishment, elopement, disillusionment. Nasty quarrel; aristocratic wife murders vicious bumpkin husband;

goes to prison; is paroled; gets work as a servant; has her true identity revealed only at her death.

But anyone who has come this far will now have to acknowledge a distinction greater than any of the above-listed similarities. "What the Papers Revealed" is no less and no more Mme. Reybaud's story than it is Reade's. In this third version of the tale, the aloof young lady is Gabriella Heath (a.k.a. Marie de Malepeire, Irène de Groucy) and, in her servant latter-days, Nancy (a.k.a. Marian, Catherine). Her suitor is not the Marquis de Champaubert or the Comte de Pontorlais but this time Sir Edward Ashly. Her peasant husband is now James Wynn, though he's still a wrestler. (Is this the only sport the different writers of this tale could think of? Or is wrestling forever the rustic sport of literary choice? One suspects they had all read *As You Like It*.)

As is clear from the characters' names, the thing that most sets "What the Papers Revealed" apart from *Mlle. de Malepeire* and "The Picture" is its locale. The 1867 version is set in Wales, and a good deal later than the versions set in France. In fact, the book that gives Gabriella Heath her radical-chic sentiments is not *La Nouvelle Héloïse* but "a history of the first French revolution." The new setting makes for even more improbabilities than those contained in the original. Gabriella's father still talks like an *ancien régime* aristocrat, not a nineteenth-century Welsh landowner: " 'From this hour remove your accursed presence, your tainted person, from the roof to which your shame has brought undying dishonour and disgrace. Go!' " And since the good citizens of Wales never staged any post-Enlightenment revolution, the wrestler's fellow rustics have to assault the big Heath house more in a spirit of raillery than revolt. But it is still on the night of the village festival that they are marching toward the mansion where the local lady is in a clandestine clinch with her proletarian swain.

The *St. James's* version of the story is far shorter than Mme. Reybaud's and about half the length of Reade's. It lacks the narrative filters through which the other two are presented. There is no primary narrator recalling a youthful visit to his uncle, nor is there any visit from an uncle's old friend to get the story-within-a-story rolling. Rather, "What the Papers Revealed" has the suitor tell his own story (announced as "The Narrative") after several pages of omniscient third-person "Introduction." What's more, in this most condensed rendition of the tale, the aristocratic beauty turned servant-crone has actually been working for the very teller of the tale, her old suitor. This should make for the best version of all — *there she's been all the time, right under his nose!* — but it doesn't really work. The telling is too rushed for the reader to appreciate the ironies and reversals, and too much depends on the papers found with poor old "Nancy" (whose ugliness here is truly traffic-stopping: she's the "most repulsive sample of womanhood I ever beheld," a "faithful old monster" with a face that is "seamed and scarred . . . ghastly, fossilised"). Also, the former suitor gets his surprise near the *beginning* of this version, ahead of the reader and guests, and something is lost when the one who has the biggest shock to get gets it first.

In most narrative and descriptive respects, "What the Papers Revealed" is so bad that it makes one recall why Victorian parents looked down on novel-reading in the way their descendants scorn television. Indeed, it seems too crude to have inspired in Reade a desire to steal it. Well, that's not true, either. Reade's years of obsessive prowling from theater to theater, in Paris and London, trained him to look for *plots,* those great engines of events in sequence. They were what one needed. No matter how clogged a good plot got in a bad writer's pen, it could be brought to full life by one who understood narrative economy, knew how to paint emotions in primary colors — and how to stop just short of the threshold of risibility, something the *St. James's* writer didn't.

So, yes, it seems for a moment possible that Reade got the plot of "The Picture" from "What the Papers Revealed" and made it into something much better. But J.B.S. is wrong. There are too many vivid elements in Reade's story — the banns, the wrestler's gambling away of his mother's money, the gunshot fired by the girl's father on the night of the elopement — that do not appear in the *St. James's* version. That of course doesn't mean anything in itself; Reade could have added them after his own invention. But he didn't, because all those elements are in *Mlle. de Malepeire.* That was Reade's real source for "The Picture," just as it was the source of the anonymous author of "What the Papers Revealed," who dropped those above-mentioned exciting touches, along with some others, for reasons of space. Like Marie de Malepeire herself, Mme. Reybaud had at least two pursuers, occupying two very different strata, at least in the literary world: one an anonymous contributor to an undistinguished magazine, the other a novelist whom contemporaries often mentioned as being second only to Dickens.

An ad hoc posse of American readers were soon in pursuit of Reade.

In the February 28, 1884, issue of the *Nation* (price 10 cents; the front page advertising the works of Tennyson, Arnold, and a four-dollar octavo work called *Hereditary Genius: An Inquiry into its Laws*), the editors noted receipt of a letter directing their attention to what the correspondent thought were "striking resemblances between Mr. Charles Reade's story in the March *Harper*, entitled 'The Picture,' and a Novel, 'Where Shall He Find Her?' translated from the French and published anonymously by the American News Co. in 1867." This may be the same as the Crowen Publishers' translation, from which all quotations from *Mlle. de Malepeire* have been taken for this chapter. The Crowen title page is indeed anonymous, saying only that it was "from the French" and by one I.D.A.; it is, of course, William Walsh's *Handy-Book of Literary Curiosities* that tells us this was a translation of Mme. Reybaud's *Mlle. de Malepeire*. But when the Reade scandal was breaking, a decade before Walsh's book was available, the initial investigators, alert to the similarities between "The Picture" and *Where Shall He Find Her?*, didn't know, in the case of the latter, whose work they were actually dealing with.

By mid-March things were sufficiently complicated for an academic to step in. Professor Charles Mills Gayley of the University of Michigan did not name the author of "What the Papers Revealed" or, more usefully, of *Where Shall He Find Her?* Instead, he suggested two additional sources for Reade's "Picture":

> The plot, the essential phases of dialogue, and the accessory descriptive padding, to the minutest detail, are abstracted from "The Portrait in My Uncle's Dining-room," a story which appeared in No. 11 of the *Month*, London, probably 1869; and in *Littell's Living Age*, November 6–November 27, 1869.

The staff at the New York Public Library are sufficiently brisk to allow patrons to file three different request slips at once; so one may ask for the relevant volumes of the *Month* and *Living Age* together. One waits for the slips to travel through the pneumatic tubes to the stacks, and then, just minutes later, the pink number matching one's ticket lights up on the board in South Hall, and there, at the counter, are the books: a miracle of ingenuity and municipal munificence, more satisfying than the autoprogrammed cassette that records itself and keeps, like a warm dinner, in the VCR. The operation proceeds so swiftly that one barely has time to rearrange the *St. James's, Harper's* and Crowen texts of the story to make room for the two new ones at one's place in the reading room, which is rapidly beginning to resemble a game board and to encroach upon the neighboring patron's place.

The *Month* was a Victorian Catholic magazine, a popular ally of the Oxford movement, printed in London and priced at one shilling. The July 1869 number, which ran the first of four installments of "The Portrait in My Uncle's Dining-Room" (identified only, like the Crowen version, as being "From the French"), included articles on "The Prospects of Catholic Education" and "Difficulties of the Theory of Natural Selection." Nineteenth-century literary magazines printed anonymous stories and reviews as often as attributed ones. Nothing in *St. James's Magazine* is signed, and the *Times Literary Supplement* never ran the names of contributors until well into our own century. Mme. Reybaud's name wouldn't mean much to English readers in any case. One assumes that the *Month,* and Crowen Publishers in New York, acquired the story legitimately.

The *Month*'s version is Mme. Reybaud's all right, from Dom Gérusac to Babelou (the young assistant of Marion, spelled with an *o* here), and yet what appeared there in the summer of 1869 was not exactly what Crowen had published in New York two years before. Compare the opening sentence of what's in the *Month* —

> During my college life, rather more than thirty years ago, I used annually to spend a part of my holidays with an uncle of my mother's at a pretty country house in Upper Provence, a few leagues from the Piedmontese frontier.

with the first lines of *Where Shall He Find Her?*:

> During my college life, some thirty years ago, I was in the habit
> of spending part of my vacation with an uncle on my mother's
> side, who lived in a pretty house at Upper Provence, some leagues
> from the frontier of Piedmont.

There are no more differences here than what you would get
from two students set to translate the same passage, but there
are enough to prove that one translator was at work in England
and another in America. (The English one was somewhat more
careful: in London Marion is "certainly the ugliest creature" the
narrator has seen; in more open-minded America she is only
"perhaps the ugliest creature" he's beheld.) *Réellement*, Marion
"*était bien*" the ugliest, according to *Revue des Deux Mondes* for
August 1854, home of the genuine article that a decade or so
later began its international odyssey of translation and kidnap.

Littell's Living Age, a durable Boston miscellany, had already
seen 1,327 issues by November 6, 1869, when the first of four
weekly installments of "The Portrait in My Uncle's Dining-
Room" appeared. It is not acknowledged as first having appeared
in the *Month,* though its having concluded a four-month run
there in October would seem to have allowed it time to be noticed
and reprinted. The only origin given is "From the French," that
by now familiar phrase whose vagueness would infuriate any
agent of our time pushing for the kind of name recognition that
would allow his client to have her breakthrough into a new market. In any event, the *Living Age* isotope of the story is exactly
that of the one in the *Month:* "During my college life, rather
more than thirty years ago, I used annually . . ."

With so many versions already on the table, the tale is beginning to have the familiarity of a bedtime story, and if you're not
careful you may nod off — even with the noise of the salsa band
on the library's steps drifting up into the reading room on this
hot summer afternoon. You have to revive yourself by turning
back to the transcription you had made from the microfilm of
Professor Gayley's stern academic letter to the *Nation,* which
informs the public he is trying to outrage against Charles Reade
that "The Portrait in My Uncle's Dining-room" also made an
appearance in 1870, along with some other short stories, in an

octavo volume published by Littell & Gay. Well, since Littell & Gay were the publishers of *Littell's Living Age,* there can be no doubt which version would be in the octavo, and you're glad of it, since there's hardly any room left on your share of the reading room table. As for Professor Gayley's assertion that "the same story, in company with 'The Strawcutter's Daughter,' was afterward issued by Sadlier in a 16mo volume" — we will take his assiduous word for it.

Actually, for all his zeal, he fails to note yet one more book-length rendition of the story, this time called *Marion: Or, The Picture in My Uncle's Dining Room,* published in 1870 by Kelly, Piet & Co. of Baltimore and included in volume 490 of the Library of Congress's catalog of pre-1956 imprints. Kelly, Piet may ring a soft bell in the visually observant: the firm's name appears on the covers of the *Month.* It was that magazine's American distributor. (You now remember the Catholics settling Maryland, and the Baltimore catechism from which you learned the seventh — Protestant eighth — commandment.) And since the last line of the *Month*'s cover reads "All rights of translation and reproduction reserved," you assume they ceded the rights they had to the story to Kelly, Piet, as they perhaps did to *Littell's Living Age,* despite that digest's lapse in acknowledgment.

This makes eight incarnations of that wretched Rousseau-reading girl. And yet, returning to Professor Gayley's long letter, and considering it along with those of common readers like J.B.S., you have to remind yourself that *no one has yet identified the author Reade robbed.* "What the Papers Revealed" was an anonymous plagiarism, and *Where Shall He Find Her?* was merely "From the French," just as the versions in the *Month* and *Littell's Living Age* were, albeit from someone else's (somewhat better) French. If it were not for Walsh's *Handy-Book,* we wouldn't know her name either.

Professor Gayley makes a stab at guessing the original author in his letter to the *Nation.* He reminds readers, quite legitimately, that he hasn't had time to come up with proof and, unconsciously anticipating the professors of New Criticism who in a few decades will take over posts like the one he has in Michigan, avers that knowledge of the author's identity is "not essential" in any case. But he goes ahead and guesses. He considers the 1870 Sadlier's edition, which "puts 'The Portrait in My Uncle's Dining-room' into covers with one of Lady Georgiana Fullerton's novels," noting that "the American Catalogue classes it ["The Portrait," that is] twice among her writings." He argues that there is both stylistic and historical evidence to support the attribution, but however glad we are to know of Lady Georgiana Fullerton, Professor Gayley has rounded up the wrong victim.

Which was a pity for readers of the *Nation,* because the incriminating parallel columns he ran in this lengthy letter to the editor make the case against Reade even more airtight. He invited readers to compare not only the plot and characters of "The Picture" with "The Portrait," as it appeared in the *Month* and *Littell's Living Age,* but some of the descriptive passages as well. Here is just one of the eight that he offered with the assurance that there "is scarcely a paragraph in 'The Picture' in which such amusing coincidences with 'The Portrait in My Uncle's Dining-room' as the preceding do not occur":

Original Version [the translation in the *Month* and *Living Age*]	Mr. Charles Reade
Vases of Japan China, always filled with fresh flowers, decorated the corners of the room, and each frame of the gray wainscoted walls was enlivened by a landscape painting of some historical scene. ... On the walnut sideboard stood some ancient pieces of plate of exquisite workmanship. ... A portrait which Dom Gérusac had hung up over the pier-glass of the chimney piece.	Chinese vases five feet high and always filled with flowers, guarded the four corners of the room: vast landscapes were painted on the walls and framed in panels of mellow oak: many pieces of curious old plate glittered on the sideboard. ... Over the mantel-piece of the dining-room hung a picture in an oval frame.

But Professor Gayley still hadn't identified the corpse, as it were, and he had something like a kind word for the perpetrator's cleverness. Noting that "the original substance has been considerably condensed as well as vilified," the professor, in a ghastly foreshadowing of the language of his present-day successors in academe, urged readers to "bear in mind ... Mr. Reade's allotropic modification of the story."

The second installment of "The Picture," the last thing Charles Reade would publish in his lifetime, was on newsstands in New York late in March. Appearing in *Harper's* just after an anonymous poem called "A Tell-Tale of Spring" ("Ah, fairest Spring's spring-tide, / 'Twas thankless and bold / To spy out your secret. / I'm sorry I told!"), it brought the story to the conclusion it had already reached on Mme. Reybaud's writing table thirty years before. The episode opens with the mademoiselle's father (a marquis, not a baron, in Reade's peerage) firing his gun at the daughter's peasant suitor. She makes her declaration of love; is denounced; flees. At this point in the narrative the curé is told by Suzon (her junior servant, Mme. Reybaud's Babelou) that Catherine (Marian) is sick. After attending to her, the curé returns and tells the story of Mlle. de Groucy's marriage to her rustic wrestler: his womanizing, his nasty mother, his gambling, his insolence. To make a long story short, which is just what Reade did, one can report that, yes, the peasant is a gambler, and that, yes, he loses the money his mother gives him, and that following a rough quarrel he's murdered by his aristocratic wife. After the usual round of *éclaircissements* (with the exception of one for the curé, who in Reade's version has known Catherine's real identity all along), the portrait makes its way from uncle to narrator-nephew. Below the story's concluding paragraph in the April *Harper's* was another anonymous poem, "The Godmother's Gift," whose third stanza read:

> 'This is the kiss shall ope the eye
>   And stimulate the brain
> To see what others never saw,
>   And he can ne'er attain.'

Both installments of Reade's "Picture" contain some good, even original, touches. Before the village festivities, for instance, he has the mademoiselle suggest that her aristocratic suitor wrestle the peasant. And when she comes to her senses and excoriates her bullying bucolic husband, she directly echoes the imprecation her father uttered upon her elopement. "Rot on your dunghill, all of you!" she cries to her in-laws, just as M. de Groucy had cursed her by saying, "Since you can fall no lower . . . marry your peasant, and live on his dunghill with him." Irène does in her boorish husband not with the undescribed knife put in her hand by Mme. Reybaud but with a weapon more symbolic of economic determinism, "an instrument ladies used in that day for embroidery." And, ever the litigant and polemicist, Reade gives to his mademoiselle what none of her other creators, translators and kidnappers did, and what certainly they could not have composed so well: an impassioned speech, in her own defense, to the jury at her trial. "I gave up father, friends, rank, wealth, everything for him, and I loved him dearly. He gave me a bitter provocation. . . . How can you punish me? Imprisonment cannot add to my misery, and death would end it. Therefore I ask no mercy: be just." But skillful touches first require something there to be touched. And what Reade used to operate on Mme. Reybaud was really the same instrument he allowed Irène for killing her husband, an embroiderer's tool. He in fact changed little, and most of that needlessly.

Until late in March all the complaints against Reade's theft had occurred on the American side of the Atlantic, far enough away from his lonely house on London's Uxbridge Road that he may not even have heard them. He had more serious business to attend to at the moment than one more controversy. Since the death of Mrs. Seymour, ailments had found him more and more defenseless, and as Easter approached they were closing in for the kill. But with the appearance of the March 29 issue of the *Academy*, a London magazine, the sounds of disapproval were tapping at his door, and if his waning consciousness permitted him to hear them, he must have felt a little like M. de Malepeire as the torch-carrying mob made its way to the château.

At the front of the assault was Miss E. J. Marshall, whose letter of March 22 was printed by the *Academy* in the following week's number. "May I venture," she began, "to call attention to a story entitled 'The Picture,' by Mr. Charles Reade, now appearing in *Harper's Monthly*, which bears a most extraordinary resemblance to Mdme. Charles Reybaud's *Mademoiselle de Malepeire*, a one-volume novel published by Hachette at Paris in 1856?" (In *The Eighth Commandment* Reade paid tribute to "M. Hachette, a French publisher" who "has never published or translated any English book [since the 1851 treaty], without paying the author.") Miss Marshall offered succinct plot-and-character comparisons of "The Picture" and *Mlle. de Malepeire* before going on to some word-for-word ones in the manner of Professor Gayley. The difference between her parallel exhibits and his, however, is that her left-hand columns come from the truly original story and not the subsequent English versions Gayley assumed Reade was using.

She concluded her report to the *Academy* in a briskly neutral tone: "I might quote many more passages which are equally parallel, but fear to trespass on your space. To say the least, as no acknowledgment is attached to the publication of Mr. Reade's story in *Harper's,* some explanation seems to be called for." The editors of the magazine appended a note to her letter, announcing the findings made by Miss Marshall's fellow sleuths in New York; but the important thing was that the author whom Reade had plundered had at last been identified, and the *Academy* congratulated itself by congratulating Miss Marshall on "having traced this multiform story to its original source." Multiform, indeed: Mme. Reybaud's tale, with its wonderfully tragic sequence of romance and comeuppance, its local color, its remoteness in time, its mysterious secret solved in a purloined-letter-like way, was a *pièce* to which translators, adapters and (by 1884) two plagiarists could show no *résistance*.

The "People Who Are Talked About" column in the *New York Times* for March 30, 1884, carrying "Social, Dramatic and Literary Gossip of London," reported news of Miss Marshall's letter along with other transatlantic items such as the impending question in Parliament about the Duke of Connaught's unwise attendance at an elephant fight presented by the Rajah of Bhurtpore. So Miss Marshall was certainly having her effect. But readers of the next week's issue of the Boston *Literary World* would discover that a third woman (assuming J.B.S. to have been one) was also avenging Charles Reade's violations of the sex and, though her letter probably reached print a little later, had in fact scooped Miss Marshall's discovery of Mme. Reybaud as the *originale.*

This correspondent to the April 5 issue of the *Literary World* was no less a person than Mary Chesnut of Camden, South Carolina, whose Civil War *Diary from Dixie* would create a sensation upon its posthumous publication in 1905. A wit, a feminist, antislavery but passionately antebellum, Mrs. Chesnut, daughter

of Senator Stephen Decatur Miller, was educated at Madame
Talvande's French School for Young Ladies in Charleston, and
was well equipped to read *Mlle. de Malepeire* in the original
French anytime she wanted to. This is apparently just what she
did in 1883, even though she was also in possession of yet one
more English translation of the story. She asked the editor of the
Literary World for permission

> to say a word of Mr. Charles Reade's "Picture" in the March
> number of *Harper's*. It is from the French of Madame Charles
> Reybaud. I read it in the original a year ago, and recognized it
> instantly, in its new form.
>
> Before my eyes as I write, I have the New York *Albion* of January
> 3d, 1857, from which I copy: "Enter according to act of Congress
> in the year 1857, by Wm. Young & Co.," etc., etc., "Mademoiselle
> Malpeire. By Madame C. de Reybaud. Translated for the *Albion*."

Unfortunately, this time when the clerk in the reading room
flicks on the pink light corresponding to your ticket number, the
one you hope will bring up issues of the *Albion* from the months
before the Buchanan administration got under way, it is to inform you that the *Albion* is available only on microfilm, and not
over in North Hall, either. It's kept in the NYPL Newspaper
Annex at 521 West 43rd Street, between Tenth and Eleventh
avenues.

This means a walk, on a hot summer day, to Clinton (or, in
Charles Reade's day, Hell's Kitchen), all along 42nd Street by
way of Times Square, where all the movies have the same plot,
but some of whose titles possess the lunatic invention setting the
inspired parodist apart from the mere porno-plagiarist: HANNA
DOES HER SISTERS, ON GOLDEN BLONDE. The Newspaper Annex is
a plain place, more warehouse than library, close to the huge
garages of the United Parcel Service and just a little to the east
of the Hudson River docks. After a minute or two the *Albion* —
"A British, Colonial, and Foreign Weekly Gazette," a miscellany
for Anglophilic American cousins — is rigged up in the microfilm reader.

Eschewing the "From the French" anonymity that the *Month*
and *Living Age* would employ a dozen years later, this 1857
number of the *Albion* (which apparently survived everything from

Fort Sumter through Reconstruction in the Chesnut attic) indeed offers a "Mademoiselle de Malpeire" by "Madame Charles de Reybaud," in a translation made expressly "for the Albion." That's just what it seems to be, too, because if on this first printed visit to America Marion is "certainly" the ugliest creature the narrator ever saw, her story begins with words not employed by either the *Month/Living Age* translator or the one for Crowen Publishers: "About thirty years since, when I was in College" is simply not the same as "During my college life, some thirty years ago" or "During my college life, rather more than thirty years ago." "Mademoiselle de Malpeire" continues in this ever so slightly original way for another four small-print installments in this weekly gazette, whose motto was "*Coelum Non Animum, Mutant, Qui Trans Mare Currunt*" ("They change the sky, not their spirit, those who sail across the sea") — Horace.

Mrs. Chesnut sent her letter "Very respectfully" to the Yankee editor of the *Literary World*, but there is an unamused curtness in its last paragraph, and perhaps a kind of contempt in her repetition of the novelist's first and last names: "Mr. Charles Reade, without altering the story at all, has condensed it somewhat. This you will find, by comparing his translation with the one to be found in the *Albion*." If she was, in fact, more disgusted than amused by her finding, it may have had as much to do with her own frustrations as any general feeling of being witness to a moral affront. The late 1870s and 1880s were difficult times for Mary Chesnut, who was trying to get a writing career off to a very late start. She was slowed down by her own poor health, deaths in the family, her husband's political setbacks and visits from financially ruined relatives. It would be no wonder if Mary Chesnut — aspiring author, daughter of the defeated Confederacy, feminist — were a bit disgusted by the spectacle of prosperous Charles Reade, from all-conquering Albion, stealing the words of a rather obscure Frenchwoman while near the height of his own fame. *Sir, you are no gentleman!*

Mrs. Chesnut did not manage to publish any fiction, but between 1881 and 1884 "she substantially completed the book based on her wartime diaries," as C. Vann Woodward and Elisabeth Muhlenfeld explain in their introduction to *The Private Mary Chesnut: The Unpublished Civil War Diaries.* Actually, there are those who have held that her diaries were so doctored between their original keeping and the publication of *A Diary from Dixie* that they do constitute a kind of fiction. "She turned third-person narrative into dialogue, put her own thoughts in the mouths of others, telescoped or expanded entries, occasionally shifted dates and often rearranged incidents to heighten dramatic impact" — enough changes for the critic Kenneth S. Lynn to accuse her of "one of the most audacious frauds in the history of American literature."

She would hardly be the first diarist to achieve fame by such a procedure, and even so, such accusations would make her not a plagiarist but a forger. In any event, what Mary Chesnut was trying to do was bring old notebooks to literary life. She was trapped in a sick body, trying to make a belletristic impression, before death came, by going back to private jottings she'd made years before. During the early 1880s she had more in common with Charles Reade than she could have guessed.

Professor Gayley, in his letter to the *Nation,* speculated that Reade's version, "The Picture," "whether it be the outcome of buying, borrowing or unconscious memory, is based upon the English [translation] rather than the French original." Let's consider, in reverse order, the three possibilities mentioned in this quotation. (1) Unconscious memory: impossible. It's one thing to remember a good story, even to have a good bedtime one sink so satisfyingly into your dreams that you think you've made it up, but the kind of word-for-word similarities that Gayley himself arranged in parallel columns are another matter entirely. (2) Borrowing: a polite synonym for stealing, the euphemism to keep uppermost in mind. Finally, (3) buying: an interesting but unlikely possibility.

Reade did, it's true, buy French *plays,* a fact he was quite proud of. In *The Eighth Commandment* he recounts how after the 1851 copyright treaty went into effect he made a deal with the French dramatist Auguste Maquet to purchase rights to his play *Le Château Grantier,* even though the loopholes of the copyright act permitted him to appropriate it scot-free. It was only because Reade was, by his own estimation, such an honorable man that he offered compensation — indeed, offered it to set an example for his fellow countrymen. After all, the English are supposed to be "merchants, not cleptomaniacs," and to anyone who saw the transaction as a commercial intrusion into the sacred realms of art, he had a retort ready: "Would it have been less vulgar to steal it than to buy it?"*

But while it might be perfectly tasteful to pay for the right to adapt and produce someone else's play, one could hardly offer to buy someone's novel in order to do a little fiddling with it before bringing it out under one's own name. That wouldn't be translation in the ordinary literary sense. No, it was another kind of "translation" Reade had in mind — "translation" in one of its more archaic, romantic senses: the secret removal of someone's child and the substitution for it of a changeling.

Back in 1856 — a few weeks after the publication of *It Is Never Too Late to Mend,* Malcolm Elwin reminds us — Reade departed London for Paris. He was looking for a test case that would help establish his position on dramatic copyright. In *The Eighth Commandment* he makes much of how he purchased the rights to *Les Pauvres de Paris,* by Edouard Brisebarre and Eugène Nus. The agreement he made with Brisebarre stipulated that Reade could produce a translation of the play in England if he gave the authors half of what he made from it. Reade, back home in England, more or less dared potential pirates to steal what he had legitimately acquired for money; this created huge opportunities for verbal and legal pugilism, which Reade discusses at length in *The Eighth Commandment.* Any reader with strong enough eardrums can turn to that book for a full, subjective account of the struggle. But what must interest us now is something else that it is reasonable to assume happened on that Paris trip in 1856: Charles Reade's purchase of *Mlle. de Malepeire* by Mme. Charles Reybaud. Not the rights to the book; just a copy of the book itself, which was making its appearance as a single volume that year, both long installments from *Revue des Deux Mondes* (1854 and 1855) having been at last issued together.

*Reade's commercial dealings apparently never involved blackmailers. That was not the case where Katherine Mansfield was concerned, according to a new biography by Claire Tomalin. Mansfield and her husband, John Middleton Murry, apparently paid her ex-lover, who knew about her plagiarism of a story by Chekhov, to keep quiet about it.

Reade probably had no other object in mind than the acquisition of a pleasant volume with which to while away a bachelor's evening in his hotel room before resuming his theatrical business the following morning.

The French of this Oxford don was excellent. He had no need to wait for any translations of *Mlle. de Malepeire*. His notebooks contain plenty of evidence of his ability to read the original with complete appreciation of its style. Indeed, the point where a trip to those notebooks is called for has now arrived. A short walk along 42nd Street won't do it this time; a flight to London is the ticket.

The notebooks are the key to Reade, his achievements and compulsions, and the key to the notebooks is, appropriately, a skeleton — one old metal sliver that unlocks two wooden cupboards at the end of the catalog room in the London Library. Most of the notebooks have been here since the First World War, when they were donated by H. V. Reade, whose letter offering them, dated February 15, 1916, says that his great-uncle used to spend "about an hour every day" on them. Along with most of the rest of the London Library, they survived a direct hit by an enemy bomb during World War II. (General Eisenhower's headquarters were in the corner of St. James's Square diagonally opposite the one into which the library is tucked.) Today the square is especially peaceful, its quiet park presided over by an equestrian statue of William IV, the whole tidy arrangement inserted into London like a well-kept secret, a couple of minutes' walk from the bustle of Piccadilly Circus and Trafalgar Square.

One of the two cupboards is beneath a diagram of the library stacks. ("French Fiction" is on the third floor, you will note, for those occasions when the notebooks will prompt you to venture up there on the slow lift.) The library's helpful director, Douglas Matthews, opens the cupboard and warns you that the notebooks are a bit unwieldy, hefty and hard to work with, and that their keeper was a bit of a magpie. No one has touched them in about five years, he says, and there's plenty of dust on them: an incongruous film of peace on top of all the dead, mad energies within.

Yes, Reade's French was more than up to a reading of *Mlle. de Malepeire*. In notebook 20, not far from a note about Coleridge

("To restore a commonplace truth to its first uncommon lustre you have only to translate it into action"), there is a commonplace-book jotting that attests to Reade's ability to absorb even scientific literature, on a subject most apropos, in its native French:

> Generation spontaneous. confuted by Mons. Pasteur.
> See an excellent article Journal des Debats 6 April 1860.
> Omne virum ex ovo.

Indeed, Mme. Charles Reybaud makes repeated appearances in the enormous notebooks. In one of them, appraised by Professor Emerson Sutcliffe as probably belonging to 1860–61, with additional entries in it from a decade later, Reade made notes for "Bonae fab." — that is, *Good Stories* and *Good Stories of Man and Other Animals*. On page 23 there is a list of titles beside their note: "Each old model story in style of contemporary writer." Among the titles on the list is "Candide. Style of Addison." The first two?

> Mademoiselle de Malespierre
> Faustine.

An *X* is next to the first. *Faustine* was another work of Mme. Reybaud's, published in 1852. On page 83 of the same notebook: "Having often given the world the fruit of my invention I am now about to give it the fruit of my reading and judgment — which are, I think, great [fresh?]." Twenty-nine pages after that, a list of "Libelli":

> Balzac chez lui
> Les [deux] corbeaux
> Mlle de Malepierre
> Les gendre
> ?Adamo nel Paradiso. Italian play.
>   Chien et chat, or the foxy father.
>   Le philosophe sans le savoir.

And then, on page 127, the jotting

> Murder will out
> _____
> Sometimes

On the back of the marbled flyleaf Reade has written, "If lost on Railway or elsewhere a handsome reward to whoever brings it."

The book in which this is written is a foot wide and about twenty inches tall; it is huge, like a ledger of birth certificates, a couple of inches thick and weighing a ton. Not even Pinatel the wrestler could take this tome with him on a train ride. The reward note provides one more occasion for wondering, as any student of Reade winds up doing with some frequency, just *what* he thought he was thinking.

He certainly gave Mme. Reybaud some thought, and on more than one occasion. In a notebook that Sutcliffe dates as being from 1876, a book full of plot ideas for fiction and plays, Reade, just six pages after a reminder to himself about Dumas ("Conscience a drama . . . is in 6 acts, 3 admirable. 3 Bosh. Cut away the 3 bosh, and invent or steal 3 quite different"), summarizes the plot of "Les Corbeaux by Madame Charles Reybaud" and then makes a memo to himself: "This is a good story damaged by petty surprises. Rewrite it: begin at the beginning." He follows this with a list of specific manipulations to be performed — the sort he hardly needed to make in the appealingly well constructed *Mlle. de Malepeire.*

But even this is not the most revealing secret in the right-hand cupboard in the London Library. That lies on a page marked "Publicabilia" in an alphabetically ordered commonplace book:

sharp novels

Reade's abridgements.   or some such general

sharp stories   title

Fabula cetacea. Les miserables.

une servante? done. Mlle de Malepierre.
Brevia novella. See, red quarto digest in voce

opuscula

Candide in the English of Addison

He never got around to this Augustan Anglicizing of Candide, though this is the second time he proposes the project to himself. And one must wonder if he was really thinking about abridgments of Melville ("Fabula cetacea") and Hugo. But there can be no doubt about the story of the "servante" having been done. The only real question is when Reade dropped his apparently forthright idea of offering abridgments on an up-and-up basis. (Typically, he fulminated against the "abridgment swindle" in

The Eighth Commandment.) "Reade's abridgements" sounds like a good commercial title, and no one could say his narrative energies were insufficient for such a project, even if *Mlle. de Malepeire* seems decidedly less in need of condensation than *Moby-Dick* or *Les Misérables.* But at some point Reade abandoned this plan in favor of simple theft. There is a wavy line through "Reade's abridgements," a 3½-peaked cross-out, like so: ∿∿∿. When did he make it? Probably not long before he started writing "The Picture," when he was sick and depressed but trying to rally. As Elwin says of him in this period:

> He returned to his old habit of work, methodically revising his notebooks and working out suggestions for stories. Many of the notebooks are marked as "looked over" on various dates in 1881 and 1882. . . . There is discernible a pathetic determination to divert his thoughts from miserable introspection by a fixed routine of work. His writings reflect nothing of the emotional workings of his mind at this time. His stories were written up from the notebooks, the posthumously published *A Perilous Secret* being largely suggested by the "baby-farming" notes which he had posted up when working on *A Terrible Temptation.*

For his novels, even *The Cloister and the Hearth,* Reade had always preferred a real-life basis to a purely romantic one, but by the time he was writing the last story he would publish, he may have been so anxious about his inability to invent that the moment came when he stopped trying to kindle his imagination with press cuttings and, instead, found ready-made warmth by opening up someone else's novel — and writing it all over again.

On the same page of *The Eighth Commandment* where Reade wrote, "The literary pirate is an intellectual and moral type, well worth the microscope," he wondered, "Out of every twenty adapters how many are ever heard of in letters except when they bray in a Frenchman's skin?" Perhaps by 1883 he imagined the French simply owed him for all his agitations on their behalf: Mme. Reybaud became the representative, the Marianne, through which the writers of a whole nation paid him back. Reade liked having opportunities to bully those he had championed; he had stood up for the rights of female physicians, too, and by being a woman Mme. Reybaud was probably performing one more class-action act of reparation.

In his last years, according to his nephew's memoir, "racking cough became his constant companion. He fell away to a skeleton. Food seemed poison." A quarter century before, in *The Eighth Commandment,* he had written: "Moral, like physical disease, has its curable and its incurable stages." He had reached the latter. Up until now most of his plagiarisms could be defended (and no one ever had more excuses than Reade) as peccadilloes, mere nickings: the real compulsion to steal was kept in check. But as his body broke down, the compulsion broke out, just as viruses carried more or less harmlessly for years, under a kind of bodily house arrest, will run riot during the last stage of a final illness. The wavy line through "Reade's abridgements" shows the moment when his conscience hesitated, wavered and then took a more headlong plunge than any it had ever before been willing to. *To hell with it,* one can hear him saying as he canceled the words. He wouldn't bother with any tedious, legitimate abridgment; he'd go ahead and publish it as his own.

The London Library is certainly a lovely place to work in any season, and goodness knows it provides more quiet comforts than the New York Public's Newspaper Annex can. But of all the libraries visited so far, from the Multnomah County Public to the Mid-Manhattan, none can compare, not even the London, to the Pierpont Morgan, at the corner of Madison Avenue and 36th Street in New York. Here, in the hushed baronial splendor of a philanthropy fed from the preunionized world to which the anti-labor Reade felt J. P. Morgan entitled, you look for the last paper crumbs along the trail that led from Mme. Reybaud's Provençal imagination to the newsstands of New York City in the winter of 1884. "The Harper Collection of Autograph Letters and Manuscripts in the Pierpont Morgan Library. The Gift of Harper & Brothers 1958 with Later Additions" contains, according to page 33 of its typewritten index:

Reade, Charles. 1814–1884.

Autograph letters signed and letters signed (9), dated London, etc., 20 February [1852] — January 1884, addressed to officials of Harper & Bros., concerning his writings and their American publication.

Is it possible that there is something incriminating to be found here? You wait for the letters to be brought to a polished table in the heavily paneled reading room while watching a woman at a computer terminal incongruously dominating a portion of it: each time she hits the return button on the keyboard the reading lamps on the table flash, but no one looks up.

The folder of letters arrives quietly and is set out on a felt cloth to protect the tabletop from the reader's pencil — the only user-friendly handwriting tool permitted here. The earlier letters are routine enough and not especially relevant to the investigation under way. But the letter Reade sends with New Year's greetings on January 1, 1881, is interesting for the apology and explanation it offers:

> I should have sent my letter on International Copyright and "Stage-right" to your weekly rather than to the Tribune; but I fancied my view was opposed to yours, and therefore I did not like to impose upon your courtesy by making you its public channel. I am so near the end of my career, and without copyright you deal so liberally with me, that I have no great personal interest in the question; but for the sake of young authors, especially American, am much pleased to find you an advocate of I.C.

Reade, you remember, had argued in *The Eighth Commandment* that American unwillingness to submit to international copyright inhibited the growth of a truly American literature, just as the "loophole" concerning drama kept the English from creating their own achievements in that genre: why invent what you can import for free?

Below this passage he turns more personal, mentioning how difficult it has been for him to work since the death of Mrs. Seymour in September 1879. He took one commission from America, he says, but grief would not let him do it justice, and "so, as I never cheat people, I declined it altogether." Still, he knows "that the guardian angel I have lost would not have me idle: so I mean to *try* and write again." He imagines attempting some stories based on actual occurrences: "true narratives, made interesting by the methods of fiction." This is the drive that sent him back, that year, to the notebooks.

In the summer of 1883 he attempted to convalesce on the

Continent. On July 8, from Heidelberg, he wrote Henry Mills Alden at Harper & Bros., explaining that his "wind spasms" were the reason he had "been so long unable to complete the second instalment & last of the story called the Picture. However I mail it to England today where it will be copied & forwarded to you." This seems both encouraging and routine. The writer's copy, like the publisher's check, is always in the mail. But the little problem with "The Picture" that Reade goes on to note is somewhat more peculiar, enough to occasion as much of a eureka as the Morgan's quiet reading room permits one to utter:

> Unfortunately I wrote the first part so long ago that I have now forgotten what names I gave to some of the people especially to the peasant whom the heroine of the tale marries, and kills. But you will attend to the MS. and supply these blanks and mend errors in general for your poor suffering brother in arts.

It is never too late to mend details of this order, and Alden or one of his assistants soon undertook the business of putting whatever had appeared in Reade's first mailing into the "blanks" he left in the second. But did it not strike that editor in New York as curious that Reade would forget the name of someone as crucial to the story as the ignoble savage killed by Irène? Did it seem likely that Reade would have forgotten the name of a character who was part of a story that had supposedly sprouted and grown in the root cellar of his own imagination?

Reade was apparently working with such inattention that he was even able to forget the rather obvious literary joke involved in the name with which he rechristened Mme. Reybaud's Pinatel, the giant wife-beating wrestler so full of "contempt for those who were not his *equals* in brute strength." That name was Michel Flaubert. More a *nom bouffe* than a *nom juste*. This whole episode, besides confirming the plagiaristic evidence of the text, and the lazy fatefulness of the canceled line in notebook 20, inevitably sets one trying to imagine the real Flaubert, on holiday in Egypt, sitting back down to a novel he'd been working on at home and scratching his head in frustration: "What was that name I picked? Bouvard? Beaujolais?"

Probably before the last part of "The Picture" could reach Harper & Bros., Reade was back at 3 Blomfield Villas in London and temporarily feeling better. On August 10 he was able to write Alden once more, "happy to tell [him] that the wind-spasms, which have crippled my pen for months are now abating and I hope to do good work." He would have had in mind the "Bible Characters" series he would be offering *Harper's*, as well as the conclusion of the novel he was writing, his last, *A Perilous Secret.*

But Reade's hopes for his health were unfounded. Six days before, on August 4, he had been seen looking "feeble and tired" at the Drury Lane — and that visit is thought to be the last he was ever able to make to a theater. That fall he continued with "Bible Characters" when he could, but he was clearly and finally failing. Elwin reports how the literary memoirist "James Payn met him one day, 'painfully ascending the stairs of the London Library, looking very old and ill.' Seeing some books under Payn's arm, he said, 'How hard you work!' . . . then added with pathos, 'so did I at your age.' " The notebooks that would be carted up the steps of the library thirty years later certainly bear that out.

In December of 1883, Reade wrote to Harper & Bros., object-ing to unwarranted editing of "Bible Characters." He managed to blow off a bit of erstwhile bombast: "Thirty years ago when I was a struggling author I always refused to be edited, and cut the work short whenever it was attempted behind my back. I am the same man at the zenith of my reputation. Why not?" He added a complaint about how the firm "again broke faith with me and shelved 'The Picture' for about four months," going so far as to ask that the manuscript be returned. Alden evidently responded with a mollifying letter. A month later the two of them were still at odds over the question of editing, but things were enough smoothed over for Reade to express his hope that "The Picture" would be "published before Easter, so that I may not lose the London season as I have lost my Christmas market."

Alden, who no doubt knew nothing of Mme. Reybaud's story, would have done Reade's reputation a favor by sending him back the manuscript instead of printing it. But print it he did, and well before Easter, too; early enough, in fact, so that when Easter morning did arrive, and readers in London were learning of the death of Charles Reade, which had occurred just forty-eight hours before, they were no doubt also talking about the last time they had heard his name: just a couple of weeks ago, wasn't it?, in connection with that nasty business involving the French-woman.

Charles Reade's study was lined with mirrors from ceiling to floor, so when he wrote, all the reflections of his many selves could stare at one another, with two of them, the policeman and the thief, locked in dynamic contradiction, each bit of light-fingeredness overcompensated for by fulmination.

"Kleptomania" is a word Reade frequently employed in his copyright crusades. He uses it in "The Rights and Wrongs of Authors," where America's refusal to subscribe to international copyright is "suicidal kleptomania." In *The Eighth Commandment,* where it is spelled with a *c,* the phenomenon is used for several pages as a kind of clinical metaphor for publishers' shortsight-edness. Reade's discussion of the disorder itself is a typical blend of the crackpot and the perspicuous:

> "Cleptomania" is a term the doctors give to a certain unreasonable itch for stealing, which affects respectable people, overpowers common sense, religion, and *their true interest.* True Cleptomania seldom occurs except during pregnancy. Some persons in that interesting state are very delicate, and cannot keep their hands off articles of commerce, so unstrung are they. They appropriate pastry, or pocket handkerchiefs, or jewels out of shops, at a fright-ful risk, with money in both pockets to pay for them.

It's not surprising that Reade, whatever the medical thought of his day, would be content to recognize this as a female disorder (consider the sex of his chief victim), but the last portion of his descriptive pathology has stood up scientifically: the kleptoma-niac isn't supposed to need to steal the things he does.

Peter Shaw, whose remarks on Coleridge have already been noted, calls kleptomania "the social crime that plagiarism most closely resembles" because of the plagiarist's "evident wish to be detected and in the circumstance that what is stolen may not be needed." Leaving obvious clues? Not needing what's stolen? Both of these are features of Reade's thefts. The notebooks were in-dexed and cherished so as to make posterity's discovery of their

incriminating memoranda inevitable. And even if Professor Elton Smith is right about Reade's frequent dependence on collaboration because of his "distrust of the creative imagination," that
didn't stop him from producing some highly original books
(*Christie Johnstone*, and even, in its way, *The Cloister and the Hearth*),
and it didn't create any remotely plausible "need" to steal one
last short story for a bibliography that had already made him
famous and wealthy. He stole because, like other plagiarists and
kleptomaniacs, he was compelled to. Neither crime is something
one commits just once.

William Dean Howells wrote at the turn of the century that
plagiarism "argues a strange and peculiar courage on the part
of those who commit it or indulge it, since they are sure of having
it brought home to them, for they seem to dread the exposure,
though it involves no punishment outside of themselves." The
degree to which "conviction" for plagiarism carries any practical
risk to an author's career beyond momentary shame from loud
accusers like Charles Reade is something to be taken up at
greater length in the next chapter. But the issue of courage is
clear in Reade's case: he had it, in pigheaded instance after
instance throughout his life. The plagiarist always needs it. After
all, he never gives up the stolen goods to a fence; he puts them
on display under his own name. Reade had courage in zany
measure, jumping into whatever ironic scrape or controversy he
could find. Trollope couldn't stop shaking his head over him:
"He means to be especially honest, — more honest than other
people. . . . And yet of all the writers of my day he has seemed
to me to understand literary honesty the least."

Was he one of those people who just can't get it? Was he like
the schoolchild who submits a published poem to a contest as
her own and when caught is baffled, since she thought her discovery of it in a book *made* it her own? Reade was capable of
making such bizarre statements about plagiarism — "A book-pirate may often escape by re-wording the matter, because in many
books an essential feature is the language" — that one sometimes
wonders whether parts of his mind were quite right or even
minimally developed. But the best argument for Reade's awareness of the wrong involved is his unceasing preoccupation with
the subject of plagiarism. It glowed satanically. The truth is that

he can be explained in the algebra of most compulsions. He stole because he hated stealing and he hated stealing because he stole.

The deathbed scene that occurred on Good Friday, April 11, 1884, is staged in predictably different styles by Reade's two biographers. The man Burns sees perishing at 3 Blomfield Villas is self-deluded and pathetic, only his egotism shielding him from final realities: "He was able to maintain his heroic self-image to the very end. He died, his letters show, believing that he was a great novelist, a great dramatist, and a true if misunderstood and unrecognized prophet. Moreover he died believing that in years to come, when the peoples of the world had become ambidextrous and London had become a city of rational roofs, his Notebooks would provide the final vindication for his 'great ideas' as well as for his 'great art.' " Elwin, of course, is the opposite, warm-hearted and worshipful, ushering out a spirit still "protesting, arguing, inquiring, intent in death, as in life, upon the unwearying quest of truth."

The Reverend Charles Graham, who had brought Reade religion after the death of Mrs. Seymour, was at his side, and it was he who reported the writer's last words to have been "I have no hope but in God. God only can create; and God only can re-create." Oh, how tempting to think it was the last dust-up of his controversial life that was on his mind and lips, that he was making a penitential whisper.

Eight days later, and three weeks after it published the accusing letter by Miss Marshall, the *Academy* ran Charles Reade's obituary, without reference to the scandal of "The Picture." Richard F. Littledale conceded that Reade's last stories "added nothing to his reputation," but took pains to mention what some of the journal's recent readers must have felt were curious talents to be singling out now. "Granted that [Reade's] was not genius of one of the higher types, yet genius is to be seen unmistakably in all his best work, marking it with *verve*, originality and vigorous action, and in particular exhibiting so much ingenuity in the construction of plots and the invention of telling situations."

Marie de Malepeire, that poor humbled aristocrat, would never find much peace in dying: someone was always resurrecting her.

Two years after Reade expired she was revived again and forced once more to stumble through her headstrong misadventure, this time on German coffee tables in the big illustrated magazine *Über Land und Meer,* which each week carried humorous stories, articles on nature and popular medicine, and engravings of royalty to the middle-class *Volk.* The four volumes of *Über Land und Meer* that were brought up from the lower depths of the New York Public Library together weigh more than an IBM Selectric typewriter and are so covered with dust that you have to imagine the Bismarckian *Hausfrauen* who subscribed to the unbound originals sternly clucking at their current untidiness. But when you open up to October 1886, you indeed find what William Walsh's *Handy-Book* said would be lurking in the magazine around that time: "Das Lebende Bild" ("The Living Picture") by one A. von Bosse, whom volume 1 of *Deutsches Literatur* reveals to have been born in 1829.

So Mme. Reybaud's masterpiece was by 1886 available to ordinary readers in the country whose soldiers were laying siege to her adopted city at the time of her death fifteen years before. But what about English readers?

Ten years after Reade's death, in London's *Temple Bar* magazine, an appreciator of Mme. Reybaud would mention what a shame it was that *Mlle. de Malepeire* was out of print. Two years after that, in 1896, this unfortunate situation was, in a way, corrected when Chatto and Windus reprinted "The Picture" in the fifteenth volume of the New Collected Library edition of the works of Charles Reade. This would presumably have pleased Mme. Reybaud, whose favorite sayings were said to include "*Il n'y a pas de mal irrémédiable.*"

3

The Epstein Papers:
Writing a Second First Novel

The best thing about New York is everything you can do
here. The worst is everything you can't do here.

— Jason Epstein

POOR Philip Russo. In Jacob Epstein's 1979 novel *Wild Oats,*
he's suffering through a job for which he has no love or
calling, teaching English at Beacham University: "Twice in the
last ten days he had fought with the urge to stand up in the
middle of class and say, 'Forget it. No one cares. I sure don't.
This is all shit. No one's prepared,' and walk out." "Blocked"
after writing five chapters of his book on Dickens, he finds insult
added to inertia when he receives identical essays from two different seniors in his Dickens seminar: "Same topic, same title —
'The Specter of Technology in the Novels of Charles Dickens' —
every idea, every sentence, every word, even every punctuation
mistake — the same." Neither of these papers is the original,
either. Russo knows this because there's a third 'Specter of Technology in the Novels of Charles Dickens' in his files. It had been
submitted, though not written, by a student who eventually got
expelled from Beacham for plagiarism.

The real author is "a computer in New Jersey. . . . Russo knew
the racket. An agency, probably a couple of college kids behind
it, a couple of hustlers, had thousands and thousands of these

essays on file — on Malthus and Plato and Rousseau and Homer and the Russian Revolution. They solicited college kids in ads placed in the back of underground magazines."

Fairly mainstream magazines, too. "Term Paper Blues?" the advertisement in *Rolling Stone* inquires sympathetically. A male model playing a frustrated student sits amid stacks of books and crumpled papers, late-night drafts that have misfired. The solution is calling a toll-free hot line to "Research Assistance" ("since 1970") in West Los Angeles: "Our 306-page catalog contains detailed descriptions of 14,278 research papers, a virtual library of information at your fingertips. Footnote and bibliographic pages are included at no extra cost. Ordering is as easy as picking up your phone. Let this valuable educational aid serve you throughout your college years." In the *New York Times Book Review* it is "Research Unlimited" advertising its services. On the bulletin board of the All-College Dining Center at Vassar College it is "Authors' Research Services, Inc." ("Backed by a solid reputation since 1973") that offers order blanks for its catalog. One dollar will get you its listing; two dollars buys that plus the "Helpful Research & Writing Tips." If you spring for the deluxe package, your catalog and guide will arrive by UPS with the firm's Chicago address, but not its name, on the envelope. The cover of the "Catalog of Research and Writing Services" looks much like that of a typical college catalog, with a picture of young men and women gaily passing under a Gothic arch at some generic alma mater. (The photo, however, seems computer-disenhanced: all the faces are too blurry to be identifiable.) Page i expresses a wish — "GOOD LUCK IN YOUR ENDEAVORS" — guaranteeing students that "all orders are absolutely confidential" and reminding them that Authors' Research Services depends on *them:* "Our business thrives on our good reputation and personal referrals." All 16,000 and more papers in the catalog have been written by ARS's "staff of professional writers, each writer a specialist in one or more academic areas."

The papers listed constitute not so much the "virtual library" described by ARS's competitors as a whole underground university of semireliable knowledge, a Montgomery Ward of academic mendacity. Let's say you need to whip up something on *Tristram Shandy*. The thing to do is put in an order for paper #2301:

Lawrence Sterne's *Tristram Shandy Gentlemen:*
Examines Sterne's treatment of time in this work.   5   6   2

The specialist who wrote this paper may not know the title of the novel, or how Sterne's first name is usually spelled, but he must know something: those three numbers at the right mean the paper has five pages, six footnotes and two sources. In fact, this production must be an exhaustive treatise compared to paper #251:

Two Centuries of Inspiration for 18th and 19th Century Writers: Joyce, Wordsworth, Coleridge, Shelley, Byron, Mill, Keats, Tennyson, Auden, and Dylan Thomas. How these writers dealt with the sense of the divine, the vision of godliness in man, and with inspiration.   8   23   8   G

Twenty-three footnotes may seem like a tedious lot, but this author has covered his daunting subject in eight pages, which means he's plumbed the imaginative wellsprings of each of his writers in an average of less than one apiece, even as he's managed to get some of them started on their careers a century ahead of schedule. You know this is an impressive production from the *G* on the right. It "indicates the study is of exceptional quality or of graduate level."

As they say on late-night television, which is probably what ARS's customers are watching when they should be in the library: here's how to order. The white form supplied with the catalog informs the buyer: "The cost of a catalog paper is $5.50 per page. The maximum charge for any SINGLE catalog paper is $93.50. That is, all papers over 17 pages are priced at a flat $93.50 each (plus postage and/or Illinois tax, as applicable). ALL orders for catalog papers MUST be accompanied by payment IN FULL. SORRY, NO PERSONAL OR COMPANY CHECKS WILL BE ACCEPTED." Well, the bursar at Old Sywash can be a bit strict, too.

On the back of the form the purchaser signs a statement acknowledging that he has received a copy of Illinois revised statute, chapter 14, §219 (1973). The first paragraphs of a letter addressed "Dear Customer" explain:

A) The First Amendment to the U.S. Constitution gives us the right to research, evaluate, criticize or write reports, reviews, etc., on any topic, idea, or concept we so choose. All U.S.

citizens have this right including our Company. Accordingly, our business is "legal."

B) Recently, there have been promulgated limitations to this right of Freedom of Speech. In 1972, Illinois passed a law which in pertinent part, can prohibit the sale of any academic materials which the seller reasonably should have known would be used fraudulently by the buyer to obtain academic credit in an accredited institution of higher education.

C) As a customer, you should realize that you must put forth an additional effort in the preparation of your paper, speech, review or study for which we are providing assistance, in order to conform to Illinois law. In that regard, to prevent the fraudulent use of materials furnished by our Company, all such typewritten or copied materials will be protected by copyright notice, and will have all pages stapled together with the title page stamped with a copyright warning to further prevent the use of said materials as original work for credit.

What this caveat emptor, once decoded, really says is this: in addition to the $5.50 per page you've already spent, you're going to have to shell out another $1.50 per to your roommate to get the damned thing retyped. No good handing Doc Bartlett something Xeroxed and festooned with little circled *c*'s; suspicions will arise.

It has been observed that no one's Hamlet is the same as anyone else's. This is what ARS customers would no doubt call a "true fact." So it's not impossible that catalog item #9753 ("Hamlet: Madness or melancholia? An analysis of this character and his motivations; the causes of his distress. Argues that he suffered from melancholia. 9 14 18"), which even lacks the coveted *G*, might seem inadequate to one's own reflections, or just a bit unoriginal and overcooked. That's where ARS's "Custom Research Order," the yellow form supplied with the catalog, comes in. What a piece of work you'll get! Just provide a description of the research you need ("Please be as explicit as possible!") and check off whether you want "Basic Level Research" (six-page minimum; $12.50 per page) or "Advanced Level Research" (eight-page minimum; $14.50 per page). Indicate, along with name, address, telephone, Visa or MasterCard number and due date, whether you'd like a bibliography (remember, it counts as a page) and footnotes.

If you've paid Authors' Research the extra dollar for "Helpful Research & Writing Tips: An Anthology," you'll be getting advice on such matters as:

Is There a FAST Way to Locate Journal Articles?
"I Just Can't Put My Ideas Down in Writing"
When Should You Use Footnotes, and What Kind?
What About Style and Vocabulary?

And hearing such warnings as:

DON'T   use books with the words "How To" in their titles, or any
         similar words. These are not scholarly books.

Authors' Research Services looks at the big picture: "The meat of writing . . . consists in organizing and presenting ideas and concepts, and *comparing and contrasting* them when necessary. This is hard to teach; it comes only with practice. But the best shortcut is READING. Start reading nonfiction books of all sorts." But even with this expansive consideration of basics, Authors' Research does not neglect the details: "Try to use many different verbs, and try to turn other words into verbs." Example:

WRONG	RIGHT
If the policeman does his job well, the offender will be apprehended and will be sent to jail. He may get a parole later.	Arresting offenders accounts for most of the policeman's time. The convicted criminals are usually depositied [*sic*] in prison, where good behavior may win them a parole.

At first you may think this is a joke, or that the columns have been reversed by a printer's error after the wrong example entirely has been put on page 6. But probably not. ARS is just doing its bit to mislead students down one more garden path, toward the popular notion that when it comes to getting on in academic life, the best thing students whose first language is English can do is write it as if it's their second.

Both Research Assistance and Authors' Research Services were founded during that time of ethical confusion known as the Nixon administration. But term-paper mills have flourished long before and since, and some detectable differences lie among the generations of "specialists" who have produced the catalog papers. In 1971 the Boston proprietors of Termpapers Unlimited, the Warren brothers, Ken and Ward, told the *New York Times* that those faculty members who worked for them were moonlighters. A decade later, with the academic job market in a terrible slump, many more were just otherwise unemployed. In December 1979 Justice Richard W. Wallach of the New York State Supreme Court charged John Magee, president of Collegiate Research, with contempt of court, since Magee had not heeded injunctions against carrying on his business. "A sad byproduct" of the business, noted the judge, "is the exploitation of down-at-the-heels Ph.D.'s who churn out specifically commissioned assignments at Grub Street rates." Reporting on the mills for the *Times,* Don Hulbert and Carole Bodger noted a new motivational wrinkle — beyond the enduring ones of panic, sloth and exhaustion — among students in school at the dawn of the entrepreneurial Reagan years. "Some students now seem to be equating education with commerce; a degree buys the good life, they seem to be saying, and when the promise of the good life is taken away, they no longer feel bound by the rules." They quoted a term-paper miller named Louis: "Knowledge is not gathering information. Knowledge is adapting to existing circumstances." Which is to say that knowledge is power, but time is money.

Epstein's Philip Russo decides not to turn in the two cheaters he's caught: "Walking down the street, on his way to meet his son, Russo was thinking: 'Who the hell am I to set myself up as some moral paragon, as if I know right from wrong. The hell with it, the kids are desperate to get good grades, they want to please their parents and get into law school, be rich guys. I might not have done something like this in my undergraduate days, but the world was different then.' " He also realizes that if he's ever really hard up, he can earn some money writing for one of the mills himself.

At Vassar College, Dean of Studies Colton Johnson has spent more than a dozen years listening to students' excuses, granting extensions, reading the riot act, patiently sorting grandmothers who are genuinely dead from ones only spuriously so, distinguishing circumstances that extenuate from those that incriminate. He's never actually had a student confess to doing business with a term-paper mill, but "from time to time" the Academic Panel — himself, three students and three faculty members charged with adjudicating plagiarism cases — has come across papers that could not have been written from resources in the Vassar library.

The chief motive of the Vassar plagiarist is panic; students become suddenly frightened by a deadline from which they've been hitherto distracted. A few simply want to get ahead, whether that means having the grades for medical school or just Junior Year Abroad, but most times, says Dean Johnson, "they're just under that pressure. . . . There is no tomorrow after that day, and instead of talking it out and buying more tomorrows they go borrow it." The paper, that is.

Though the ranks of the panicked remain largely constant in number, "there are banner years," mostly due to the conduct not of students but faculty, who, instead of taking cases to the Academic Panel (as they are required to), make ad hoc adjudications of their own. Johnson's office tries to discourage this, but he knows it happens. He has had anonymous phone calls from faculty members seeking his advice about something they suspect is plagiarism; he's told them, yes, it sure sounds like it, bring it to the Panel — and that's the last he's heard of it. The reluctance to bring cases before the Panel stems partly, Johnson admits, from the professor's fear that the process will get out of control: "You always feel a little on trial yourself. You go do all the legwork in the library. You have to make sure your documents are all correct. You get there and some student says, 'Did you tell the students exactly how not to cheat?' and you have to admit, 'Well, no, this was a senior seminar; I didn't think it was necessary.' "

An analogy with rape comes up again and again in discussions of plagiarism; in this case the faculty member is the victim being grilled by the awful defense lawyer: "Admit it! You *wanted* her to plagiarize!" And yet what professors at Vassar may forget, at least according to Dean Johnson, is that the three students on the Panel are often tougher on their peers than the three professors.

Apart from feeling reluctant to bring these squalid matters to collective judgment in the dean's office, however, the professor may feel discouraged from even gathering evidence to support his suspicions. There is no more infuriatingly tiresome job in academic life than searching for that needle in the book stacks, the elusive source you *know* young Heather must have copied but that you simply can't find. And here you are spending three hours of a Saturday afternoon in a fruitless search while Heather's back in Wyatt Hall blowing a joint and watching a Billy Idol video. Sometimes it's just easier to lie to yourself: "Well, Heather *is* a bright girl. Maybe she did come up with this on her own. It's not impossible." Often the source will be a commonly available text, but certainly not always. And if Heather has borrowed her paper not from some issue of *Modern Language Quarterly* but from her roommate Seth, it's unlikely she will ever be caught.

If a source has been detected, the professor and student must, even before a decision has been made to go to the Panel, endure the Confrontation. Edith Skom, an instructor in Northwestern University's Writing Program, has described two approaches:

> A friend of mine — I'll call her Anna — liked a dramatic Perry Mason approach. Anna told me how she confronted one plagiarist: Calling the student aside after class, she made an appointment for him to see her in her office. The time arrived, the student came to her office. He was nervous at first, no doubt because he thought she had found him out. But when she urged him to take a seat, pointed to his paper on her desk and said, "That was a good paper you wrote," he relaxed and looked pleased.
>
> "Oh, you think it's good?"
>
> "Very good," she said. "An excellent paper. Profound ideas."
>
> "Thanks," he said modestly and sat back in his chair, very much at ease now.
>
> Then quick as a flash Anna pulled the desk drawer open, whipped out the book he had plagiarized from, and thrust it into his face. "Did you get any of your ideas from *this*?" she asked, and the student all but collapsed.
>
> Anna's approach seems to me the equivalent of giving the plagiarist a stress test. A gentle approach is more my style. I'm aggressive in tracking down plagiarism, but when it comes to confronting a student, I'm tentative, embarrassed — as if *I* had plagiarized.

The second method is considerably more common. And yet, there are students who, like latter-day Renaissance poets, are genuinely baffled by the whole premium placed on originality. The machinery of academic attribution strikes them as fastidious, beside the point. Social science students, Dean Johnson notes — citing an article in the *Chronicle of Higher Education* — sometimes fail to see any purpose in paraphrasing *information*. What's the use of repackaging it? Isn't this a waste of effort and thought? Some students will plead ignorance, though Johnson insists that Vassar defines ignorance very narrowly, just as he won't listen long to the student who blames the typist for leaving off the footnotes. Almost all of the dozen or so cases brought before the Panel each year result in verdicts against the student: "We convicted a student here when one of our distinguished professors of political theory caught one sentence from Martin Luther King's 'Letter from Birmingham Jail' in the midst of a twenty-page senior term paper."

Though there is a range of more severe sanctions, this infraction would have received the one that is automatic at Vassar: an asterisk on the back of the record card. As Johnson explains: "that . . . means that if the student requests in writing a college recommendation I have the obligation to . . . summarize the hearing in as fair a manner as possible." Which is to say that whenever he's asked to provide a college recommendation, Johnson must turn the card over and see whether the scarlet P, as it were, is affixed.

But keep in mind that these recommendations are rarely required. Johnson is asked for them by "your better law schools, some brokerage houses and, oh, the Secret Service or the CIA or something like that." A convicted plagiarist applying, say, to graduate school in history would need to send the school only recommendations from individual faculty members, as well as a copy of his transcript — and only the front of that, no asterisk, would be Xeroxed and mailed. Even so, as far as Johnson can recall, every student whose asterisked record he's had to summarize has gotten into one of those better law schools. And when state bar examiners have received the explanation? Those students have been admitted to the bar, too.

Those same students may eventually become the lawyers who

will threaten to sue the college after being retained by the parents of students facing plagiarism charges. "We've had lawyers waiting outside the Panel rooms," Johnson says. But since Vassar is a private institution, it has more flexibility than public institutions, and lawyers are therefore barred. Aside from the asterisk, available sanctions include expulsion (applied only once, in Johnson's memory, to a student who appeared before the Panel four times) and suspensions, for "real sustained, systematic, or repeated offenses." But Johnson admits that suspensions aren't what they used to be. Once "you'd send a girl home to sit on the front porch of her parents' home, ashamed, and be a shame to her neighborhood, but now they only go to Aspen for a couple of weeks." It's true that those two weeks in Aspen will probably make it impossible for her to catch up in her class and she'll flunk, but something — that is, the shame — has probably been lost. Most often what the Panel decides, beyond the asterisk and short of suspension, is to invalidate the plagiarized piece of work. It may be averaged in as a zero or an F or a 59, or it may simply not be counted at all.

On the subject of the new writing technology, Johnson is definite. It has "absolutely" increased the possibility and easefulness of plagiarism, and will keep on doing so as it develops. Word processing has been "incrementally more helpful" to the production of stolen papers. A student writing on Emily Brontë can sit in the library with a book open beside the computer terminal and "type in whole hunks of it," ending up with an easily "manipulable text" — zapping in his own verbs and modifiers here and there, covering his tracks via disingenuous paraphrase: no eraser shavings, no trail of crumpled, crossed-out pages. And this is nothing compared to what "digital scanning" of books will eventually make possible. "Any time you want Professor So-and-So's essay on X," Johnson says, "you can get the whole text, and at the press of a button it's yours. Then you put Johnny Jones at the top, and then you sit with the thing on the screen and where So-and-So says a word you don't think you understand, therefore your professor knows you wouldn't use, you get your thesaurus out and plug something in." So plagiarism's fine felonious future seems assured, with fewer and fewer reasons Why Johnny Can't Fleece.

A program called "The Technology of Writing" has been co-ordinated at Vassar by Robert DeMaria, who is also the principal author of the college's handbook *Originality and Attribution,* distributed to all freshmen, which outlines the spirit and methodology through which authorities are cited and plagiarism is avoided. Also the author of a highly regarded book on Samuel Johnson's dictionary, DeMaria turns to the *OED* in explaining to students that the word "plagiarism" is derived "from a Latin word meaning kidnapper or seducer," telling them forthrightly that plagiarism "is, after all, theft, and you do not want to be accused, as Sir Robert Peel was by Benjamin Disraeli, of being 'a burglar of others' intellect' " — citing the *Hansard* from which Peel's words come.*

DeMaria lucidly gets down to practical matters of direct quotation, proper and improper paraphrase, what is common knowledge (Samuel Johnson's place and date of birth) and what probably is not (how Johnson is thought to have contracted scrofula). He steers literature students away from books of criticism in the early stages of their work on a paper, lest they fall into the temptation that "occurs when a student reads a secondary source that seems to express precisely the idea he had for the paper, only better. If this is not a temptation to plagiarize, it is often a discouragement to the completion of the project." One appealing feature of *Originality and Attribution* is the author's uninhibited use of the language of morality in this squishily relativistic, post–*in loco parentis* era of campus life. Aside from admonishing stu-

---

*Had the space in his pamphlet permitted, DeMaria might have mentioned that Peel was accused by a very grimy pot. Disraeli committed his own most famous plagiarism in a funeral oration for the Duke of Wellington: the source for his grave robbery was an article by Louis Adolphe Thiers (1797–1877) on the French marshal Laurent de Gouvion Saint-Cyr (1764–1830). The pun-filled epigram that lampooned the theft in Leigh Hunt's *Examiner* is preserved in Walsh's ever-helpful *Handy-Book of Literary Curiosities:*

> In sounding great Wellington's praise,
>   Dizzy's grief and his truth both appear;
> For a flood of great Thiers he lets fall,
>   Which were certainly meant for Saint-Cyr.

The always vigilant Charles Reade recorded Disraeli's transgression in one of his notebooks. Thiers, by the way, was a friend of Mme. Reybaud's.

dents to avoid temptation, DeMaria counsels them to practice "an act of self-examination" when they're unsure they'd be writing what they are if they hadn't consulted something first. His useful rule of thumb: "If the material that you present *can* be assigned to a source, then it probably *ought* to be assigned to a source." He tells them, in a comfortable second-person way, "No teacher will think less of you for recognizing your debt to another writer," and urges them to skirt the paradoxical trap of thinking a lot of footnotes in a paper will make the professor feel the student hasn't come up with truly "original" thoughts on the subject at hand. (This, as DeMaria mentions, is a defense frequently uttered to the Academic Panel.)

One danger inherent in handbooks explaining the do's and don'ts of paraphrase — and a reason instructors sometimes object to them — is that students may be able to infer from them techniques for theft of which they would otherwise never have schemed. But the need to distribute something on this subject, which seems often so genuinely puzzling to freshmen, is obvious to virtually every college and university, assuring the creation of hundreds of pamphlets like *Originality and Attribution* nationwide. And since opportunity doesn't have to knock very loudly when it pays a call on irony, the following UPI dispatch inevitably appeared, on June 6, 1980, in the *New York Times:*

> Stanford University said today it had learned that its teaching assistant's handbook section on plagiarism had been plagiarized by the University of Oregon. Stanford issued a release saying Oregon officials conceded that the plagiarism section and other parts of its handbook were identical with the Stanford guidebook. Oregon officials apologized and said they would revise their guidebook.

Philip Russo's chief function in *Wild Oats* is to impregnate Zizi Zanzibar, the freshman girlfriend of the novel's protagonist — wimpy, asthmatic, sweet, gallant and hapless Billy Williams, who navigates late-adolescent waters at crummy Beacham University and who, back home in New York City, must deal with his divorced, ineffectual mother; her somewhat shady boyfriend, Henry; and his own brief affair with the gum-chewing Lulu. Billy is more amiable than interesting, and the wild oats he sows are more in the nature of embarrassed little pumpkin seeds. At the age of eighteen he "hadn't succumbed to any perverse sexual demons, never seen or heard God, never gotten a girl pregnant, never run away from home, never had a head-on car crash, never been kidnapped or raped or gotten cancer." This stock-taking occurs on page 79, and in the two hundred pages that follow, none of these things will happen.

Wild Oats seems to be a harmless, modestly entertaining book. Epstein's exposition is occasionally a bit belabored ("Why, Billy wondered, so many years later could he so clearly remember things like this?"), but he is capable of small bursts of style, phrases that blip up, a bit startlingly, from the calm sine curve of his prose: "Billy started toward her, legs spastically shooting out in all directions at first, then coordinating into a groovy shuffle." Like any first novel, it had uncertain prospects for success, but the last thing this book appeared headed for, upon its publication in 1979, was trouble.

Its jacket blurb called *Wild Oats* "deceptively comic" and invoked Billy's *Bildungsromanisch* forebears: Huck Finn, Amory Blaine, Benjamin Braddock. The last, being the hero of *The Graduate*, is the only one who makes any real comparative sense, but blurbs are rarely constrained by plausibility, and probably no subgenre of the novel more regularly invokes the names of older brothers than that of initiation. On the back of the jacket, above a Woody Allen–like photo of the very young author, Lillian Hellman, whose memory would soon be questioned by Mary McCarthy, proclaimed the novel a bridge between the generations: "Once in a while, a young writer sees himself, his friends and his parents with a remarkable good-natured brilliance. When that happens it is lovely to read and brings back the gaiety that maybe we once had." Good-natured, certainly; brilliant, certainly not. But blurbs are for burbling and this puff was no more inflated than the one below it by John Gregory Dunne: "Jacob Epstein has that rarest of commodities, a sense of humor; and in *Wild Oats* he uses it to calibrate every nuance with deadpan and wickedly funny accuracy."*

---

*In his own novel *The Red White and Blue* (1987) Dunne commits an odd form of connubial plagiarism, presumably sanctioned: he appoints a character named Tuck Bradley to be U.S. ambassador to a Central American country named

The reviews of *Wild Oats* were exceptionally flattering. Holden Caulfield was added to Billy Williams's literary kin in a number of them. There were small, inevitable disagreements among the reviewers — one praising the "immediacy" ensured by Epstein's own very recent graduation from college, another saying he needed the perspective that more "distance" would bring — but the praise was strong and generally uniform. Anne Tyler, in the *New York Times Book Review,* said the Russo character was a mistake, but that otherwise the book was "unfaltering — a densely written, solid piece of work, far beyond what you'd expect of a first novel." The *Saturday Review* saw "tremendous future promise."

There were some followers of New York literary life who would say, of course, that Jacob Epstein could hardly have shown anything else, that he had, after all, been born in belletristic clover. His parents are Jason and Barbara Epstein, Jason being the editorial director of Random House and Barbara the co-editor of the *New York Review of Books.* It was certain that *Wild Oats* would be seen as the first novel by the Epsteins' son — and in this respect young Jacob was not so much a hostage to fortune as a potentially sacrificial lamb. The *New York Review of Books* is not known for gentleness in expressing its dislikes, and Jason Epstein had also made his share of literary and business enemies over the years. Of his own young life in New York, he once wrote: "At the time, one's conquest of New York seemed inevitable; less a challenge than a natural right and one never expected to grow old."

Jacob Epstein turned twenty-three the year *Wild Oats* was published. He was fresh out of Yale, where he had won the Curtis Prize for Literary Excellence, an award to juniors for "literary or rhetorical work." And no one could say that who he was had anything to do with that; entries in the competition must be submitted under a pseudonym. He seemed enough of a comer for the jacket of *Wild Oats* to herald his most recent doings in a

---

Cristo Rey. In his wife Joan Didion's 1977 novel, *A Book of Common Prayer,* the U.S. ambassador to a Central American country named Boca Grande was named Tuck Bradley. It was nice to find Tuck, a decade later, still married to his unfailingly diplomatic wife, Ardis.

more than usually grandiose way: "Before completing his senior year at Yale, he took a leave of absence to begin *Wild Oats*. The novel was written in Berlin, on Ireland's Connemara Coast, and in London, where the author was on the staff of *The New Review*." (Precious cargo in that backpack!) Jacob Epstein's debut may have been a little oversold, but one couldn't find much to be embarrassed about. *Wild Oats* garnered most of its good reviews from critics who in fact minimized the family connection and tried to concentrate on the book itself.

By early 1980 the book had made its way across the ocean and into English bookstores. British reviewers, who had less reason to care about the novelist's parents than their American counterparts, offered praise similar to what had been heard over here. In the *New Statesman,* the young critic Blake Morrison: "The novel's material might have made a lesser writer smartass or self-pitying, but Epstein has an excellent command of tone, and an affectionate, ironic stance." The *Times Literary Supplement* saw *Wild Oats* as "no bad omen. If Jacob Epstein can remain true to his age, whatever it is, when he writes his next novel, and not be prompted by praise like this to freeze his future protagonists in futile re-runs of the adolescent Billy Williams — that is, if he can avoid Salinger's nemesis — he will turn into a very interesting novelist indeed."

Despite the hopes of the *TLS*, there would be no next novel from Jacob Epstein. It wasn't the opportunity to cannibalize his own early success that did him in; it was the revelation, on October 19, 1980, that *Wild Oats* owed a little too much of its rapid success to someone else's.

The article in that Sunday's *Observer* was called, inevitably, "A Tale of Two Novels," and it was a first-person account by the young British writer Martin Amis of how he discovered *Wild Oats* to contain about fifty resowings of bits from his own first novel, *The Rachel Papers*, published in 1974. "Some months ago," Amis began, "a friend gave me a new novel to read. 'You'll like it,' he said. 'It's your kind of thing.'" In reading *Wild Oats* Amis first noted some descriptive "echoes," but wasn't much bothered by them, and as for larger similarities ("precocious hero with wayward parents, sexual initiation with 'unserious' girl, emotional initiation with 'serious' girl, obsession with bodily functions and exams, etc., etc."), they worried him "not at all." How many situations, after all, does life offer, especially to the poor, pimply adolescent?

Calmly aware that the "boundary between influence and plagiarism will always be vague," Amis nevertheless soon realized that *Wild Oats* had "decisively breached" it. It wasn't a matter of similar plots and themes; it was a case of replicated language. Forget the old mathematical illustration that if you sit enough monkeys down at enough typewriters for enough time, one of them will eventually produce *Hamlet*. Here were just two young novelists, one of them in possession of the other's four-year-old novel. "Epstein wasn't 'influenced' by 'The Rachel Papers,' " Amis concluded, "he had it flattened out by his typewriter."

He offered the following extracts for comparison, himself in quotation marks, Epstein in italics:

"I could feel, gradually playing on my features, a look of queasy hope." *He could feel, playing across his face, a look of queasy hope.*

"My legs started off, at first spastically shooting out in all directions, then co-ordinating into a groovy shuffle." *Billy started towards her, legs spastically shooting out in all directions at first, then coordinating into a groovy shuffle.*

"Emendations took the form of replacing some of the 'ands' with 'buts,' and of changing the odd 'moreover' to 'however.' " *Revisions thus far have taken the form of replacing some of the "ands" with "buts" and the odd "however" with "moreover."*

"I always tried to look tranquil, approachable, full of dear-Marje wisdom; with no results." *Billy . . . tried to appear sensible and approachable, full of Ann Landers wisdom, but with no result.*

"I wished she would go. I couldn't feel anything with her there. I wished she would go and let me mourn in peace." *He wished that she would go. He couldn't feel anything with her there. He wished she would go and let him mourn in peace.*

If one were to read *Wild Oats* unaware of *The Rachel Papers*'s existence, one would be left with a certain puzzlement: how is it that Epstein's workmanlike prose will take those occasional trampoline bounces into the realm of real style before dropping back down to the mat — and staying there for an awfully long time between leaps? Amis's exposé clears up the mystery, and after reading it, the style-conscious reader who goes back to *Wild Oats* without a copy of *The Rachel Papers* will have little trouble finding other plagiarized lines, ones left unmentioned in the article. All he really need do is look for the passages that whistle instead of hum. No reviewer mentioned this unevenness at the time *Wild Oats* was published; perhaps they took it as a coltish display of the writer's extreme youth.

Throughout the seventies and early eighties Martin Amis developed a reputation as a literary bully boy. An *Esquire* profile from 1986 carried three epigraphs by three separate people (a novelist, an agent and a TV producer), none of whom wished to be identified: each one characterized Amis as "a little shit." Actually, he was gentle in his exposure of Epstein. He praised him as "a genuinely talented writer" with "a marvelous ear, even when he is merely translating my dialogue into American." Before publishing the *Observer* piece, he rejected the idea of suing, as well as the advice of friends who "cheerfully suggested blackmail as an option." Corlies Smith, who was for a time Amis's American editor at The Viking Press, recalls lunching with Amis and his American agent, Peter Matson, at the time Amis became aware of the plagiarism. To his credit, Smith says, Amis was "reluctant to do anything" even though "it was clearly eating at him." Smith suggested to Amis that he have somebody else write a letter exposing Epstein. Indeed, some journalists Amis knew offered to do just that. But Amis chose, reluctantly, to announce his own discovery. Seven years later he said, "All I wanted to do was put it on the record" — and have done with it. It seems clear that what motivated him to write the *Observer* piece was an abstract sense of literary justice as well as the inevitable sense of violation experienced by the plagiarized writer. He did not seem out to bully Epstein: "I had met Jacob a couple of times and found him a likeably nervous character. The last time I saw him, in New York, I apologised for not yet having read his novel. 'Oh, that's okay,' he said tremulously. 'I'm a great admirer of your work, by the way.' "

*

Let us do briefly what Jacob Epstein seems to have done at length: look at *The Rachel Papers.**

Charles Highway is, in British parlance, both literally and figuratively a wanker. He's got asthma (like Billy Williams and like Charles Reade) and spots and he's puny as can be. Just before turning twenty, Charles goes to London for an A-levels cram course and moves from boredom with Gloria, his utility girlfriend, to something like ecstasy with Rachel Noyes, the object of his meticulous seductions, before getting disillusioned in a Swiftian fit: one morning Rachel's underwear proves her to be as grossly corporeal as the rest of us. None of this would be very interesting — like most *Bildungsromans, The Rachel Papers* begins and ends in the foul rag-and-bone shop of the crotch — except for two things. Martin Amis is immensely skillful at grossing out the reader, and finally, *The Rachel Papers* isn't so much about coming of age as coming of page. As surely as *Madame Bovary* or *Flaubert's Parrot* (or, for that matter, *Mlle. de Malepeire*), this is a novel about reading, one in which the hero takes all his behavioral cues from books, and who methodizes whatever he learns in an unending series of notebooks, files and diaries. If Charles Reade's notebooks were the arsenal from which he weaponed his assault on literature, Charles Highway's are the supply line through which literature fuels an assault on life itself.

When he's not jotting, Charles is usually busy being disgusting. "There was no reason to believe that with her clothes off she would smell of boiled eggs and dead babies," he says of his sister. A large pimple is "a fine double-yolker"; when he wants to get rid of one of these he doesn't do anything deft: "For five minutes I savaged it with filthy fingernails." A rubbish bin is "the colour of baby's crap," and someone's cheeks swell "as if to contain a mouthful of prancing vomit." He propounds an aesthetic of grody-ness: "The nastier a thing is, the funnier it gets." Before a reader sniffs that Amis "overdoes" it, he should stop to think how well, and very nearly peerlessly, he just does it: "The hall smelled of boiling cabbage — or, let's be accurate, it smelled as if someone had eaten six bushels of asparagus, washed them

---

*The Vassar College library — like, no doubt, some others — owns one copy of *Wild Oats* and none of *The Rachel Papers.*

down with as many quarts of Guinness, and pissed over the walls, ceiling and floor." Nothing succeeds like abscess: in *The Rachel Papers* Martin Amis, that filthy little boy, made himself the prose-poet laureate of bodily discharge. Almost every phrase has an unpleasantly gifted spin: "We rolled about hugging and tickling each other, and laughing, in an evasive cross-fire of bad breath." It's the sort of thing another writer might wish he could do himself.

Charles is sufficiently organized and self-important to give titles to his different notebooks. One is *Highway's London;* another folder is *Conquest and Techniques: a Synthesis:* "When I get a good idea, or a detail worth elaborating on, then I turn it into a full-dress sentence (and circle it with red ink). The section entitled, simply, 'Gloria,' I now see, is done in a rather pompous mock-heroic style, like Fielding's descriptions of pub brawls — the sort of writing I usually have little time for." He goes through about seven diaries a year, adding them to the ever-growing pile of incunabula he carries about: "I snap open my dinky black suit-case and up-end it on the bed; folders, note-pads, files, bulging manilla envelopes, wads of paper trussed in string, letters, car-bons, diaries, the marginalia of my youth, cover the patchwork quilt. I jostle the papers into makeshift stacks. Ought they to be arranged chronologically, by subject, or by theme? Patently, some rigorous clerking will have to be done tonight." He re-searches and cross-references each date and orgasm and can get an erection reading the write-up of a bed session with Gloria. He is so dependent on his memoranda that he finds his success at ad-libbing through a surprise encounter with Rachel ("Didn't have a single note-pad on me") something remarkable: "Postur-ing, wordy, inept, if you like — but not bad for a viva." He'll paraphrase Marvell in a sex-begging letter; see his experience buying condoms as being "*too* much like low-brow American fiction"; and realize that he can see things only as others have seen them again and again: "In my world, reserved Italians, heterosexual hairdressers, clouds without silver linings, ignoble savages, hard-hearted whores, advantageous ill-winds, sober Irishmen, and so on, are not permitted to exist." When he con-siders suicide, he concentrates on the right wording for the note — and is dissuaded by the realization that he hasn't ap-pointed an executor for his notebooks.

The reviews of *The Rachel Papers* surpassed any young writer's most wanking critical fantasies. A cavil here, a carping there, but mostly heaps and heaps of praise. "Remarkable" (the *Listener*); "very funny indeed" (the *Spectator*); "tight, bright and full of talent" (*Books and Bookmen*); "scurrilous, shameless, and very funny" (*TLS*). Amis had managed to shoulder two burdens of the past: the specific one of his father Kingsley's reputation as the youthful creator of *Lucky Jim*, and the larger, longer one of being original in a mode older than Juvenal and in a genre started before Sterne. In *Encounter* Clive Jordan wrote that his characters were "described with the detached, excessively detailed physicality common to satirists down the ages. What holds the attention are not these limited characters, but the author's verbally inventive scrutiny of them; any time-travelling in this narrow environment can only be in the language itself."

The language itself: the author's fingerprint. Plots and characters and outlooks are almost too few to mention. The author's originality really lies in how he configures the infinitely varied molecular matter of the words. Amis fit his individual talents into the larger tradition and thereby earned the right to be considered an original.

The Rachel Papers won the National Book League's Somerset Maugham Award and crossed over to America, where all reviews begin with *New*. And as such, with the exception of the *New York Times Book Review* ("not really one to give a novelist father the sweats"), was it proclaimed: "Perhaps the best teenage sex novel I've read since Philip Roth's *Goodbye, Columbus*" (Eliot Fremont-Smith in *New York* magazine); "Some wildly funny lines. . . . Less a work of fiction than a collage of brightly malicious cinematic takes about that hoary first-novel chestnut, young love and early sorrows" (*New Leader*). On July 18, 1974, the summer before Jacob Epstein started Yale, it was praised as "nasty, British, and short" by Karl Miller, writing in the *New York Review of Books*.

Born on August 25, 1949, Martin Amis was not yet twenty-five when his novel was published. His father has recalled how he "read nothing but science fiction till he was fifteen or sixteen. It was his stepmother who took him in hand and said, 'How do you expect to get anywhere if you don't read books?' I didn't think he was university material." Indeed, Amis *fils* says he "flirted . . . with expulsion" at more than one grammar school, committing one offense of a literary sort. It was more a matter of forgery than plagiarism:

> I suppose the worst thing I ever did was to steal the diary of a fat, speechless classmate and fill it with a year's worth of bestial, obscene and quite imaginary antics. . . . The father of this unhappy boy found the diary, brought it to school and confronted the headmaster with its contents. The headmaster, as he flexed his cane, told me that he would not permit "the sewer vocabulary" to gain currency at his school. I got six of the best, and they hurt a lot; but I was allowed to stick around.

He eventually made it to university, where, if the memoir he contributed to a collection called *My Oxford, My Cambridge* is to be believed, he was of sufficient sexual backwardness to indicate that Charles Highway was actually given a bit of an aphrodisiacal pump-up from whatever autobiographical basis he may have had. What the memoir shows Amis and Highway sharing at Oxford is a preoccupation with character types and literary behavior — all youthful action being made possible, or just interpretable, through fictional precedent. Amis recalls "writing malarial, pageant-like, all-night essays," the first of which was accomplished via "eighty-four hours with Roget . . ."

The thesaurus is part of any young writer's passage, a sort of confetti'd version of the term-paper mill: the words one assiduously gets from it don't belong to anyone in particular, but they're not really one's own, either. Refuge in *Roget's* betokens a natural lack of confidence; it's the normal, neurotic defense mechanism of which plagiarism is perhaps the sick mutation. The rest of the sentence in which Martin Amis talked, a decade later, about his early reliance on forced synonymity shows the unstrained idiolect of the bona fide stylist; the compound adjective, one of Amis's staples, helps him fill out his freshman routine: ". . . lone sconce-dreading dinners in hall (i.e., college), a begowned sampling of lectures and libraries, tentative don't-mind-me sorties into the town." By the time he was writing *The Rachel Papers* he'd taken himself to London for work as an editorial assistant on the *TLS*. After the novel made its prize-winning splash, his days as a self-described "gnome" were behind him.

*

The New York press was quick to pick up the *Observer* story. Two days after it appeared in London, the *New York Times* ran a three-column article, "New Novelist Is Called a Plagiarist," which summarized the charges and announced Jacob Epstein's reply to them:

> Reached in Manhattan, Mr. Epstein, with some chagrin, asserted that the paragraphs in question had been excised from the second edition of his novel, but that these corrections were too late for the recent British publication.
>
> "I've been dreading this for months," Mr. Epstein told a London reporter. "It is the most awful mistake, which happened because I made notes from various books as I went along and then lost the notebook telling where they came from. The first edition should never have been published. I wanted to write to Martin at the time, but was advised against it. I shall certainly be writing to him now to explain."

Whoever advised Epstein not to write Amis when the notebook supposedly turned up did him no service. Amis still maintains that if Epstein had done that then, in the summer of 1979, that would have been the end of it. He would have accepted the apology, however implausible the explanation accompanying it might be. But more than a year went by without Epstein's doing anything — hardly a sign of good faith.

In October 1980 Epstein fleshed out his explanation in a letter to the *Observer*. He'd found the notebooks in his closet after returning from his year abroad ("The novel was written in Berlin, on Ireland's Connemara Coast . . ."), but *Wild Oats* was already out. Thirteen plagiarized items — "images and phrases" — were deleted from the second edition. ("There aren't 13 bits," Amis would say, "there are 50 odd bits from my book.") But *all* of the offending replications appeared in the British edition published by Secker and Warburg; Epstein says he wrote to tell them they should make up their edition from the revised version of *Wild Oats*, but his letter somehow never reached them and the British edition wound up being printed from the original, as it were, American one. He and his agent tried to keep the books back until revisions could be "somehow pasted in," in Epstein's words, but it was too late.

So Epstein's apology finally came to Amis on the pages of the *Observer*, one week after Amis's exposé. He told the story of the notebooks and declared: "I do not know any good way to apologise for this, nor the way to explain to you how my respect for your writing became something so lacking in respect."

To some extent the history of plagiarism is a history of notebooks, from the whirlpool of Coleridge's, through the overregulated cupboardfuls of Reade's and down to almost every contemporary dispute over a book involving research. In the fall of 1978, Alex Haley, the author of *Roots,* agreed to pay large damages to Harold Courlander and Crown Publishers for taking some material (and exact wordings) from Courlander's novel *The African.* Haley excused himself by saying that many people, including student volunteers at colleges where he lectured, contributed bits of "amorphous material" to him while he was preparing *Roots.* "Somewhere, somebody gave me something that came from 'The African.' . . . That's the best, honest explanation I can give." Eight years later Britain's Princess Michael admitted taking, for her book *Crowned in a Far Country,* some material on the French empress Eugénie word for word from a biography by the late Harold Kurtz. A spokesman clarified things for the press: "It seems that, when she read her notes a long time after making them, she forgot that she had written down actual phrases from one of the books she was using."

Epstein's explanation would have been slightly less implausible if there had been, in fact, even *more* exactness in his replications of Amis. But there was at least one "smoking gun," ruling out inadvertency, among the handful of examples Amis cited in the *Observer:*

> *The Rachel Papers:* I always tried to look tranquil, approachable, full of dear-Marje wisdom; with no results.

> *Wild Oats:* Billy . . . tried to appear sensible and approachable, full of Ann Landers wisdom, but with no result.

The British columnist Marje Proops can't become intelligible to American readers until her name is consciously changed to its American equivalent. Epstein had to do this deliberately, the way an American traveler in London must remember to change the voltage on his electric shaver.

In 1985 June and William Noble published a distasteful little book called *Steal This Plot: A Writer's Guide to Story Structure and Plagiarism,* which included a Q-and-A chapter with such practical advice as this:

> *Question:* What if I want to use characters from an old work — say, John Oakhurst and Mother Shipton from Bret Harte's *The Outcasts of Poker Flats?*
>
> *Answer:* This story was written in 1870 and the copyright has long since run out. Use the characters — steal them. *BUT* — if we use them *as they appear in a revised edition* which still has copyright protection, we'd have problems. The bare plot anyone can steal at any time.

The sleazy specificity of this prescription for stealing one is surprising, because the Nobles really don't know what a plot is; otherwise they wouldn't write, about *Wild Oats* and *The Rachel Papers,* that "it's pretty clear that Epstein *did* steal Amis's plot," which they define as: "Three months in the lives of two young men; both away at school, sexual encounters and promiscuity; preoccupation with biological functions, ludicrous coping with the urge for self-respect and adulthood; first serious love relationship." These things are subjects, situations, motifs, themes perhaps. But a plot involves these things in relation to a *sequence* of events, the maintenance of which is perhaps the hardest part of composing any novel: no one who has ever written one can any longer be mystified by the job of the "continuity" person on a film; he can only wish he had one sitting by his desk. Epstein's sequence is not suspiciously similar to Amis's at all, even if a few particular situations do seem improbably duplicated. (Visits to sympathetic dentists occur in each novel. What are the odds of finding two sympathetic dentists in the same county, much less in two different novels?)*

One peculiar thing about *Wild Oats* is that the subject of plagiarism doesn't come up just once (the Russo business) but twice. In the *Observer* Amis drew attention to how Epstein has Mark, the disturbed son of Billy Williams's mother's boyfriend, get

---

*In his *Observer* piece, it should be noted, Amis also used the term "plot" to describe the kinds of elements discussed by the Nobles.

caught, by his father, plagiarizing *Winnie the Pooh:* "Mark at first denied that he had plagiarized, but when Henry said, 'For God's sake, Mark, you can't do this. Do I have to drag you to a bookstore to prove this thing to you?' Mark ran down the hall and locked himself in his room and wouldn't come out."

Peter Shaw, in his *American Scholar* essay, says it's also suspicious that the hero of *The Rachel Papers* is a "verbal plagiarist" — Charles Highway's notebooks — particularly when Amis admitted in the *Observer* to lifting an occasional line himself. Amis pointed out in his exposure of Epstein that the description of some surviving templar tufts of hair on a bald head as "two grey-coloured wiry wings," which Epstein took from *The Rachel Papers*, was in fact taken (by Amis) from a description of Podsnap in *Our Mutual Friend.* He also admitted to once having taken "a whole paragraph of mesmeric jargon from J. G. Ballard's 'The Drowned World,'" and acknowledging it to his friend Ballard only after one of Ballard's fans complained to his publisher. "The lapse," Amis explained, "was evidence of laziness, and a kind of moral torpor." Shaw claims that these admissions help put Amis, along with Epstein, among those committing "inadvertent, yet somehow purposeful, self-exposure."

But this really won't hold up. As Shaw himself says, "An accusation of plagiarism normally arises only where there has been a *pattern* of improper conduct." An individual lapse, or a fit of cheek, which seems to be what Amis can be called to account for, is hardly the same as compulsively borrowing dozens of passages. Charles Highway's being a "verbal plagiarist" is no more reason to be suspicious of Amis than Jean Valjean's being a thief is reason to doubt the probity of Hugo: verbal plagiarism is the very subject of *The Rachel Papers*, which is a piece of writing about reading in the way that *Don Quixote* is. If plagiarism-as-subject is a matter of "self-exposure" in *Wild Oats*, it's because of its more incidental role — in light of what Epstein was doing. It was a hint, a compulsively dropped clue to what the author was engaged in. And what that was, finally, was not so much becoming Martin Amis, who cannot reasonably be called a plagiarist, but Charles Highway, someone whose literary life ended after a single novel.

*

F. R. Leavis once said that the self-promoting Sitwell family belonged to the history of publicity, not poetry, and it may well be that the Epstein affair does, too. His agent, Lynn Nesbit, insists that the press exaggerated the whole thing, and most people who work in the world of publishing — including Martin Amis's former American editor, Corlies Smith, would agree: "It was blown out of proportion . . . by people who wanted to get Jason." Or Barbara, for that matter. It was one thing for *Publishers Weekly* to make the incident the lead item of trade news in its November 7, 1980, issue, but other publications didn't so much write the story as cackle it. "Life seems to be imitating art in the plagiarism flap involving writer Jacob Epstein, son of local literary lights Barbara and Jason Epstein" went a lead paragraph on *New York* magazine's "Intelligencer" page. Even the good gray *Times* put it into the Week in Review section's "Headliners" column, that group of Sunday snippets-as-sniggers accompanied by photographs that serve almost as mug shots for what are, as often as not, achievements *Esquire* would call dubious: the flap over *Wild Oats* was titled "Against the Grain." In the *New Republic*, R. D. Rosen rather witlessly joined the pack in a piece called "Epping," which carried a bio-line identifying himself as "the author of *Pride and Prejudice, To the Finland Station*, and the screenplay for *Guns of Navarone.*" Rosen defined "Epping" as a confessional fad supposedly set off by Epstein:

> Fleming Arleutter, a Chicago writer with five out-of-print novels and no following to his credit . . . called a press conference at the Palmer House to announce that sections in each of his novels had been lifted *in toto* from sources that include *A Sentimental Education, The Tin Drum,* Time-Life's *Recipes From the Cooking of Spain and Portugal,* the US House of Representatives 1973 Subcommittee Hearings on the Role of Franchising in Small Business, and an as yet unpublished novel by Joyce Carol Oates. As a result of this startling disclosure, Arleutter's publisher is reissuing his books in an omnibus edition and has signed him to a lucrative contract for two forthcoming novels based closely on Iris Murdoch's oeuvre.
>
> . . . several authors have reported that their latest manuscripts have been turned down by their publishers with the explanation, "It's terrific stuff, but we haven't read anything like it before."

Any grain of satiric validity in this owed nothing to Epstein: publishing, like other businesses, has always worked according to received retail truth — give the customer more of what he wants.

The *Newsweek* story of November 3, 1980, reported that the paperback edition of *Wild Oats*, which was reaching store shelves as the plagiarism news broke, totaled 110,000 copies. This is certainly far above the average for first novels, but it still didn't put *Wild Oats* in the megabucks world of plagiarism litigation. From Corlies Smith's point of view, one reason coverage of the case has to be seen as overblown is that it was really a matter of "one book that didn't sell plagiarizing from another book that didn't sell." Not long before *Wild Oats*'s exposure, there had been some large, well-publicized out-of-court settlements. Gail Sheehy, the author of the phenomenally successful *Passages,* paid a substantial sum to a California psychiatrist whose scientific research she had popularized without enough attribution. The amount of the agreement between Alex Haley and Harold Courlander was not disclosed, but the *New York Times* guessed it involved "hundreds of thousands of dollars." These big settlements reflected the vast sales that had lengthened the authors' royalty statements. Amis never had any intention of suing, whatever the sums at issue might have been. He remains aware that what happened with Epstein was "a very special case" and that the reaction it incited was perhaps vindictive: people were probably "extra tough" on him because of his parents. The case was so magnified by publicity that a half-dozen years after his *Observer* piece was filed Amis was "still not sure" he should have done it.

In the years since the episode, Amis has written with considerable wit about literary success and fame in America, where the "uncontrollable nature" of the latter ensures that "multiple rapists and winners of ugly-contests are promptly bombarded with love-tokens, marriage-offers, and so on." According to Amis, "When success happens to an English writer, he acquires a new typewriter. When success happens to an American writer, he acquires a new life."

Pondering why "American writers tend to hate each other," Amis has wondered whether some of it has to do with the hugeness of the place: "In England writers mix pretty well: they have a generally middle-class, generally liberal unanimity. In America writers are naturally far flung (Alabama, Washington, Chicago,

New England); to come together, they have to traverse great distances; it isn't surprising, when they meet, that they seem so strange to one another." Perhaps, but the Epstein incident was in most respects a very local affair. The perpetrator's parents were high-profile figures in a city that, with some justification, still thinks of itself as the Apollonian sun around which the literary asteroids of outer America spin. Like most great capitals New York is a very provincial place; there is really only one literary party in town, and if you show up at it on any given night, for a few hours of *Schadenfreude* and logrolling, and you mention to your fellow writers a work-in-progress on plagiarism, you will be asked not about Coleridge or ethics or word processing but, inevitably, "Are you writing about Jacob Epstein?"

To come back to the business of notebooks: there are writers who do manage to use them responsibly, for storage and for practice. Martin Amis's father, Kingsley, told the *Paris Review* how he uses one:

> It's not a very fat notebook. It contains things like scraps of dialogue that one overhears or thinks of . . . very short descriptions of characters . . . comic incidents seen, or conceivably invented. But I don't write synopses. I used to at one time. I mean, I kept a very thick and detailed notebook for *Take a Girl Like You* — about a hundred pages. But I think that was partly nervousness, because I knew that its theme, and using a female protagonist, was going to put a severe strain on my resources. And I was limbering up, as it were, to write that.

Robert Louis Stevenson said that as an undergraduate in Edinburgh he had

> always two books in my pocket, one to read and one to write in. Whenever I read a book or a passage that particularly pleased me, in which a thing was said or an effect rendered with propriety, in which there was some conspicuous force or happy distinction in the style, I must sit down at once and set myself to ape that quality. I was unsuccessful and knew it. I tried again and was again unsuccessful, and always unsuccessful, but at least in these vain hours I got some practice in rhythm, in harmony and construction and coordination of parts. I have thus played the sedulous ape to Hazlitt, to Lamb, to Wordsworth, to Sir Thomas Browne, to Defoe, to Hawthorne, to Montaigne, to Baudelaire and Obermann.

For all Stevenson's youthful exuberance the distinction between his two books remained clear, whereas with Epstein, at some point, the two blended into a system of double-bookkeeping, a form of embezzlement he may at first not have fully realized he was engaged in. The accountant moves the first fateful figure into the wrong column, as yet unwilling to admit to himself what he's doing. Volition is present, but awareness of it hasn't yet completely risen from the fingertips to the brain. The conscience can still deny what's going on, but down below, on the page, the line has been crossed, and the right hand knows what the left hand is doing. In his book on the Chicago 7 conspiracy trial, Jacob Epstein's father, Jason, explained: "Under what is known as the doctrine of 'conscious parallelism,' the existence of a conspiracy may be inferred by the jury from the similarity of purpose suggested by the overt acts of the defendants, unless the defense convinces the jury of a less sinister interpretation." Whatever Jacob Epstein claimed, *Wild Oats* looked like a convincingly sinister conspiracy between the part of him that was reader and the part of him that was writer.

A few weeks after the press din in New York, a single, ringing defense of Epstein by Darryl Pinckney, called "Spooking Plagiarism," appeared in the *Village Voice*. Nearly as young as Epstein, he made a well-written but poorly reasoned effort to invalidate the confession Epstein himself had made. When *Wild Oats* appeared in 1979, Pinckney said, he read it with pleasure; a year later, as the reports of plagiarism came out, it "was still in [his] mind — so much life this side of the Atlantic in it, unthinkable as significantly derived from an English work. Regardless of confession."

Pinckney's essential argument for appealing the verdict is that most of *Wild Oats* is *not* plagiarized. This familiar defense is one that, in this case, cannot be summarized without risibility: "In reading the two books — Epstein's first edition — I would confirm Amis's charge of 53 lines or phrases that echo, sometimes with changes, sometimes not, *The Rachel Papers*. It was a hard task, collating these two books, but my feeling that *Wild Oats* was essentially Epstein's book led me to do this." That feeling was never destroyed by hearing the fifty-three echoes: "He is not a criminal, he is a writer. He wrote *Wild Oats*. It is his." Question: If the police enter the house of a suspected thief and find fifty-

three stolen objects amid, say, two thousand legitimately purchased by the occupant, should they not proceed to arrest him?
As Judge Learned Hand wrote, "No plagiarist can excuse the
wrong by showing how much of his work he did not pirate."

About what might be called, to adapt a British phrase, the
"naughty bits," Pinckney writes, "I cannot excuse the lines —
they are too foolish and unhelpful to the composition." Indeed,
he insists, "Most of the 'lifted' lines are casual descriptions, what
one would call dead lines, not always striking, and in that sense
a wonder." This is hardly true, but one way of pleading for a
lighter sentence is to devalue the stolen goods. (Watergate, you
recall, was called a "third-rate burglary.") The fact remains that
he who steals Amis's prose steals flash, not trash. *The Rachel
Papers* was good enough to plunder.

Pinckney thinks that what Amis calls "chunks" may be "situa-
tional matter, expressed here and there in similar language,"
though it will be clear to most readers of Amis's *Observer* piece
that "chunks" is a relative term — verbatim passages larger than
the other bits. But Pinckney undertakes comparison of what he
surmises to be two of the "chunks." Here is his second, or "Exhibit B":

> ... the description of an orgasm. Amis's is longer and far more
> bravura than Epstein's. On top of and inside Rachel at last,
> Charles: "I grow old I grow old shall I feel her fingernails hear
> her neigh give me strength O my people affirm before the world
> and deny between the socks not long for the garden where end
> loves all ten more five more the bathroom in the garden the
> garden in the desert of drouth, spitting from the mouth the with-
> ered apple-seed." On top of his summer fling, Lulu, Billy:
> "... Anything to keep his mind distracted from the matter at
> hand, or below him ... a baseball player stealing second, Martin
> Luther King, oh God ... I have a dream ... here it comes ... Lit-
> tle black boys shall walk hand in hand with white girls ..." I'm
> afraid, alas, that Epstein's Billy "surfs" on Lulu's climax, just as
> Amis's Charles "surfs" on Rachel's climax. And all four surf like
> Molly Bloom. Yes.

Clever, but disingenuous, too. Instead of wondering about something Amis only may have had in mind, why not quote some of
the absolutely word-for-word passages side by side? Or the Dear

Marje/Ann Landers lines? Pinckney says that "kinship is not thievery," and he's right, of course. But no one had been talking about kinship; Amis himself described any overlappings of plot and character as unsuspicious, even inevitable, remaining aware that such overlapping still didn't produce books that were, atmospherically, very similar. In fact, the books don't feel, overall, very much alike; it's just that they are, sometimes, exactly the same.

G. K. Chesterton, in his own warning against plagiarism surveillance, wrote that "to see the similarities, without seeing the differences, seems . . . a dangerous game." It leads, he thinks, to mad obsessions with notions like the one that has Bacon writing Shakespeare. All this seems so reasonable that one is likely to forget that plagiarism sometimes *does* happen and that, in any case, no one has been talking about suspicious similarities; the subject is irrefutable identities.

When Pinckney admits that the "trouble is serious," he seems to be thinking of the trouble Epstein, unfortunately, is in. He views him as the victim, and the detection of plagiarism, rather than plagiarism itself, as the disreputable activity ("These two books, which I have laboriously scoured, scraped, scanned — better work for ambulance chasers and out-of-work attorneys"). Though Pinckney can say he knew Jacob Epstein only slightly when he wrote "Spooking Plagiarism," he seems to take the latter's problem personally, saying that this particular accusation of plagiarism, coming in a season of them, "hit me the hardest." He treats *Wild Oats* as if it were a sacred text ("He wrote *Wild Oats*. It is his"), even referring to the book's recent "defacement." And even if Pinckney was not involved with the *New York Review of Books* at the time this essay was published (he later would be), "Spooking Plagiarism" does sound a bit like a *New York Review* alarm against McCarthyites being spotted under every bed: "Careful, all you people at the typewriter. Careful, indeed. Watch your drinking and keep that copy of Edgar Allan Poe's essay, 'Mr. Longfellow and Other Plagiarists,' under the beaten pillow. Careful with your hallucinations over the page late, late at night."

In the early and mid-1840s Poe leveled a number of charges against Longfellow — most seriously that he had stolen from Tennyson. In 1845 there was an extended exchange in the *Broad-*

way Journal between Poe and the pseudonymous "Outis," who defended the white-haired bard of "Hiawatha." After some months of fighting "Outis," Poe seemed to recant, concluding that "all literary history demonstrates that, for the most frequent and palpable plagiarisms, we must search the works of the most eminent poets." This apparent reversal, declaring that Longfellow's near duplication of others' words resulted not from "moral delinquency" but the unconscious osmosis inevitable in someone with "poetic sentiment," is the only essay that Pinckney chooses to quote. In acquitting Longfellow of willful theft, Poe may have honestly regretted the sometimes vituperative tone of his charges, but he was probably also tired of being under "suspicion of malevolence or discourtesy" — the suspicion with which Pinckney regards Epstein's detractors ("ambulance chasers"). One of the many quite rational things Poe has to say about plagiarism is this:

> When [it] is committed and detected, the word "littleness," and other similar words are immediately brought into play. To the words themselves I have no objection whatever; but their application might occasionally be improved.
>
> Is it altogether impossible that a critic be instigated to the exposure of plagiarism, or still better, of plagiarism generally wherever he meets it, by a strictly honorable and even charitable motive?

Explanations involving osmosis, which we'll discuss in a minute, have a certain plausibility, and so do those of coincidence, which Longfellow himself cited on one occasion: "One cannot strike a spade into the soil of Parnassus, without disturbing the bones of some dead poet." But it is simply not conceivable that Epstein put so many of Amis's lines into his manuscript without once hearing a bell of recognition sound.

What Epstein was doing was committing literary suicide. Martin Amis recognized this from the beginning. In the *Observer,* just before calling attention to one of *Wild Oats*'s telltale plagiarism scenes, he declared the psychology of plagiarism to be "fascinatingly perverse: it risks, or invites, a deep shame, and there must be something of the death-wish in it." Epstein would call that explanation "cruel and vindictive," but psychiatrists interviewed when the incident broke agreed with Amis. Dr. Arnold Cooper, head of the American Psychoanalytic Association, commented on the plagiarist's unconscious "need for public punishment. The person, in one way or another, can be inviting shame." One thinks of the "tremulousness" Epstein displayed in meeting Amis before the latter had read his novel, and of his inability to write the letter of apology that would have forestalled his public denunciation, and one must wonder if it was all less a matter of self-aggrandizement than self-destruction. Dr. Robert Michels, of Cornell University Medical College, says that when those lacking in self-esteem "finally achieve a great success, they devalue or even undermine it. . . . Their success is destroyed because it had built into it the seeds of defeat." And Peter Shaw, you remember, says that the criminal to whom the plagiarist compares most closely is the kleptomaniac, "both in his evident wish to be detected and in the circumstance that what is stolen may not be needed. (With kleptomania, lack of need, we are told, is absolutely central.)" Reade's theft from Mme. Reybaud occurred long after his reputation was solidly made, and the notebooks he left behind are like an indexed confession just waiting for a policeman to come along. Epstein didn't "need" the fifty or so bits in the way the desperate student, the night before the due date, needs the stolen term-paper material. Without them *Wild Oats* would have been remembered as a fair-to-middling first novel instead of a scandalous curiosity.

Shaw notes that plagiarists tend to be especially vehement toward other plagiarists and "tend to suffer from the delusion that they have been plagiarized from." Coleridge, of course, overfills this bill, and the same sort of guilty righteousness seems to extend to the plagiarist's cousin, the forger. The British book dealer Thomas J. Wise, who early in this century secretly specialized in passing off pirated facsimiles as first editions of Romantic and Victorian writers, also "developed an obsession for unmasking forgers," according to John Whitehead, "an obsession which again brought him into the limelight and earned him many more admirers due to his success as a literary detective."

Back in 1902 in his essay "The Ethics of Plagiarism," Brander Matthews pronounced "the amateur literary detective . . . an almost useless person," declaring that "a ready acceptance of the charge of plagiarism is a sign of low culture, and that a frequent bringing of the accusation is a sign of defective education and deficient intelligence." He reminded his readers that language is "finite" and plots even more limited, before making the curious assertion that "in any discussion of plagiarism quite the most important question is the relative value to the borrower of the thing borrowed. If he has flocks of his own, he may lift the ewe lamb of his neighbor, and only laborious dulness will object." What's odd (aside from the fact that Matthews uses the phrase "laborious dulness" without any attribution, though thirteen pages earlier he's quoted it from Scott) is why it should be all right for an imaginatively rich man, but not a poor one, to steal — as if lots of talent excused rapacity any more than lots of money. But even if one accepts Matthews's sense of justice, one can't use it to acquit Epstein: the swag from Amis outshone what setting he was able to give it.

Matthews admitted there exist "cases of absolute necessity" that justify the use of parallel columns: "It is plagiarism for an author to take anything from another author and reproduce it nakedly," but if "the second comer can improve on the work of the first comer, if he makes it over and makes it better, and makes it his own, we accept the result and ask no questions." This is where reasonable writers continue to differ: what strikes one as blatant leaves another blasé. The British author D. M. Thomas has been in trouble twice over plagiarism, once for his translation of Pushkin and another time for his novel *The White Hotel.* The critic John Bayley (in the *New York Review of Books*) put both instances in a favorable light:

> He has been accused of borrowing from previous translators, even of copying from them instead of working from the original.
>
> The charge of plagiarism was also made against his best-selling novel *The White Hotel,* and in both cases seems equally unfounded. Apart from not admitting his theft, the plagiarist hides behind the material he has stolen. Thomas handsomely acknowledged the use he made in the novel of Kuznetsov's memoirs of Babi Yar. His translations acknowledge a debt to Professor John Fennell, whose Penguin selection gives the best plain prose rendering available of Pushkin's verse.

The *Atlantic*'s reviewer of Thomas's subsequent novel, *Ararat,* was none other than Martin Amis, who was customarily sensible on the subject of possible plagiarism. He was untroubled by the Pushkin translations, but not so comfortable with what Thomas had done with — or to — Kuznetsov: "It wasn't a case of plagiarism; but it was clearly a case of something. When the reviewers spoke of the transports and crackups they weathered as they checked out of *The White Hotel* ('I walked out into the garden and could not speak,' and so on), it was Babi Yar that had assailed them. The testimony is unbearably powerful; it is the climax of the novel; it is, in plain terms, the best bit — and Thomas didn't write it." To acknowledge something on the copyright page is all well and good; neglecting to put quotation marks around much of what is used is something quite different. If young Heather — to return for a moment to academic life — lists a book in her bibliography, that doesn't mean she can let exact words from it go without a footnote and inverted commas. Call them ewe lambs or anything else: the words are all.

When it is clear that plagiarism has occurred not from absent-mindedness but avarice (be it for money, approval or disgrace), then a kind of emergency damage control is in order. In 1972 Graham Greene's agent complained that two pages from *Bound to Violence*, by the West African writer Yambo Ouologuem, contained passages that were almost word-for-word reproductions of Greene's 1934 novel *It's a Battlefield*. William Jovanovich, Ouologuem's American publisher, agreed to get rid of the 3,400 copies of the novel still available from Harcourt Brace. "Even if Mr. Greene were to say that he just wants an acknowledgment, we would still go ahead and destroy the copies. . . . If I can not warrant it, I can not publish it."

Even if he doesn't indulge in imitation as a deliberate exercise, a young writer with even the smallest promise has to be able to absorb the rhythms of writers who excite him. What's hypnotic becomes osmotic, necessarily and happily so, for no one will ever amount to anything unless his early reading leaks into his first writing. As, yes, Brander Matthews put it in "The Duty of Imitation": "The artist can be individual, he can have an accent of his own, he can separate himself from his fellows, only as his own personality manifests itself, which it is not apt to do in youth and which it cannot do until the artist has learnt his trade. Only by imitation can he acquire it; and imitation is therefore his duty, — independent imitation and not slavish copying."

The scientist usually peaks early if he peaks at all; the artist is allowed a much longer period of discipleship, rebellion and general foolishness. Countless writers, would-be and/or eventually real ones, grow up imitating a strong stylist of choice. Joan Didion says reading Hemingway taught her "how sentences worked. When I was fifteen or sixteen I would type out his stories to learn how the sentences worked.* I taught myself to type at the same time. A few years ago when I was teaching a course at Berkeley I reread *A Farewell to Arms* and fell right back into those sentences. I mean they're perfect sentences. Very direct sentences, smooth rivers, clear water over granite, no sinkholes." Didion is herself a stylist so original and recognizable that she lends herself to parody (and self-parody) as easily as any writer you can think of; but if you peel back what's irreducibly hers, you can spot beneath it some underground springs of Papa, particularly the laconic refusal to let any sentence or paragraph go on too long.

When I began writing in the 1970s, Hemingway was largely out of fashion among the young. Very much in fashion was Joan Didion herself. I can look back on things I've written as late as a few years ago and hear an occasional Didionesque hum coming through the walls of margin around my own inferior prose. In most ways we couldn't be less alike as writers. Anyone who has come this far will classify my style as loquacious, parenthetical, deliberately (and sometimes presumptuously) "friendly." None of these is a hallmark of Didion. And yet her work is one of the underground streams running beneath my own writerly shop. A student of mine once approached me with a paragraph I'd written (originally part of a speech) about the experience I had rereading my college diaries. It concerned advice my thirty-three-year-old self would offer his nineteen-year-old precursor: "First, stop confusing the relative values of love and self-respect. The difference between the two is something like the difference between luxury and necessity, perfume and oxygen." My student suggested this was an awful lot like a sentiment expressed in an essay by Didion ("On Self-Respect") we'd read in class — the

*Epstein explained that he kept his fifteen blue notebooks with their extracts from Amis, Nabokov, Turgenev, Goethe and others "to see how writers got things to work."

term before I wrote those sentences. Well, on reflection I supposed it was; but this *was*, after all, my own behavioral code, independently arrived at, just as others had similarly won that hard conclusion before Didion. And, in any case, there was my arresting perfume-versus-oxygen analogy, which I could recall being quite pleased with when it swam into my ken and down through my pen. So I could call that my original contribution to the subject. Or could I? I went back to the Didion essay and found her recommendation for reducing one's sense of self-importance: putting one's head in a paper bag and cutting off the air supply to the inflated brain. No contrast to perfume, and in fact no use of the word "oxygen." But I had to wonder: was the analogy really my own, or was it rising, unbidden, from one of those underground streams?

If I looked closer at the rest of my retroactive prescriptions to my adolescent self, I could probably spot other models and heroes: something of Mary McCarthy in the listing of things, maybe something of Orwell in the actual numbering of the list's items. Again, two writers I'm utterly unlike, whose very wastebaskets inspire my envy; but unlike them as I may be, they're somewhere in my inkwell, however diluted, however misapplied. The risk of aping, consciously or unconsciously, is of course reduced if one has a whole pantheon of idols. (Matthews quotes the French writer Legouvé: "The only way not to copy anybody is to study everybody.") The greatest danger remains getting a very recognizable stylist too deeply under the skin of one's own writing bump. Speaking of "the risk of verbal infection," S. J. Perelman noted: "The kind of words I use are liable to become imbedded and fester, like the steel wool housewives use."

One of the writer's occupational fears is that he will plagiarize unwittingly (a fear that swells into a paralytic case of Caesarean wifeliness while writing a book on this subject). In April 1925, just before publication of *The Great Gatsby*, F. Scott Fitzgerald sent Willa Cather a letter, along with two pages of his manuscript, and expressed his distress over the similarity he noted between a passage from her novel *A Lost Lady* and his own description of how Daisy's voice affects the men who hear it. He'd written his lines before he read *A Lost Lady* (the manuscript pages he sent Cather, from chapter 1 of *Gatsby*, have Daisy still being called

Ada), and friends like Ring Lardner told him he shouldn't delete them because of innocent coincidence — after all, it's not even a voice Cather describes; it's the effect of Marian Forrester's eyes on Niel Herbert. But Fitzgerald, on the verge of seeing his masterwork in Scribner's windows, was nervous nonetheless. Cather's understanding reaction is recounted in Phyllis Robinson's biography: she "sent a gracious reply, complimenting Fitzgerald on *Gatsby* and denying that she had detected any plagiarism. The only way to describe beauty was to describe its effect, not the actual person, she told Fitzgerald. It was what she had been telling people for years when they charged her with drawing her characters too closely from life."

Every novel is probably a roman à clef. Some may require a whole key ring to get the reader through a maze of interlocking chambers, but what he will never find inside the smallest cask in the innermost room is whole cloth. Our imaginations are only the jumble of what we see and hear; creativity lies more in the mixing than the making. And for each character a novelist stirs up from five or six living souls (some he's not even consciously remembering), he may use half a dozen lines of dialog he's heard in a variety of real-life circumstances, and for each of which he now finds a convenient use in his book. Fitzgerald's notebooks contain plenty of things he seems to have picked up on the street or at parties, oral ephemera from strangers who passed in and out of his life. But he didn't neglect household words either. Zelda Fitzgerald complained that in *The Beautiful and Damned* she could "recognize a portion of an old diary of mine which mysteriously disappeared shortly after my marriage, and also scraps of letters which sound vaguely familiar. Mr. Fitzgerald seems to believe that plagiarism begins at home." Kenneth Halliwell, the lover of playwright Joe Orton, felt his contributions to Orton's work (which included the title for *Loot*) were insufficiently acknowledged — one of the many scores he settled by hammering Orton to death in the summer of 1967.

The theft of what is merely spoken or gesticulated is usually not so violently resented. In fact, we generally give those plagiarists points for cleverness. The familiar story goes that when Wilde and Whistler were together and Whistler said something particularly apt, Wilde exclaimed, "I wish I'd said that, Jimmy," and Whistler responded, "Don't worry, Oscar, you will." As the anecdote rolls down through the decades, it tends to gather from posterity more affection for Wilde's nerve than Whistler's wit — just as Milton Berle is beloved for stealing other comedians' jokes. When Gary Hart seemed to be mimicking John F. Kennedy's gestures during the 1984 primary campaign, a few voters and commentators expressed irritation, but it was no big deal; the body language that would cause him real trouble lay three years in the future.*

The most famous political plagiarist of our time is Senator Joseph Biden of Delaware, whose undoing got going on September 12, 1987, when the *New York Times* ran a front-page story, "Biden's Debate Finale: An Echo from Abroad," that reported how the senator's peroration in a recent Iowa debate had closely resembled a speech Labour party leader Neil Kinnock had used in a television commercial during the previous May's election campaign in Britain. The crucial passages ran as large-type captions under photos of Kinnock and Biden:

Why am I the first Kinnock in a thousand generations to be able to get to university? . . . Was it because our predecessors were thick? . . . Was it because they were weak, those people who could work eight hours underground and then come up and play football, weak? It was because there was no platform upon which they could stand.

Why is it that Joe Biden is the first in his family ever to go to a university? . . . Is it because our fathers and mothers were not bright? . . . Is it because they didn't work hard, my ancestors who worked in the coal mines of Northeast Pennsylvania and would come up after 12 hours and play football for four hours? . . . It's because they didn't have a platform upon which to stand.

Never mind whether you agree with the government-as-bootstrap philosophy, and never mind that the Kinnocks of a thousand generations ago, had they gotten government grants, would have been commuting to university by dinosaur. The original was an awfully good speech.

*In "The Duke and His Domain," Truman Capote reminded readers that "many critics reviewing [James] Dean's first film, *East of Eden*, remarked on the well-nigh plagiaristic resemblance between his acting mannerisms and Brando's."

Any student of plagiarism reading that newspaper article would have known one thing for sure: there would be more "revelations" to come. And indeed, the compulsive factor, like other classic features of the crime, would soon show itself. Four days later there was a report that Biden had also appropriated words from his acknowledged political idol, the late Senator Robert F. Kennedy, without attributing them. "The gross national product does not allow for the health of our children, the quality of their education or the joy of their play. It does not include the beauty of our poetry, or the strength of our marriages, the intelligence of our public debate or the integrity of our public officials," said Kennedy. Biden noted the inability of material standards to measure exactly those things, in exactly that order. Lifts from Kennedy's onetime rival, Hubert Humphrey, were also discovered; borrowings from John F. Kennedy were then revealed, too. Most damaging of all came the report that at Syracuse University Law School, in 1965, Biden had been accused of plagiarizing a paper.

The classic features of the case:

"*Of all people!*": as usual, there was the irony that Biden, among the lackluster pack of Democratic candidates, had probably the smallest need to steal speeches. He was the one, it was generally agreed, with the best oratorical abilities.

"*How could he have taken something so obvious?*": people do get over to England pretty frequently, and they're not unlikely to turn on one of fifty million television sets running the same commercial. Nor is Robert Kennedy so distant a memory that some of those active Democrats attending the California state convention at which Biden used Kennedy's remarks weren't going to notice.

Plagiarizing the apology for plagiarism (think back to Sterne and Burton): on October 23, 1987, *National Review* pointed out what many who had heard Biden's withdrawal from the presidential race had noticed — the similarity of his words to Tom Joad's (or, if you like, Henry Fonda's) in *The Grapes of Wrath:*

> "Then it don't matter. Then I'll be all around in the dark. I'll be everywhere, wherever you look. Wherever there's a fight, so hungry people can eat, I'll be there. Wherever there's a cop beating up a guy, I'll be there." (John Steinbeck)

There will be other presidential campaigns. And I'll be there out front. I'll be there. There'll be other opportunities. There'll be other battles, other places, other times, and I'll be there. And I'll be there. (Joseph Biden)

Not word for populist word, perhaps, but the melody lingered on.

If the one element missing from the perpetrator's pattern was the tendency to accuse others of plagiarism, perhaps this is because politicians have so many other opportunities for self-right-eousness that every one seized doesn't have to be compulsion-specific.

Certainly the reaction to Biden's exposure followed standard lines. The Greek messenger — that is, the Dukakis campaign — was blamed for sending around an "attack video" of the theft from Kinnock, a modern, electronic equivalent of parallel columns. Paul Kirk, chairman of the Democratic National Committee, insisted that Dukakis "make certain that this kind of practice is ended by his campaign." Soon afterward, Dukakis's campaign manager was forced to resign for what a *New York Times* editorial later quoted someone describing as "spreading vicious truths."

The usual "tempest-in-a-teapot" defenses were offered for Biden, and it was further pointed out that nearly all "original" political speeches are, after all, plagiarized — composed by paid ghostwriters before delivery in the first person by the candidate himself: a universally accepted form of mutual hack-scratching.* Why not blame Pat Caddell for giving Biden Robert Kennedy's lines? Well, precisely because the conventions of political speech-writing *are* universally accepted. The pol can steal from the staffer, but neither should steal from the party's gods. Biden must have spoken the Kennedy lines knowing where they came from; he once described Kennedy as "the man who I guess I admire more than anyone else in American politics." And when it came to finding reasons for direct blame, there was Biden's increas-

*The tendency to refer to oneself in the third person ("Why is it that Joe Biden . . . ") is common enough among politicians, but no one showed it more frequently in the early Democratic debates of that year than Biden did. One has to wonder, seriously, if he was so used to thinking of himself as an object that his sense of responsibility for his own actions wasn't blunted.

ingly visible pattern of mendacity — lies about his scholastic record and, at the least, misleading statements in the Kinnock adaptation itself: Biden's father had a Chevrolet dealership in Wilmington, Delaware. The ancestral miners he had in mind turned out to be generic Irish ones of somewhat distant racial memory.

Biden, of course, has guilty bedfellows among his own political victims. Does one blame Theodore Sorensen or John F. Kennedy for getting "Ask not what your country . . . " from Oliver Wendell Holmes ("It is now the moment . . . to recall what our country has done for each of us, and to ask ourselves what we can do for our country in return")? (In between Holmes and Kennedy it was used by Warren Harding.)

Politicians begin training themselves early in finding excuses for what they do. Governor Mario Cuomo of New York, an even better orator than Biden, once recalled how when he was accused of breaking St. John's prep school rule against smoking, he denied his guilt, even though he was holding a lit cigarette. Young Mario's defense to the accusing priest? "Father, I have shoes on, and yet I'm not walking." But the older Cuomo apparently had been reading — Robert A. Caro's biography of Lyndon Johnson, in which the same excuse is made by LBJ to the dean of his no-smoking college when the future president is found with a lit pipe. In fact, Cuomo once told Caro that he did indeed read and enjoy *The Years of Lyndon Johnson: The Path to Power;* so it would seem he was at the very least a victim of an unconsciously fulfilled I-wish-I'd-said-that fantasy. And no one could deny his political talent for denying even smoking guns.*

Politics is not so serious and dirty a business as literature. On January 12, 1988, Senator Biden met Neil Kinnock for the first time and gave him a bound copy of Biden speeches. "I told him he was welcome to use them whenever he liked," the senator said, "with or without attribution."

*

*During his 1986 reelection campaign, Governor Cuomo used the slogan "Leadership that's working" — the same slogan President Reagan had used two years before. In 1988 the president's trouble came less from plagiarism than forgery, when his spokesman Larry Speakes admitted to inventing certain remarks that he attributed to Reagan.

It is the theft of the written that troubles us more than that of the oral, and not just because the former is more documentable than the latter. It also has to do with the fact that although there's too much of both, there's far more talk than writing in the world; and writing (despite what they say about the radio waves of our utterances winging endlessly through space) is more demonstrably eternal than speech. To put one's theft into print is to have it forever on the library shelves, guiltily stacked just an aisle away from the volume it victimized, a stain that doesn't wash but forever circulates. The well-intentioned writer may have a terror of unconscious plagiarism partly for the same reason the fastidious one trembles at the possibility of committing an error in print: because the deed will always be around. That is the heart of the erratum, and it is the added shame of plagiarism.

If one's published errors are an eternal punishment, it's because being in print at all is supposed to be an eternal reward. Children and fame are the only kinds of afterlife most people believe in now, and even in more theistic times, authors often thought that heaven could wait. The Victorian critic Francis Jacox wrote an essay called "Self-Seen in Print," reminding his readers of Dickens's first experience of that condition:

> His first "effusion" was dropped stealthily one evening at twilight, with fear and trembling, into a dark letter-box, in a dark office, up a dark court in Fleet Street; and when it appeared in all the glory of print, he walked down to Westminster Hall, he tells us, and turned into it for half an hour, "because my eyes were so dimmed with joy and pride, that they could not bear the street, and were not fit to be seen there."

It is the arrival, not the journey, that often matters in these things. Sylvia Plath, who confided to her journal an "itch to emulate," wondered about the purity of her artistic ambition: "I dimly would like to write (or is it to *have* written?) a novel, short stories, a book of poems." Both Amises, elder and younger, have acknowledged the motivating power of vanity. Kingsley agreed with George Orwell about "the desire to be thought clever, to be talked about by people he had never met." Martin, asked to reveal his Christmas wish for 1985, humbly told the *New York Times Book Review* that it was "for a new short story that would ease or illuminate a single reader's day" — but only after he'd indulged a fantasy of being granted "a 20,000-line blank-verse epic poem, so funny, moving, true and beautiful that the days following its appearance would be a spontaneous global holiday."

In a lecture called "How to Fail in Literature," Andrew Lang (who in 1910 edited the first version of *The Cloister and the Hearth,* titled *A Good Fight*) pointed to the young writer's desire to "astonish his relations," and recommended plagiarism as a reliable route toward that end: "When you are accused of being a plagiarist, and shewn up in double columns, you may be pretty sure that . . . you have failed to fail, after all. Otherwise nobody would envy and malign you, and garble your book, and print quotations from it which you did not write, all in the sacred cause of morality."

But this isn't very funny or true where Jacob Epstein was concerned. A decade has passed since *Wild Oats,* and no novel has appeared with his name on it in all that time. We should not rule out a literary comeback, surely; probably the least perceptive line Scott Fitzgerald ever wrote was the one about there being no second acts in American lives. From John Adams to Richard Nixon, American lives seem to consist of nothing but, and there's always the book to be written about how you picked yourself up off the ground. Still, even though he must have succeeded in astonishing his relations, no one could claim Epstein's notoriety did him anything but harm.

In the fall of 1980, there must have been young writers, ones a little older than Jacob Epstein, who were not making it and beginning to doubt that they would, who allowed themselves the self-consoling jeers of the thwarted. Little Jacob, who had gotten too much too soon, and no doubt gotten it as a result of his fancy parents, had now gotten what was coming to him. This was the equivalent of a younger Kennedy's being arrested; people could pick which generation to feel pleased against.

In the mid-eighties, the young doctor-writer Perri Klass (also the child of writers), whose essays in the *New York Times*'s "Hers" column and whose book of stories (*I Am Having an Adventure*) elicited a good deal of admiration, came in for what she calls "a certain amount of 'superwoman' publicity (she writes! she goes to medical school! she has a baby!)," which she could "imagine engendering a very natural desire to find feet of clay." Late in 1986 that "natural desire" found a diseased host, a person who began an anonymous hate campaign against Klass, which included unsigned, misspelled charges of medical incompetence as well as gift-wrapped packages of excrement sent to her at work.

Perhaps the most potent weapons in the deranged arsenal unleashed against her were false charges of plagiarism. However unconvincing they might be on examination, they were contrived with a good deal of effort. One of them, mailed to publishers and editors, concerned an essay by Klass in which the weary, overworked doctor is "feeling sorry for [herself] and fantasizing about changing places with a patient" as she struggles, late one night, to get through a thirty-hour hospital shift. The anonymous mailing claimed to show how Klass's article was very similar, in wording and in movement from topic to topic, to an article supposedly written by one "Maisie Wilson, Nurse-Probationer" for a British nursing journal during the Second World War. Klass, it would seem at first glance, had simply plugged in some modern, American nouns and experiences. The anonymous correspondent said that the Maisie Wilson article "came out of a scrapbook kept by his mother, who had been a nurse in England." He included a photocopy of the purported cutting, "a closely typeset newspaper column, surrounded by injunctions to observe the blackout. There was an apparent fragment of a date ('44) on the top but no periodical name — but after all, it had supposedly been cut out and pasted in a scrapbook 40 years ago." A previous mass hate-mailing by the writer had also involved "a xerox of a xerox" and an inability to produce the name of the original publication.

What Perri Klass was apparently up against was someone sufficiently swelled with hate "to go to all the trouble of rewriting and retypesetting [her] little article." But this possibility, while it's the real explanation, seemed improbable and frightening enough for Klass to begin doubting her own honesty. Already suffering from the common syndrome that makes hard-working, successful people with much responsibility worry every so often that they've somehow been faking it, Klass saw her ordinary self-doubt start cooperating with the emotional sabotage being conducted by her tormentor: "I knew I was actually doing O.K., I knew I was closely watched and my superiors were satisfied, and I knew that many, if not most, other interns felt as insecure as I did. But I still felt a little like a fake doctor — and so it was hard to dismiss letters that accused me of being a fake writer." The metaphor of rape, so often used by the victims of plagiarists and by their just accusers, was now employed by Klass in a description of panic over being falsely accused: "When I first saw the letters, the accusations, what I really wanted was to keep them secret. I felt, I think, a little bit the way the victim of a rape must feel — I didn't want too many people to know what had happened, I didn't want to spread the word any farther. Accused of crimes I hadn't committed, did I even feel momentarily guilty? Not exactly. . ."

Writing about this ordeal in an essay for the front page of the *New York Times Book Review* ("Turning My Words Against Me") was an act of moral, and maybe even physical, bravery. A psychiatrist warned her not to give her assailant the reaction he was craving; she should avoid "any kind of public response," rather in the way one is told by the phone company never to talk back to an "annoyance caller." But Dr. Klass rejected the psychiatrist's advice: "I am writing about this because the person who wrote those letters wanted to take away my voice, wanted to claim it wasn't really mine, and I am not willing to let that happen. I am writing about it, in part, to lay claim again to all my words." Ironically, she had been made to suffer the fate of a real plagiarist's victim: her own words had been taken from her. If this thief came up from the cellar, instead of through the library door, the effect was weirdly similar.

No one could dispute the justice of what she was trying to do in her essay. But one danger — aside from again setting off a crazy person — that she doesn't mention is that of being publicly observed in a miasma. As the Greeks knew, pollution spreads indiscriminately. The internal effect of this phenomenon is to make the victim feel guilty, but the external one involves the short, fuzzy memory of the public. When Perri Klass's essay appeared one Sunday morning in 1987 readers up and down the East Coast of the United States felt sympathy for her and told each other, over coffee and croissants, "How awful!" But we retain little, and what we do retain we mix up. Several years later some of those same sympathetic readers will no doubt be at cocktail parties where her name will come up, having been spotted over some new essay that morning. And just as surely some of them will say, "Oh, Perri Klass, she's a plagiarist, isn't she?"

One writer aware of this is Martin Amis, who in *Money* makes a few crucial appearances as himself. The appealingly loathsome narrator, John Self, at one point gets in touch with Amis about doing rewrites on a film, *Money*, telling the reader that his producer, Fielding Goodney, "had heard of Martin Amis — he hadn't read his stuff, but there'd recently been some cases of plagiarism, of text-theft, which had filtered down to the newspapers and magazines. So, I thought. Little Martin got caught with his fingers in the till, then, did he. A word criminal. I would bear that in mind." Today the real Martin Amis says he has "no complaints," but concedes that once a plagiarist is exposed, the victim gets "vaguely tarred by the same brush."

Jacob Epstein's family background is interesting not just in terms of publicity but in its psychological implications as well. If your parents are important editors in New York, what, after all, is the worst possible thing you can be caught doing? Your plagiarism can accomplish a sort of Oedipal slaying before, in keeping with tragic models, it becomes the instrument of self-slaughter. When the story broke one critic told a reporter from *Newsweek:* "If he were my kid I'd horsewhip him . . . but for God's sake don't use my name." If the case recalled any father-son situation in literary history, perhaps the one that came first to mind was that of Samuel Ireland, the eighteenth-century bookseller, and his son, William. William's crime was forgery, plagiarism's more glamorous inversion, in which the perpetrator claims not that what he hasn't produced is really his own, but that what he indeed has created is actually somebody else's. The younger Ireland began bringing home biographical relics of Shakespeare, which he was supposedly acquiring from a "mysterious old gentleman." In fact, he was — with considerable skill — counterfeiting the relics himself. He kept upping the forged ante (surely a demonstration of the death wish) until he was claiming to be in possession of an unproduced play of the Bard's, a heroic political drama called

Vortigern. Ireland had actually written the play himself, mining a great variety of Shakespeare's extant plays for dialog he could mix up and adapt — sort of a forgery based on borderline plagiarism. The "discovery" of *Vortigern* created a predictable sensation (James Boswell, always emotionally susceptible, came to London to kiss the manuscript). The first two acts of its premiere at the Drury Lane, on April 2, 1796, went down well enough, but during the third the audience began to hear a rat. Ireland's exposure, carried out chiefly by the scholar Edmund Malone, came inevitably, his worst humiliation occurring when the father he had been so eager to impress, and whose credulity was so great toward the Shakespearean bones his son was supposedly retrieving, refused to believe young William had the talent to have forged *Vortigern* himself. His son bitterly protested: "The Vortigern I wrote; if I copied anyone it was the Bard himself; in no one paper, book or parchment was I furnished with language by any one living — if there is Soul or Imagery it is *my own.*" They were never reconciled, and the younger Ireland eventually made his way as a novelist writing under a number of pen names. Pseudonymity would be a special form of hell for an exposed plagiarist; for a forger it probably offered some familiar comfort.

The plagiarist is more likely to suffer hell's permanence than the forger. Given the greater creative dash involved in his brand of wrongdoing, the forger may just pass through a purgatorial probation before emerging into posterity's regard and renown. William Ireland is admired, if not quite honored, by later generations of readers, and Chatterton is a romantic martyr. Future ages may even discover a soft spot for Clifford Irving. But plagiarism is irredeemably sleazy, and Jason Epstein probably did have the right to feel sorely tried by his son's *Wild Oats,* even if before and since that time the senior Epstein has been touched by other controversies involving both plagiarism and forgery. During the late sixties, when he was writing a series of articles about the city and its schools for the *New York Review,* he was also editing a book by David Rogers (*110 Livingston Street: Politics and Bureaucracy in the New York City School System*) for publication by Random House. Epstein showed one of the pieces to Rogers, who, according to Philip Nobile, "became distressed about what he felt was the similarity of ideas and logic between his manuscript and his editor's. . . . 'I feel I taught Jason a lot,' says Rogers."

As a captain of intellectual industry, Epstein gets involved in more than his share of editorial dust-ups. One of them occurred a few years after his son's troubles and involved forgery by an author just signed up at Random House. Timothy J. Cooney didn't forge the manuscript of his book (on moral philosophy, titled "Telling Right from Wrong"); what he faked was an endorsement by Robert Nozick, chairman of the Department of Philosophy at Harvard, urging that Random House publish the book. Cooney felt sure the book would not have been accepted without the forged letter, though Epstein says he had "pretty much decided to publish" before getting it. When news of the forgery reached the public in September 1984, Cooney professed pride in what he'd done, reportedly telling Nozick he did it not only to advance his manuscript's fortunes but to impress his ex-wife, too. Random House, after several weeks, decided that it couldn't go ahead with publication. Epstein explained: "I have tried to reconcile Mr. Cooney's forgery with the kind of trust that ought to prevail among authors, publishers and readers, but after much thought I've been unable to do so. . . . It ought to be published, but not by us."*

One additional feature of his son's transgression, seemingly designed to complicate anyone's psychological speculations about the case, was the fact that he picked as his victim someone who was, like himself, the son of a prominent literary parent. If Jacob Epstein really did have a "death wish," the choice of someone who shared with him an essential feature of identity was a good one: even before being detected, while waiting for the boomerang to ride the whirlwind, he could be hurting himself by beating up on a kind of transatlantic twin. Whether or not this was so, both Amis senior and Epstein *père* loyally came out like dads to the playground, to side with their respective scuffling sons. Jason asserted that what Jacob did "was not plagiarism. . . . It is very common for accidents like this to happen, especially among young writers." But Kingsley insisted it was "a flagrant case. It takes one back to the days before copyrights."

---

*One is reminded of Sterne's letter to Garrick endorsing his own work — composed by Sterne but sent out by somebody else.

Not that he would adopt Martin's style for his own. He has even expressed a distaste for its "terrible compulsive *vividness*," admitting that he can't read his way through to the end of a paragraph of it: "It's too ornate." And yet in Martin's earliest days practicing the family business — the time, in fact, of *The Rachel Papers* — the influence of Kingsley was visible in some of his own style's smallest components. The satirically phonetic speech in that first novel — "The Imbenkment," "*Perry-dice* Lost" and "U-word," meaning "You heard" — is classic Kingsley, family stock-in-trade Martin has showcased in some nonfiction as well: "*Turds, ee-bait, inner-stain* and *wide-ass,* for instance, are [Capote's] renderings of 'towards,' 'about,' 'understand' and 'White House.' " His international and sexual politics also seemed, fifteen years ago, much like his middle-aged dad's: the Loyalists of the Spanish Civil War, for whom Rachel's father is supposed to have fought, are, to alter ego Charles Highway, the "Trendy Cause," and women are pretty much all diminutively alike: "Naturally, them being girls both, Rachel had hardly set foot in the house before Jenny confided in her." None of this, of course, constitutes plagiarism, but the writer whom Epstein chose to plunder was himself someone who labored under the anxiety of influence. Most of us come around to our fathers' opinions later, not sooner, but Martin Amis has grown less like Kingsley Amis in the decade and a half since *The Rachel Papers.* His opinions, like his style, have become sufficiently alien from his father's to provoke a certain parental irritation. By the mid-eighties Martin Amis was passionately opposed to the bomb. Not so his father: "Anyone who has read my father's work will have some idea of what he is like to argue with. When I told him that I was writing about nuclear weapons, he said, with a lilt, 'Ah, I suppose you're . . . "against them," are you?' "

As he's moved out of his father's more rotund shadow, Amis has also taken what seem to be special pains to acknowledge received influence and indebtedness, perhaps enough of them to satisfy even Peter Shaw. In the introduction and acknowledgments to *The Moronic Inferno* Amis informs the reader that he got the title phrase "and much else, from Saul Bellow, who informs me that *he* got it from Wyndham Lewis." Bellow is perhaps Amis's chief literary hero, and he is present once more in the author's note to *Einstein's Monsters,* in which Amis cites some influence on each of the volume's five anti-nuke allegories:

> May I take the opportunity to discharge — or acknowledge — some debts? In order of composition: "The Time Disease" owes something to J. G. Ballard; "Insight at Flame Lake" to Piers and Emily Read and to Jack and Florence Phillips; "The Little Puppy That Could" to Franz Kafka and to Vladimir Nabokov; "Bujak and the Strong Force" to Saul Bellow; and "The Immortals" to Jorge Luis Borges and to the Salman Rushdie of *Grimus.* And throughout I am grateful to Jonathan Schell, for ideas and for imagery.

When asked if his part in the Epstein affair, and being "vaguely tarred by the same brush," makes him now supersensitive to the business of acknowledgment, Amis says "not really," describing these statements as simply a courtesy he's happy to perform. He notes in conversation that one of the *Einstein's Monsters* stories, "The Little Puppy That Could," takes a specific bit or two from Kafka for the legitimate literary purpose of helping the well-read reader realize that a metamorphosis (puppy into handsome soldier) is going to take place. But he wonders with a laugh if he shouldn't "have kept [his] mouth shut" about influences: "You're asking for trouble" from reviewers by such acknowledgments, practically inviting invidious or exaggerated comparisons that otherwise might not have occurred to them at all. Despite his denial of special pains, one has to remark upon the specificity of Amis's good manners, and wonder whether or not, after his own justifiable whistle-blowing against Epstein (and perhaps things like Shaw's rather severe comments about himself), there isn't a bit of compulsive caution in his current imaginative make-up. *Einstein's Monsters,* whatever influences may shadow it, is highly original work marked by Amis's own stylistic trademarks.

How far does one take acknowledgment, homage and disclosure? In an essay on Steven Spielberg written in 1982, Amis told readers of the *Observer:* "Film-makers today — with their target boys and marketing men — tie themselves up in knots trying to divine the LCD among the American public. The rule is: no one ever lost money underestimating the intelligence of the audience." Would every British reader recognize Mencken here? Probably not. Should Amis have mentioned the source for some of the wording? Maybe, maybe not. If he thought they *ought* to recognize Mencken here, and he was damned if he was going to slow down his own paragraph with a pedantic parenthesis, that was fair enough. After all, one could put an end to literary allusiveness altogether if one feared the footnote police were waiting to lunge from behind every punctuation mark. The point at which a writer's expectations of his current readers must give way to acknowledgment of his printed precursors is a matter for individual common sense and conscience; if Amis was a bit casual about "sources" as late as 1982, by the middle of the decade he was unusually fastidious.

Every writer can reasonably be expected to know at least one writer's work backwards and forwards; that writer is, of course, himself (the writer Proust said was the hardest to avoid plagiarizing). His normal instinct and delight is to see his work stay in print or come back to life in another form. After speaking in the introduction to *The Moronic Inferno* about how he did some revision of its contents between their appearance in periodicals and resurrection between covers, Amis jokes: "I should have worked harder, but it was quite hard work getting all this stuff together (photocopying back numbers of journals can be a real struggle, what with the weight of the bound volumes and that Xerox flap tangling you up and getting in the way)." The passage is really an expression of writerly delight in discovering that the presumed perishables have been in the freezer all along.

No writer wants his work to have just one temporary or inconspicuous life, and just as he probably has favorites among his own books, he will also have individual passages and sentences of which he's particularly fond, things he'd like to display again in a new context. Amis himself has shown the tendency to recycle old personal favorites. In one story in *Einstein's Monsters,* he has a character refer to the readers of supermarket tabloids as the sort of people who know, among other things, "how President Kennedy is alive and well, living with Buddy Holly on the planet Krypton." Five years before the anti-nuclear *Einstein's Monsters,* when Amis seemed to view missile attacks mostly as a part of his harmless obsession with video games, he published a whimsical book called *Invasion of the Space Invaders,* in which he made the point that belief in extraterrestrials was not confined to "cranks, readers of the *National Inquirer* [*sic*], fantasists who think that President Kennedy is alive and well, living with Buddy Holly on the planet Krypton." You can bet he didn't have to look the sentence up when a few years later he gave it another minute of airplay: he *liked* it, and could remember it down to the comma. This isn't so much "osmosis" as the circulation of one's lifeblood.

There are certain writers of such longevity, and who are held in such affection, that the reading public positively wants them to keep repeating themselves — rather in the way we like film stars to keep playing themselves or nightclub singers to close with their biggest hit. Perhaps the best authorial example is P. G. Wodehouse, who brilliantly wrote essentially the same book for a half century or more. As Richard Usborne points out in *Wodehouse at Work:* "Situation comedy in good hands can stand a great deal of repetition and, when you get a good cast of actors together, their sameness from story to story can be half the fun." Wodehouse sometimes reproduced things not just essentially but exactly. A sample from Usborne: "*Ice in the Bedroom* (1961) is in many respects a re-run of *Sam the Sudden* (1925), with several of the same characters, with Valley Fields . . . a frequent setting, and indeed Mr. Cornelius singing its praises (to Sam in 1925, to Dolly Molloy in 1961) non-stoppably in the same sixteen lines of Walter Scott's verse."

But there is a difference between old favorites and instant replays. In the May 1987 issue of *Esquire,* the novelist Nancy Lemann reported on her train trip from New York to New Orleans, aboard the Southern Crescent, in order to cover the corruption trial of Governor Edwin Edwards of Louisiana:

> In the North, the mood among the passengers was strictly business, showing signs of industry and progress; but once we passed the capital and went through green Virginia, a sort of feverish alcoholic atmosphere became the norm, and everyone seemed to go into crisis. Styles of dress became eccentric and unkempt, as did modes of behavior, particularly in the club car, which was extremely active at all hours once we crossed the Mason-Dixon line.
>
> Throughout the afternoon, oddly enough, a black woman was singing a sort of jazz love song to a diminutive white man with a black patch over one eye. It was extremely odd, and later devel-

oped into a sort of riot. I would characterize the atmosphere as smoldering.

In that same month, May 1987, one could find at the same newsstand the current issue of *Spy*, in which Nancy Lemann had another piece, this time on the more generalized theme of being someone from "Dixie in Manhattan." Without mentioning the purpose (or recency) of her trip, she recollected

> being on a train from New York to New Orleans, the *Southern Crescent*. In the North the mood among the passengers was strictly business, showing signs of industry and progress. But once we passed the capital and went through green Virginia, a sort of lumbering alcoholic atmosphere became the norm, and everyone seemed to go into crisis. Styles of dress became outmoded and unkempt, as did forms of behavior — particularly in the club car, which was extremely active at all hours once we crossed the Mason-Dixon line. Throughout the afternoon a black woman was singing a kind of jazz love song to a diminutive white man with a black patch over one eye. It was all extremely odd, and later developed into a steaming caldron of Southern hedonist squalor.
>
> I would characterize the atmosphere as smoldering . . .

If one thinks one has already said something adequately, one can argue, there's little point in reconfiguring it. But there are problems with drawing two checks quite so close together where a chunk as juicy and substantial as Miss Lemann's description is involved. And there is also the question of the slippery slope: if one doesn't feel the need to cite one's own words, and doesn't mind repeating them because they don't seem in any particular need of improvement, how long will it be before one starts paying someone else the same backhanded compliment?

The tendency to steal from oneself probably starts at the seaside: who has ever sat down to write a half-dozen postcards to the folks back home without reprising himself (the choicest bit or two) before getting to the bottom of the stack? Similarly, who has not caught himself late at night, deciding to utter again some term of endearment for the simple reason that it worked the last time?

At the age of forty, Martin Amis can now, if he chooses, rework bits and pieces from an increasingly large and well thought of body of his own work. The slap-in-the-face titles and themes of *Dead Babies, Success* and *Money* have given way to the thoughtful fables of *Einstein's Monsters* and the upcoming *London Fields*, a full-length novel of nuclear anxiety. By contrast, *Wild Oats* remains, ten years after it appeared, Jacob Epstein's only published novel. "It ruined his life," remarks one frequent contributor to the *New York Review of Books* of the plagiarism episode. Actually, this is something of a *New York Review* definition of a ruined life: Jacob Epstein works these days in Hollywood — a place where, as we will see, accusations of plagiarism usually end in expensive litigation. He has been executive story editor of the popular and critically successful TV show *L.A. Law;* his name has been the first to roll on the closing credits each week. One of the actors in the series says, "This show is about having it all. . . . But it goes further and deals with a more important issue: What is it like when you get there?"

4

Quiet Goes the Don:
An Academic Affair

> Plagiarize,
> Let no one else's work evade your eyes,
> Remember why the good Lord made your eyes,
> So don't shade your eyes,
> But plagiarize, plagiarize, plagiarize —
> Only be sure always to call it please "research."
>
> — Tom Lehrer, "Lobachevsky"

O N MANY American university campuses, modern buildings "quote" older ones in a sririt of witty homage. The Gothic turrets of the old library will be dimly discernible in the stream-lined tips of its recent extension. Whether this signifies cultural continuity or exhausted imagination is debatable, but it is certainly a wide current in contemporary design. At Texas Tech in Lubbock, the newer buildings on the enormous campus (1,839 acres) harmonize with the Spanish Renaissance architecture that has been the university's prevailing style since it opened in 1925. The new portion of Holden Hall, from the 1970s, is typical: less ornamental than what it's connected to, it is still graceful, earth-toned and low to the ground.

Among other parts of the school, it houses the Department of History and the office of the dean of the College of Arts and Sciences. On a lawn nearby is an equestrian statue of Will Rogers, whose connection to the university eludes anyone you ask. But

Lubbock's conservative spirit permits continuing enthusiasm for this kind of realistic statuary: near the downtown civic center, native son Buddy Holly, complete with his guitar and eyeglasses, is on a pedestal, and on the Tech campus, not far from Will Rogers, is a new statue of Preston Smith, the Lubbockite who served as governor of Texas from 1969 to 1973, a period in which American universities generally continued to overbuild themselves and in which Texas indulged with special ardor its appetite for new "facilities" (always easier to pry out of the legislature than raises in faculty pay). The base of Smith's statue urges the viewer to "look around" at all the buildings he got built for Texas Tech.

The "Tech" is by now a misnomer. The university may offer a master's in animal breeding and attract great numbers of foreign students to its petroleum engineering program, but it turns out Ph.D.'s in English and fine arts as well. The setting for this multitude of endeavors is hailed in the university catalog for its climate: "Summers are dry and not extremely hot, while winters are dry and moderate (average annual rainfall is only 18 inches). An average annual temperature of 60° coupled with the average noon humidity of 46% combine to make Lubbock comfortable year round." What goes unmentioned amid these statistics ("over 3,550 hours of sunshine every year") is the season called spring, when howling dust storms can turn afternoon skies dark brown, torturing contact-lens wearers and sending people home depressed, somapsychologically, by the fall of the barometer.

But the spirit of Texas Tech is generally optimistic, combining as it does practicality and salvationism. The approximately twenty-two thousand undergraduates are generally right wing and religious. In December 1986, the *Lubbock Avalanche-Journal* was welcoming the new Tech football coach, Spike Dykes, in front-page articles; the "Viewpoint" page of the *University Daily* carried a piece titled "Media Unjustly Blames Reagan," as well as some letters concerning the nature of Jesus Christ and the putative existence of hell. One communication was headed "Man Controls His Own Actions."

When Texans used the term "oil crisis" in 1986 they were talking not about high prices but low ones. Lubbock may not have seen its confidence sink to the depths of Houston's, but like the rest of boom-and-bust Texas it was more than aware that the gaudy gushing seventies were gone. During the Ford and Carter years bumper stickers urged the proper treatment of Yankees — "Let The Bastards Freeze In The Dark" — while some of the bastards skulked southward to jobs in the sunbelt. Yankees were by no means undesired by departmental hiring committees at Texas Tech, whose more progressive members saw in the national economic recession — a full-blown depression in the academic job market — a chance to deprovincialize the university and increase its stature in the state and nation. Earlier generations of faculty at Tech had been largely grown at home or in the region. The early seventies brought a wave of scholars from the big universities of the Midwest, and within a few more years the origins of young faculty members were even more distant and fancy. In 1978 the English Department, for example, welcomed new Ph.D.'s from Berkeley, the University of Pennsylvania and Harvard. The money that Preston Smith had used to build all those neo–Spanish Renaissance buildings was now purchasing a lot of sheepskin carpetbaggers who couldn't find work anywhere else. They arrived either arrogant or grateful, to be welcomed by senior colleagues who were generally hospitable but also a bit edgy. As Buddy Holly once tremulously sang, "Maybe, baby, I'll have you; maybe, baby, you'll be true." Would these mail-order marriages last for the usual forty or so years of a teaching career?

Jayme Aaron Sokolow's *vita* did not mark him as one of these indisputably blue chips, but when he arrived at Holden Hall to join Tech's History Department in the fall of 1976, he was still something of an eastern novelty. Born in 1946 in Perth Amboy, New Jersey, he had gotten a B.A. from Trenton State College in 1968 and a Ph.D. from New York University four years later, after writing a dissertation on the abolitionists William Lloyd Garrison and Henry Clarke Wright. James E. Brink, a specialist in Renaissance France, arrived in Lubbock (from the University of Washington) the same semester Sokolow did and can recall "the way he described going to graduate school. . . . I mean it was like rush, rush, rush, night classes, never on the campus."

Sokolow was part of the last wave of Great Society Ph.D.'s, whose superabundance caused an embarrassing market glut when everything slowed down in the seventies, rather like some of those unnecessary buildings that now had to be heated with expensive Arabian (or Texan) oil. While at NYU, and for a few years before coming to Texas Tech, Sokolow taught in the New York City public school system, but by the time he came to Tech his ambitions for a university career were strong and visible. He seemed to offer the department a chance to make itself a more cosmopolitan place. A few years before he arrived, an outside review of the department had been conducted, one of the reviewers supposedly remarking, "What this department needs is a good New York Jew." To be a Jew in aggressively Christian Lubbock can be an uneasy experience, but this recommendation, however crudely put, was intended and understood as a prescription admiring brains, energy and sophistication. There were some in the department who thought the arrival of Jayme Sokolow meant they were getting just what the outside doctors of philosophy had ordered.

It "was not a harmonious department . . . never had been," says Professor John Wunder, who has since become the director of the Center for Great Plains Studies at the University of Nebraska. As in most departments at Tech, the gulf between older and younger faculty members in history was not only geographical; it was widened by different expectations about scholarship. In the buyer's market of the seventies, new faculty were expected to publish far more than the professors who hired them had. Sokolow was very insistent about making a virtue of this necessity. Wunder says he was "the point man" for publishing zealotry and "very much disapproved of those who weren't publishing scholars."

He made his go-gettingnesss as conspicuous as he could. "He used to do his research in $8\frac{1}{2}''$ by $11''$ spiral notebooks," recalls Jim Brink, "and always he was carrying two or three of these around and they each represented a different writing project. . . . I was always amazed not only at how quickly he was turning things out but at how many different irons he had in the fire at the same time." Others had the same feeling. Professor Allan J. Kuethe says, "I think in the back of my mind I had wondered how anyone could be a publishing expert on such a wide variety of topics." Sokolow's pride in turning out material was so great

that he became, says Kuethe, "increasingly abusive in the classroom. I was graduate advisor at the time and he was conducting
a graduate class on teaching methods for the new teaching assistants. He had reduced at least two of them to tears, berating
them for 'stupidity.' "

This contempt extended to his senior colleagues. Otto Nelson
found nothing wrong with Sokolow's ambition, but notes that he
"had a reputation for being harsh toward people he didn't like.
. . . He had nicknames for some of the people in the department." Sokolow was not without friends at Texas Tech — among
them Jim Brink, a burly, genial man with a strict sense of fairness,
who was afraid that Sokolow might be penalized for failing to fit
into Lubbock's tight and alien mold: "I had been a great champion of Jay. . . . Jay's lifestyle and some of his characteristics were
not endearing and I maintained that that made no difference."
Soft-spoken Alwyn Barr, who was chairman of the department
in the early eighties, was a protective patron. Others were less
forbearing. A member of the English Department says Sokolow
"had a kind of ruthless presence. . . . You could tell you were in
the presence of somebody who didn't recognize normal sorts of
rules and decorum." At a party one time when Sokolow, whose
marriage had come apart, made advances toward a young instructor, this same English professor recalls feeling that it was
"kind of like [watching] a shark and a teddy bear."

By the fall of 1981 Jayme Sokolow had been at Texas Tech
for five years and had published articles on topics ranging from
the eighteenth-century American scientist Benjamin Thompson
(Count Rumford) to antebellum Jewish abolitionists to the influence of Benjamin Franklin on Tolstoy. In the *Dictionary of American Scholars* he listed his research areas as "Antebellum America"
and "19th century Europe." He was primarily a student of social
history and ideology, and the most important piece of work he
would offer for his colleagues' consideration was a book-length
manuscript called *Eros and Modernization: Sylvester Graham, Health
Reform, and the Origins of Victorian Sexuality in America,* which had
been accepted for publication by Fairleigh Dickinson University
Press. All these materials were submitted in the course of his
evaluation for tenure and promotion to associate professor of
history.

John Wunder says that by October 1981 "everyone had geared up for a battle over the tenure decision," but Allan Kuethe thinks Sokolow's research record made his tenuring a "certainty." The personality problems could presumably be offset by the publications. But as the review of Sokolow proceeded, it became apparent that he was going to defy the academic profession's conventional wisdom by becoming someone who could publish and still perish — if only locally.

Barbara W. Tuchman characterizes the German historian Leopold von Ranke as one of those "who set the historian's task: to find out *wie es eigentlich gewesen ist,* what really happened, or literally, how it really was. His goal is one that will remain forever just beyond our grasp." To attempt an exact account of the Sokolow case one must pursue what Ranke instructed his nineteenth-century colleagues were essential: original documents. Tenure cases and academic files are confidential, and the litigiousness of recent university life inspires caution, so the paper trail of an investigation into Sokolow's fate in Lubbock is not without its gaps. But crucial items do come to light (the Xerox machine being the greatest threat to confidentiality since the larynx), and some of the principal players prove to be remarkably forthcoming, motivated by their own scholarly devotion to *wie es eigentlich gewesen ist,* and by chagrin. Writing about Ranke, the historian G. P. Gooch declared, "In his dramas there are few heroes or villains." The same can be said of what went on in Holden Hall during the 1981–82 academic year.

Professor Jacquelin Collins, a boyish, energetic specialist in British history, may have been the first member of the department to become seriously suspicious of Sokolow, after someone showed him a brief article in the fall 1979 issue of *Canadian-American Slavic Studies* entitled "On the Putative Influence of Benjamin Franklin on Tolstoi." The four-page "note" by Harry Hill Walsh took vigorous exception to a 5½-page note that Sokolow had published four years before in the prestigious journal *American Literature.* Sokolow's title had been " 'Arriving at Moral Perfection': Benjamin Franklin and Leo Tolstoy," and his note contended that "Franklin played a crucial role in the development of the young Tolstoy's goals, values, and subject matter.

The Russian studied Franklin at an important stage in his adolescent development. Franklin's example and values steadied
Tolstoy and encouraged his autobiographical works, which
formed the basis for his later masterpieces." Walsh attacked Sokolow for having both his facts and his interpretation of them
wrong: "Sokolow's assertion that Franklin played an important
role in the creation of Tolstoi's masterpieces, and his statement
that Tolstoi at the end of his life 'ended his career by returning
to the source of his literary and philosophical themes,' meaning
Franklin, are too ludicrous to require comment." In the course
of his note — the interpretive validity of which is beyond our
concerns — Walsh mentioned that Sokolow's "opinions about
this purported relationship are similar to those expressed in an
earlier study by Eufrosina Dvoichenko-Markov." Not so similar
that Walsh added a charge of plagiarism to those of inaccuracy,
but enough to prompt Collins to track down the article by Dvoichenko-Markov ("Benjamin Franklin and Leo Tolstoy") in the
April 1952 *Proceedings of the American Philosophical Society* and
underline several passages where Sokolow's argument and language, a generation later, ran curiously parallel. Sokolow had
mentioned Dvoichenko-Markov's article in a footnote to his own,
but only as one of a number of sources in a large omnibus
citation. He acknowledged no exact debt to any particular portion of it. What Collins had in fact come upon was a less flagrant
example of what would soon be seen as Sokolow's habitual modus
operandi: mention a source, amid a number of others, giving an
impression of both wide-ranging scholarship and the customary
proprieties, while not indicating the extent or specificity of indebtedness.

Barbara Tuchman first achieved popular recognition for her
book on the fateful Zimmermann telegram, which helped push
American forces into the First World War. In 1981 the undoing
of Jayme Sokolow really began, like most of modern life's catas-
trophes, with a telephone call, from Collins to Ralph D. Gray, an
old friend from graduate school who was teaching at Indiana
University. Collins was calling in response to an invitation to the
wedding of Gray's daughter. During their conversation Gray
brought up the name of Jayme Sokolow. Asked for an impression
of his colleague, Collins now recalls responding with some re-

mark on the order of "I hope you haven't lent him any money" — a barb resulting partly from the comparison of Sokolow's Tolstoy article with Dvoichenko-Markov's.

Why had Gray inquired about Sokolow? Because he was the editor of the new *Journal of the Early Republic,* to which Sokolow, whose by-line identified him as a member of the Texas Tech history faculty, had recently submitted an article called "Thomas and Mary Nichols and the Paradox of Antebellum Free Love," about a husband-wife team of anti-marriage theorists in 1850s America. The article had been sent to Lawrence Foster, then assistant professor in Georgia Tech's Department of Social Sciences, for evaluation, and Foster had felt compelled to inform Gray that it appeared to have been blatantly plagiarized from the work of Professor Stephen W. Nissenbaum of the University of Massachusetts at Amherst, whose book *Sex, Diet, and Debility in Jacksonian America* Foster was in the process of reviewing for the *Journal of American History.*

The result of this conversation, which got started because of Miss Gray's intention to enter the institution so deplored a century and a quarter before by the free-love Nicholses, was that Professor Collins and his colleague Professor Brian L. Blakeley began to do some private investigations into the scholarship of Jayme Sokolow. When it came time some months later, in the fall of 1981, for Sokolow's application for tenure and promotion to be reviewed, Collins and Blakeley would be ready to present the departmental committee conducting the review with some materials they thought it would be interested in seeing. Among the items they could show them was a copy of Stephen Nissenbaum's dissertation, which Collins ordered from University Microfilms after reasoning that there was a distinct possibility the original might soon find a way of disappearing from the Texas Tech library.

As Sokolow's undoing got started in Lubbock, Stephen Nissenbaum was informed of the pilfering by Lawrence Foster. In a letter written on December 18, 1980, Foster said it appeared to be "the clearest case of plagiarism I have ever seen," telling Nissenbaum that he had "called this fact to the attention of Ralph Gray, and he is carrying it from there. I did feel, however, that since you were the original writer of the analysis I wanted to be sure that you were apprised of the situation." Like the patriotic whistle-blower who hopes against hope that there's some reasonable explanation for the apparent skullduggery he's discovered, Foster almost pleaded to be told this wasn't really happening ("Please do let me know if my supposition is unfounded about plagiarism"), or that there was some reason for it ("If . . . there is some valid explanation for the extraordinarily close correspondence of these two pieces of work, I should wish to know that"). He even suggested a situation where massive ignorance might have been more the case than deliberate theft: "If Sokolow is a student of yours, I should think that it might be well to let him know of the very serious implications of plagiarism for his scholarly career."

Foster went on to say that some of his colleagues at Georgia Tech had advised him not to do anything beyond telling Ralph Gray; had in fact suggested he not even tell Nissenbaum. This tendency, not so much to cover up as simply to shut up, to keep the dirty secret from spreading through the extended professional family, and perhaps above all, to keep from getting sued, would keep Sokolow alive professionally for years. That Lawrence Foster resisted it is greatly to his credit.

Throughout 1981, as Sokolow prepared the dossier of materials he would submit for tenure, Stephen Nissenbaum, his unacknowledged quarry, was put through an absurd form of torment. Three university presses approached him with requests that he act as outside evaluator of the manuscript of *Eros and Modernization,* which Sokolow was seeking to publish. As the recognized authority on Sokolow's subject, Nissenbaum was the obvious person to call upon. Each time he told the press about the plagiarism, sometimes supplying supporting documents; each time the result was the rejection of Sokolow's manuscript — but without any further action by the press, not even an explanation to Sokolow of the reason.

On January 15, 1981, Weldon A. Kefauver, director of the Ohio State University Press, offered Nissenbaum a $50 honorarium to evaluate Sokolow's manuscript. On February 4 Nissenbaum telephoned and told him why he couldn't do it. Kefauver followed up with a letter confirming their "somewhat unsettling

telephone conversation," thanking Nissenbaum "for the candor
with which you reported those circumstances that must impinge
upon your decision on whether or not to act as our Editorial
Board's adviser during its consideration of Dr. Sokolow's book."
The following week Nissenbaum responded bluntly to Kefauver's nervous delicacy:

> In the light of this messy business, it is clear that the question is
> not whether I should act as an outside consultant for Sokolow's
> manuscript. The question is whether you should be sending it to
> anyone at all. I hope the answer to that question is as clear to you
> as it is to me. Publishing this manuscript is not in your interest. It
> is not in my interest. Most of all, it is not in the interest of Jayme
> Sokolow. This sorry business should be stopped, quickly and per-
> manently before any damage is done.

Nissenbaum sent Kefauver some Xeroxes, in which Sokolow's
clonings were underlined and color-matched with their progen-
itors. To take two examples:

Sokolow's article on the Nicholses	Nissenbaum's *Sex, Diet, and Debility in Jacksonian America* — adapted from the Ph.D. dissertation *Careful Love: Sylvester Graham and the Emergence of Victorian Sexual Theory in America* (University of Wisconsin, 1968)
Appropriating the rhetoric of Jacksonian democracy and laissez-faire capitalism, he continued by stating that the "human passions must have freedom for development, freedom of action, freedom of enjoyment." God had left these passions free so that they might "act by His attraction." But by creating the artificial institution of marriage, society "bound and starved" the passions by a "system of restraints and behavior."	"Human passions," Nichols insisted, appropriating the rhetoric of American democracy and laissez-faire capitalism, "must have freedom for development, freedom of action, freedom of enjoyment." God has left these passions free, Nichols went on, so that they might "act by His attraction." But by inventing such artificial institutions as marriage, society has "bound and starved" them by "a system of restraints and repressions."

Yet it would be completely misleading to see Thomas and his wife Mary as nineteenth century critics of Victorian sexuality who glorified sexual intercourse. Their defense of sexuality was rooted in the very spirit which it appeared to reject.

But, for all that, it would be profoundly misleading to see the Nicholses as a kind of nineteenth-century anticipation of Masters and Johnson. What is even more striking about them than their ostensible modernity is the fact that their attitudes were, in the last analysis, rooted in the very spirit they appeared to reject.

As Nissenbaum noted, "To begin with, it is odd that both Sokolow and I have included a chapter about Thomas and Mary Nichols in works about Sylvester Graham." He pointed out not only repeated parallels in language but similarities in "subject, organization, and interpretation" — parallels that ran even straighter between Sokolow's manuscript and Nissenbaum's dissertation. It had been seven weeks since Nissenbaum had first heard from Lawrence Foster at Georgia Tech, and by now he was understandably exasperated, the matter having already poisoned his winter vacation and the start of the new term.

Kefauver wrote him one more prim letter from Ohio, on February 23, 1981. About the "perplexing and disturbing circumstance" — that is, Sokolow's ripoff of Nissenbaum's work — he could assure Nissenbaum that Sokolow's manuscript was being returned to its putative author. He also said that in his rejection letter he would "of course" not mention the "distressing matters" that he and Nissenbaum had discussed. The "of course" is what's most significant here. Until one considers the words fully, one thinks: why ever *not*? Surely it's time to confront him, to get this out in the open? But one meaning of "of course" is "as a matter of course," and in that sense Kefauver was being less astonishing than merely truthful. In the matter of Jayme Sokolow, for years, standard procedure was to reply to words he had stolen with words that were minced.

What *would* Kefauver say in his rejection letter? "I shall merely indicate that we have been led to our decision through receipt of the information that a book on the subject Sokolow undertakes to treat was published last year, and that our consultants and advisers have found no reason to recommend publication of a second work on the same topic." Like a Sokolow footnote, this proposed "indication" contained so much less than half the truth as to be, in effect, a lie.

The State University of New York Press in Albany was the next to ask Nissenbaum for assistance in considering the work of Jayme Sokolow. He told them the same story he had told Ohio State. In August Nissenbaum returned from a vacation to find a third request, this time from Mary Livingston, director of Northern Illinois University Press. She asked him if he would undertake a reading of Sokolow's manuscript ("It is fairly well written") for $100. His reply, dated August 17, 1981, was an expression as much of disgust as outrage. After accusing Sokolow of plagiarism ("I use the word carefully, in its legal sense"), he explained to Livingston:

> I wish there was a way of cutting short this sorry ritual without having to play it out again and again. For me, it has already begun to turn from a horror into a drag. So, instead of demonstrating the plagiarism once again, I will simply pass along the names of the two publishers with whom I have already dealt, and suggest that you contact them before taking any other steps.

Stephen Nissenbaum, like Jayme Sokolow, came from New Jersey. Born in 1941, he was five years older than his word dog, and his academic pedigree was more choice: a B.A. from Harvard and an M.A. from Columbia before the Ph.D. from Wisconsin. His entire teaching career had been spent at the University of Massachusetts at Amherst, where he became a full professor before he was forty. When Sokolow finally sold *Eros and Modernization* to Fairleigh Dickinson University Press (after it was also rejected by Kent State University and the University of Pennsylvania), Nissenbaum no longer had to worry about being asked to serve as an outside evaluator of the manuscript. But events in Texas during the fall of 1981 would guarantee Sokolow's continued presence in his life.

On October 2, Professor Alwyn Barr distributed a memorandum to tenured members of the Texas Tech history faculty. It stated that between October 5 and October 21 Sokolow's book manuscript, publications and student evaluations would be available for inspection in the department office. The peer evaluation committee's report would be in the same office from October 19 to October 23. At 1:30 P.M. on that day, a Friday, all tenured associate and full professors would meet to discuss his candidacy and to receive ballots, which were to be returned to Barr by the following Tuesday, October 27.

Barr is described by one colleague as "a very cautious man," and by another as "probably the most cautious person I know." He was, according to Professor John Wunder, protective of Sokolow (the outsider, the Jew) in a way that was proper and even admirable. Wunder speculates that Barr selected for the "peer evaluation committee" — the small group that would report its findings to all the tenured members of the department, who would then function as the "tenure committee" — colleagues who were, as deliberations began, reliably neutral or generally well disposed toward Sokolow. That committee eventually consisted of Professors Benjamin Newcomb (once head of the Lubbock chapter of the American Civil Liberties Union), John Wunder and Allan Kuethe.

If Newcomb today cannot recall who was the committee's chairman, it may be because at the start their work promised to be more or less routine. But on the afternoon of October 12, Brian Blakeley, a specialist in modern British history, asked Kuethe to meet with him, Jack Collins and Otto Nelson "to discuss matters relating to the Sokolow tenure case." This last quotation is from a log that Kuethe, accustomed to the use of documentary sources, began to keep of his participation in what he soon realized would become a vexing piece of departmental history. On the morning of the fourteenth the meeting took place, and he was given the results of Collins's independent investigations. He then "called Ralph Gray to obtain authorization to use copies of Gray's and Sokolow's correspondence concerning the submission of Sokolow's manuscript to Gray's journal."

Five years later Kuethe recalled reacting with "a mixture of dismay, anger, and dread, but not really surprise." Aside from the suspicious polymathy of his research interests, there "had also been much bluff and bluster in Sokolow's character." But having his vague suspicion confirmed offered Kuethe no intellectual pleasure. He realized what would happen now: "dirty, trying, but necessary work" without any "thrill of the chase." Moreover, with the committee's report due by the nineteenth, Kuethe felt "the weight of the world" on him. He undertook an examination of Sokolow's dissertation; another article was given to Otto Nelson for investigation. On the evening of the fourteenth Kuethe met with Newcomb and told him what was going on. Kuethe's log reads: "Resolve to await return of Wunder from Western Hist. meeting." In the meantime, Newcomb was to undertake the comparison of Sokolow's book manuscript and Stephen Nissenbaum's dissertation.

The meeting of the Western History Association in San Antonio was attended that week by a number of Tech History Department members. On Friday the sixteenth, Kuethe was still conducting and delegating comparisons, which, like distressing medical tests, kept coming back positive. That evening he called John Wunder's wife, Susan, leaving a message asking John to meet him on Saturday. Wunder recalls getting a page at the airport and a 1 A.M. phone call from Kuethe before the two of them met with Newcomb on Saturday morning at 10 A.M. At that meeting they decided that the peer evaluation committee had to recommend against giving tenure to Sokolow, and that consideration also had to be given to a course of action even more serious. From Kuethe's log: "Wunder, Newcomb and I also agree to urge Barr to investigate the possibility of dismissal. Newcomb calls Barr home to discover expected time of his return from Western Hist. meeting."

At 10:30 P.M. that same Saturday, the committee met with Barr. It was decided that as department chairman he would request a meeting with Lawrence Graves, at that time dean of the College of Arts and Sciences, and before that a teaching member of the History Department. (Graves had, in fact, appointed Barr chairman.) The meeting couldn't be arranged until the morning of Tuesday, October 20, and on Monday, the day the peer evaluation report was due to be ready for the inspection of other tenured members of the department, Barr advised Kuethe to delay it. In the meantime the peer evaluation committee members continued to gather up copies of the sources for Sokolow's dissertation, book manuscript and published articles with a view toward placing all of these items on a table in the chairman's office, next to Sokolow's own writings. If the connections between the two *opera* had been made insufficiently plain by Sokolow, the committee was now, rather frantically, arranging things for all to see.

What would become the most serious and voluminous part of the evidence against Sokolow — the manuscript for *Eros and Modernization* — had been assigned to Newcomb, who went about underlining, in red ink, scores of passages in it that were inadequately attributed to Stephen Nissenbaum's 1968 dissertation. The list of handwritten columns of parallel page numbers — only numbers, not quotations — runs to more than four pages.

Nissenbaum's book *Sex, Diet, and Debility in Jacksonian America: Sylvester Graham and Health Reform* had appeared in 1980, a good while after Sokolow had used the 1968 dissertation ("Careful Love") that was its basis. Sokolow may have been surprised when the book appeared a dozen years after its earlier version got Nissenbaum his doctorate, and he may first have learned of its impending debut from his friend and colleague Jim Brink, who said: "I remember the day that I saw the announcement for the book in one of my journals, and I took it to Jay and I said, 'Did you see this? This is coming out on a subject exactly the same as yours.'" Although Sokolow seemed enough surprised to make Brink feel this was the first he'd heard of *Sex, Diet, and Debility*, "he looked at [Brink] and he said, 'Oh, well, I don't think it'll be any problem.'" Brink still "can't help but think it would have been shocking to see that something you thought would have lain dormant, as so many dissertations do, suddenly comes to print at about the same moment you intend to use that material." Unless, of course, you don't shock easily.

In any case, it was from Nissenbaum's dissertation that Newcomb did his work, coming up with a concordance that could leave no one unconvinced. If one were unpersuaded by all the undocumented similarities in organization, subtopics, interpretations and sources, there were time and time again the words themselves: exact duplications, and small, transparent rearrangements.

Sokolow never published his dissertation, "Revivalism and Radicalism: Garrison, Wright and the Ideology of Nonresistance," which in 1972 he submitted "in partial fulfillment" (the phrase has seldom been truer) of his Ph.D. requirements at NYU. He dedicated it to his parents, his wife and three advisors (including neoconservative Irving Kristol), thanking them as the people "who made this dissertation possible."

It was also made possible by books like William Haller's *Rise of Puritanism* (1938). The first footnote in chapter 1, on page 11, is to Haller's book, or at least the first five pages of it. The technique is typical of Sokolow. One sees that footnote and has the ordinary expectation that he is indebted to a considerable bit of background information by Haller, which has been incorporated, *passim*, into his own argument. In fact, in the opening pages of this chapter, called "The Possessed," he has repeatedly stolen Haller's exact words without putting them in quotation marks. About Puritans, Haller says on page 3 of his book:

> Chaucer met one on the road to Canterbury and drew his portrait. No better and no very different picture of the kind of man we shall be dealing with in these pages was ever drawn by any of the numerous pens which attempted the task two centuries later. The parson, Chaucer says, was a learned man, devoted to teaching and caring for his people . . . his real business was to lead men to heaven by fair words and good example. He was discreet and benign of speech.

Sokolow:

> Chaucer met a Puritan on the road to Canterbury and drew his portrait. The parson, Chaucer indicated, was a learned man who was devoted to teaching and cared for his people. His business was to lead men to heaven by fair words and good example. He was discreet, benign of speech.

Sokolow quotes about a dozen lines from *The Canterbury Tales* relating to the parson — the exact lines Haller quoted in 1938 — and follows the footnote to Haller, pages "1–5," with one to Robert Pratt's 1966 edition of *Selections from the Tales of Canterbury*, a book Sokolow had no need to consult except to find the page numbers for the material Haller had already given him. To apply another quotation from Chaucer to Sokolow himself: "Gladly wolde he lerne, and gladly teche." Who wouldn't, if it were this easy?

The theft from Haller is so conspicuous — *The Rise of Puritanism* being more or less a classic text among historians of early America — that one wonders if one doesn't have to begin applying the "death wish" theory, at least partially plausible in cases like Coleridge's and Epstein's, to Sokolow's as well. John Wunder, who remembers the dissertation violations as "less clear cut than the others" — which may be true.   ⅃ may be taken as an index of the breathtaking predations against Nissenbaum — thinks the death-wish theory "has a lot to lend itself to in this case."

Perhaps. Jack Collins, who ordered a copy of the dissertation from NYU after he had been alerted to Sokolow's conduct by Ralph Gray, actually recites some of the Haller passage to his classes at Tech; it's famous enough for that. So why didn't he catch Sokolow right when they were hiring him? Because he didn't read his dissertation. Allan Kuethe says he "was more than a little peeved with my colleagues in the field of U.S. history. . . . As senior department members had they not read his work and if so why had they failed to spot his method?" — read it, that is, in the years before the tenure deliberations. Collins, it should be noted, is a specialist in British, not American, history, and it should be remembered that he more than anyone else was responsible for Sokolow's exposure at Texas Tech. What he's confessing to — not having read the dissertation before Sokolow was hired — is neither unusual nor heinous. Candidates for assistant professorships usually send along only a chapter from their dissertations, but it would not be feasible for every member of a large department to read all the chapters that even just the finalists are submitting. Those sample chapters tend to arrive in the closing, and busiest, weeks of the semester, just before Christmas vacation and the annual professional conventions, at which most preliminary job interviews take place. The process is fast, chaotic and onerous, and it depends to some extent, like all scholarly activity, on a presumption of honesty. With respect to the dissertation, Sokolow didn't need a death wish so much as a hunch he could sneak it through. And when, a decade after it was submitted to NYU, the dissertation joined the rest of the evidence in the chairman's office in Holden Hall, he didn't react like a suicide; he tried fighting it out.

Before Sylvester Graham was guarding American potency, Benjamin Thompson, Count Rumford, was keeping urban folk warm back in the mother country. The thumbnail biography of this one of Sokolow's scientist subjects, from *The New Columbia Encyclopedia,* reads in part:

> Rumford, Benjamin Thompson, Count, 1753–1814, American-British scientist and administrator, b. Woburn, Mass. In 1776 he went to England, where he served (1780–81) as undersecretary of the colonies, conducting significant experiments with gunpowder in his spare time. Later he entered the service of the elector of Bavaria as an administrator. He was knighted in 1784 and in 1791 was created count of the Holy Roman Empire. He chose his title from the name of the town Rumford (later Concord), N.H., where his wife was born. Returning to England (1795), he introduced improved methods of heating and cooking, and developed a more accurate theory of heat.

It was an account of Rumford's interdisciplinary achievements that caused the Sokolow case to spill across departmental lines at Texas Tech. "Count Rumford and Late Enlightenment Science, Technology, and Reform" was a twenty-page article written for *The Eighteenth Century: Theory and Interpretation,* a quarterly journal edited by two associate professors in the English Department, Jeffrey Smitten and Joel Weinsheimer. "I blame it on Joel," says Smitten, years later, with a laugh. "Joel knew Jayme about as well as I did, I guess; maybe a little better. And he and Joel talked about . . . having an article on Count Rumford, and so Jayme agreed to write this thing; and so it was a solicited article. We occasionally do that. Not anymore, as a result of this, however." Smitten did not really know Sokolow well, and what social impressions he had of him were negative, yet the presumption of scholarly honesty obtained. One assumes the integrity of a colleague's work and so does not send articles solicited from campus colleagues to "outside readers" for prepublication review and approval: if you've requested somebody to write something, you have already expressed confidence in his ability to do it well. Sokolow's Rumford article came in and appeared "reasonably well written" to the editors, and so it was published in the winter 1980 number of *The Eighteenth Century.*

Nearly two years later, when Sokolow's bibliography was beginning to crumble, the peer evaluation committee decided naturally enough to look into the Count Rumford piece. This particular task of investigation was assigned to Otto Nelson, the department's German history specialist and later associate dean of the College of Arts and Sciences. A cherubic man who speaks with softness and precision, Nelson had already endured the experience at Texas Tech of having John Hinckley, President Reagan's would-be assassin, in his class on the history of the Third Reich.

"The role of [the Rumford article] in the whole Sokolow caper was rather minor," says Nelson. "In fact, it was very minor." Nevertheless, he went about his work carefully, using a copy of the article that had been given to him earlier by Sokolow himself, with the inscription "Otto — this is a study of an American scientist in the Germanic states. I thought you might be interested in it. — Jayme." The element of self-promotion in this seems characteristic, since it is clear that, even before he got into trouble, Nelson never felt much personal friendship or professional regard for Sokolow.

Nelson annotated the article as he checked it against sources. His chief finding was that Sokolow had failed to acknowledge the extent of his indebtedness to Sanborn C. Brown's 1962 study *Count Rumford, Physicist Extraordinary*. Sokolow's technical descriptions are often very close or identical to Brown's: "tannic acid, obtained by soaking powdered nutgalls in water" — Sokolow's explanation of Rumford's invisible ink — matches Brown's ("gallo-tannic acid, which was obtained by soaking powdered nutgalls in water") almost word for word, without any footnote. And here's Sokolow on the Rumford fireplace, which, he reminds us, earned a place in Jane Austen's *Northanger Abbey:* "a very narrow throat and smoke shelf which separated the hot air in the chimney's entrance from the cold air in back of the chimney. He also introduced a damper which would shut off the outside air when the fireplace was not being used. . . . He beveled the back and the sides." Brown on the same invention, unfootnoted by Sokolow: "the narrow throat and smoke shelf which separated the hot air in the front of the fireplace from the cold air which must take its place in the back of the chimney. . . . He also introduced the damper for shutting off the outside air when the fireplace was not in use. . . . He beveled the back and sides."

One can argue that the task of technical exposition offers fewer possibilities for linguistic variation than do narrative and argument. Still, it seems clear that, even with allowance for "sloppiness," Sokolow was taking a free ride on somebody else's physics: scientific descriptions that seem to enter the article with comfortable authority are in fact desperately dependent on someone else's genuine understanding of what's being talked about.* (Could Sokolow really have explained the operation of a Rumford fireplace to someone who just dropped into his office and asked for a bit of oral elaboration?) If the classic question about presidential culpability was "What did he know and when did he know it?" the earliest question that some people had about Sokolow was simply "How does he know so *much*?" Allan Kuethe's suspicion — "I think in the back of my mind I had wondered how anyone could be a publishing expert on such a wide variety of topics" — was excited precisely by articles like the one on Rumford.

Nelson was able to come up with enough things "in about an hour's time" to damn the Rumford article in a memorandum to his colleagues:

> Under other circumstances, the article might be dismissed merely as slovenly. Viewed in connection with other matters, however, it forms part of a pattern that should lead people to question seriously the author's commitment to scholarship.

Jeffrey Smitten, one of the editors of *The Eighteenth Century,* was shown the parallel passages in the course of the History Department's investigation, and in the spring 1982 issue of the journal, an honorable retraction was issued, concluding as follows:

*See Norman Fruman's discussion of Coleridge's use of Maass (*Coleridge: The Damaged Archangel,* pages 76–77). And consider this from Michael Holroyd's biography of Lytton Strachey: "The most extraordinary piece of plagiarism is provided by Edith Sitwell's *Victoria of England,* in which, as Geoffrey Grigson rightly observed (*Times Literary Supplement,* February 11, 1965, page 107), the author looked up Lytton's quotations and merely extended them, modifying Lytton's accompanying comments, or sometimes paraphrasing them word for word, substituting a synonym for each in succession." (*Lytton Strachey,* volume 2, Holt, Rinehart & Winston, page 431.)

This failure to acknowledge sources escaped the notice of the editors, who of course do not condone such practices. The University, Texas Tech Press, and the editors of *The Eighteenth Century* apologize for this oversight, to the academic community in general and especially to Dr. Brown.

In the retraction Sokolow is never mentioned by name; nor was the title of his article. Nor was Sokolow himself asked to apologize. The embarrassment of the injured more or less ensured that. "As editors," Smitten says, "we ended up feeling tremendously guilty. It's, you know, not unlike rape. . . . The victim feels as bad, as guilty, as the victimizer." The metaphor may be extreme, but as we've seen, it's also standard.

Otto Nelson says, "Had there been any [outside] review of this, it never would have been accepted." Smitten, while happier with his new policy ensuring that, isn't so certain. After all, hadn't some of Sokolow's other articles passed through outside reviewers? In fact, he could proudly claim that before being printed at least nine of them had.

Smitten was surprised that the editors' apology received absolutely no reaction: "Nobody ever said anything about this to us — subscribers, contributors. . . . Nobody wrote to us and said, 'What a scandalous thing to have happened' or 'You people are idiots for not having caught this.' " Perhaps there's always enough scandal around to assure some of its being overlooked. That was almost the case with the Rumford article vis-à-vis the rest of Sokolow's troubles. Almost before Nelson could finish his investigation, it was clear, to use his own words, that this was "only a very small nail in an already closed coffin." And the apology issued by Smitten was only the first of three involving Sokolow to run in different scholarly journals.

By 8 A.M. on Tuesday, October 20, Alwyn Barr was at last meeting with Lawrence Graves and working out what would come to be known in Allan Kuethe's log as the "advised course of action" — a procedure about which Graves thinks the university's lawyers may already have been consulted.

Graves's handsome tanned face, thick white hair, sturdy gold-rimmed glasses and equally strong voice make him very much one's idea of what a West Texan ought to look like. But he didn't come to the state until 1955, after being raised in upstate New York and taking his Ph.D., like Stephen Nissenbaum, at the University of Wisconsin. During his time in administration Graves kept pretty much out of History's affairs, even though it was his own department. He had appointed Barr department chairman ("I was well aware of his capabilities as a scholar as well as an administrator"), and during the Sokolow affair, once he heard about it, Graves "depended upon him to have a consensus" within the department. He did not meet with either Sokolow or the peer evaluation committee.

Acquainted with the problem through Barr, Graves thought that the proper course of action would be for Sokolow to withdraw his application for tenure and resign at the end of the year. He was eager to keep the affair at a low level: "We discussed it at some length, and so I reminded him that it should be handled in the department and not brought to the College level unless it were necessary." What would have made it necessary? Graves says that in order to make him dismiss Sokolow immediately, or get him to resign at the end of the fall term instead of the end of the academic year, there would have had to be a *pattern* of abuse. "If I had had further information, and further evidence, that it was something that had happened before and was likely to happen again," he says, then he would have proceeded differently. But "on the basis of the evidence I had, this was a one-time affair," and if Sokolow had been immediately dismissed because of it, Graves reasoned, "he might have brought a lawsuit."

A one-time affair? Graves's memory tells him that all he was shown was the manuscript of *Eros and Modernization* ("My recollection is that that's all"), not the rest of the questionable articles, not the dissertation. He doesn't want to give the impression that Barr kept things from him, but he feels more severe action would have had to be taken ("to protect the profession") only if what he had seen was more flagrant than it was. All he can remember seeing was the manuscript, and he thought Sokolow "would certainly have sense enough not to try to publish this kind of thing."

Barr went from Graves's office to meet with Newcomb, Wunder and Kuethe, whose log for the morning of October 20 says that he "learned that the advised course of action was now to complete tenure report and postpone dismissal action." Presumably, if Sokolow resisted resignation, dismissal would be attempted. Wunder called George Flynn, Sokolow's friend and bicycling companion, and told him it might be a good idea for Jayme to resign.

The peer evaluation committee now had to present evidence to the rest of the tenured members of the department, the ones still scheduled to discuss Sokolow and receive ballots on Friday. What they offered was both circumspect and overwhelming. Newcomb says the committee decided that "the report would be brief on this matter of publication, and it was very brief, and then we said the evidence was in the chairman's office for those in the department to go look at. And that way we thought we were in the clear, in the sense of [not] trying to prejudge what we had found. . . . As I remember, we said nothing at all, and when the report came out people came up and said to me, 'What does this mean? What do you mean by this?' . . . and I said, 'Well, the information's in the chairman's office' and so we never really tried to push people into thinking. . . . They could just go look for themselves." The word "plagiarism" was never used.

Earlier in 1981, about six months before the crisis in Holden Hall began, Jayme Sokolow asked Jim Brink to read the manuscript of *Eros and Modernization,* which was then making the rounds of university presses. Brink's field of expertise is sixteenth-century France, not antebellum America, and Sokolow wanted him to evaluate the work's stylistic merits — "not necessarily the content," Brink says. Graceful and witty writer that Brink is, one still wonders — recalling other descriptions of Sokolow, and the personal inscription on the copy of the Rumford article given to Otto Nelson — if there wasn't also an element of flattery in the request. Brink, after all, would have a vote on Sokolow's tenure: even though they had arrived in Lubbock at the same time, Brink, a very popular teacher and sound scholar, had elected to "come up" early and had been granted tenure during the 1980–81 academic year.

There is a certain boot-camp camaraderie that endures between assistant professors who have begun their long years of probation simultaneously, and when one of them pulls ahead of the other on the tenure track, a certain awkwardness can result, as if one's teammate were becoming a referee. This, added to Jim Brink's good nature and protective championing of Sokolow, made his later examination of the tenure materials especially distressing.

Brink was scheduled to attend a meeting of the Western Society for French History in Colorado on Friday, October 23, the day Alwyn Barr had scheduled a vote on Sokolow. Since he would be unable to be with his colleagues in person, he expressed his view of the evidence in a letter he wrote on the morning of the twentieth, immediately after he had examined the material in Barr's office. Part of it reads as follows:

> The perfidy of plagiarism is so detestable that immediate dismissal from the faculty and explicit description of the reasons for this dismissal to the press considering publication of this writer's work is mandatory.
>
> I want to personally state that this is a grievous blow to me but that I am convinced after close examination of the evidence made available to the faculty, that Jayme Sokolow is culpable. I see no other recourse left to the department than to counsel immediate resignation by Mr. Sokolow or, barring his unwillingness to accept our counsel, to seek his immediate dismissal from Texas Tech University.

This genuinely anguished letter remains one of the most clear-headed and forthright documents in the Sokolow case — an affair that would have enough staying power eventually to qualify it as a saga. But even here there is one contradiction, or at least confusion: first he says Sokolow must be dismissed, then he says he should be offered the option of resignation. There is, of course, an important distinction between the two. But what is consistent in Brink's view is that Sokolow had to go *immediately* — not at the end of the term and not at the end of the year and not at the end of the additional lame-duck year usually available to unsuccessful applicants for tenure. This was as hard a line as anyone would draw that month in Lubbock, and it came from someone known not only for great, if casually worn, integrity but also for a kindly disposition toward the man who'd just been caught.

At 3:30 P.M., a few hours after finishing his letter, Brink was visited in his office by Sokolow, who by this time knew he was in trouble. Brink recalls that the meeting "was very short. . . . What I said was I was very disappointed and I was convinced that the evidence condemned him, and as I recall there was some slight hesitation or hitch in his voice, and he said . . . that he was preparing a reponse." It was made available to the department the next morning, Wednesday the twenty-first. Brink, with the hope-against-hopefulness common to responsible people learning of enormities, felt he could change his own letter "if convinced" by anything Sokolow might have to say in his own defense.

He wasn't. Sokolow's nine-page letter (beginning "Dear Tenured Faculty Members") was unconvincing in the extreme. It changed no minds, and may even have hardened some feelings against him. After a paragraph defending his teaching performance, he expressed perplexity over "the Peer Evaluation Committee's report on my scholarship both for what they say and for what they omit." The committee might have said the same thing about this letter, which confessed little and explained away much. His general defense was the same one that Darryl Pinckney employed for Jacob Epstein: "I . . . am not impugning the Peer Evaluation committee. I simply believe that their search for parallels . . . has made them overlook the finer qualities of these articles." In other words, in finding what was plagiarized they failed to appreciate what wasn't. Insofar as there was plagiarism, it could be put down to "unconscious echoes, coincidental phrasing on similar subjects, and yes" — again, like Epstein —"some sloppy notetaking." Notebooks, always notebooks, from Coleridge to Reade and on to the New (sort of) World.

He dealt with selected specifics. He denied similarities between his Tolstoy-Franklin article and Dvoichenko-Markov's by noting their overall differences in "style, organization, argument, or documentation," and by contrasting two quotations that were, in fact, rather weakly paralleled by the committee. He didn't deal with the more compelling resemblances, choosing instead to offer two nondefenses: that when Harvey (*sic*) Hill Walsh's article attacked his arguments it didn't accuse him of plagiarism, and that when the editors of *Canadian-American Slavic Studies* asked for revisions they didn't accuse him either. But reminding a policeman that his fellow officer up the street failed to catch you is a less than convincing way of avoiding arrest.

The committee's accusations concerning the Rumford article were the result of a "similar misunderstanding" — the committee's, that is, not Sokolow's. His defense was also similar: to combat some weaker parallels while ignoring more blatant ones.

He reminded his colleagues, with somewhat poignant redundancy, that the committee "perhaps could have commented on [his] other articles." This is a macro version of the some-of-it-isn't-plagiarized defense; again, it doesn't occur to him that it is not standard procedure for an investigative body to comment on incidentally adequate conduct in the bill of unpleasant particulars it finds itself forced to compile.

He was most willing to admit wrongdoing — but only to the extent of "sloppy notetaking" — in the matter of his article on the Nicholses. Quoting Ralph Gray's cautious rejection letter ("it is with regret that we must decline your article"), he admits the truth of it, saying that indeed there were in the article "passages that could have caused trouble." That is, it would seem, trouble not for Nissenbaum but for Sokolow. As for the dissertation, he says it was easy for the committee to find the overlapping of Haller and others, because he "guilelessly footnoted the exact pages." Should he craftily have avoided any citation, just as he avoided all quotation marks? Even when making his grudging confessions, Sokolow had a way of making culpability seem more *tua* than *mea*.

About the manuscript of *Eros and Modernization* and Nissenbaum's dissertation, he again dismissed the weaker reflections and ignored the blinding ones. Finding that "the offensive matter appears rather puny," he vowed to correct it before the book went into production. He noted that in those readers' reports he received from presses rejecting the book (the University of Pennsylvania, Kent State University) there was no mention of impropriety. Perhaps these two presses, which didn't call on Nissenbaum for his evaluation, never found any; but, one must wonder, even if they had, would it have made a difference? At least two of the presses that knew of the theft didn't tell Sokolow they were on to him.

On the last page of his letter Sokolow admitted "some glaring examples of sloppy work" but pleaded with his colleagues to look at the big picture:

> None of those errors . . . were deliberately foisted upon unsuspecting readers. The question is one of balance. If you read my nine articles and manuscript, what appears more compelling, the small number of admitted errors or the author's research and contributions to his field?

He informed them that he was now writing another book, to be called *Fourierism and American Utopianism: The North American Phalanx, 1843–1855*. One wonders if by this point any of his colleagues were hoping the letter would end with an academic version of the killer's anonymous plea: STOP ME BEFORE I WRITE AGAIN.

It was up to them to add Sokolow's arguments to their assessment of his scholarship and professionalism. The three misspellings in the letter are perhaps better left to a psychiatrist. They are all of the same root word, in different noun and verb forms: "plagerism," "plagerizing" and "plagerized."

By Friday Sokolow realized he was without support and threw in the towel. He would leave at the end of the year, and he promised to make changes in the *Eros and Modernization* manuscript before publishing it. This was the largest price exacted for what was, by anyone's reckoning, a good deal. Not only was Sokolow not dismissed, but he also never received a negative tenure vote. He was simply allowed to withdraw his application for tenure. No "turn down" exists on his record.

No move was ever made toward dismissal, though there was some informal discussion of the possibility after the resignation was accepted. "I think there were still some people who said we ought to go for dismissal," Newcomb says, "and my advice at that time was no, because the practical effect would not have been any different. There was no point in having a big trial with everybody taking their time to testify and having to go over all this stuff and not getting any more than you'd already got. Now, had he just failed of tenure and been given a terminal contract for a succeeding year, which is the way we do it, then I would have supported a move to dismiss him." Dean Graves probably had one more meeting with Barr, about whether there was a need to do something more. But Graves's recommendation was still that "unless there were some critical need for it . . . we should simply allow his resignation to take effect and close the matter, without attempting to do more. And that's what basically happened."

Newcomb recalls a "basic unanimity" among department members about the handling of the matter, but Wunder says there was "no consensus" about whether any further action should be taken once Sokolow's resignation had been accepted. As Newcomb says, after the deal "some people talked about: 'Well, should we write Professor Nissenbaum? Should we write his publisher and send him this stuff?' . . . I decided I wasn't going to do it — I don't know what other people thought — on the ground that the department didn't, and I think they had legal advice on this." He can't recall any discussion about whether NYU should be informed that it had awarded Sokolow a Ph.D. for a plagiarized dissertation. "No," says Newcomb, who points out that the plagiarized book manuscript was much more on his mind than the dissertation. "I don't believe we did, and I'm not sure why. I guess it just slipped our minds." But Wunder recalls at least some informal discussion of this, and thinks it should have been taken further, just as he and Brink felt the Fairleigh Dickinson Unversity Press should be alerted. (Alwyn Barr, Wunder says, was opposed to this.) Kuethe was in favor of notifying everyone — Nissenbaum, Fairleigh Dickinson and NYU: "I believed that we had an obligation both to the profession and to the plagiarized author to set things straight."

There seem to be two main reasons none of this occurred. First, as Newcomb says, was a desire to avoid giving anyone the opportunity to say that Sokolow was being persecuted. But, more important, as always, were the potential legal consequences. Kuethe still thinks the word about Sokolow should have been spread to all the interested and injured parties, but these steps "had to come from the proper institutional authorities." And no institutional subdivision of the university — the History Department or the College of Arts and Sciences — was willing to take them. One ironic reason for treading softly was shared by Wunder and Kuethe during the tenure proceedings. There were people so livid, says Wunder, that he and Kuethe feared the department might, in the haste anger causes, do something against "procedure," thereby giving Sokolow the grounds for counterattack, opening up the possibility that some appeals body would overturn the department's decision and anchor him, like Preston Smith's statue, forever in their midst.

For the rest of the academic year the department would have to live with its decision in an uncomfortably literal way. "He wasn't around much," Otto Nelson recalls. "He came and met his classes. As I would pass him in the hall he and I would just say hello. We never had a confrontation or harsh words. I don't believe I was one of those persons whom he disliked, although I think there were a number of them. . . . I think everyone probably had a very cool, kind of frosty relation with him." One proviso of his resignation's acceptance was that Sokolow not be permitted to teach any upper-division courses that spring. As Newcomb, who was assigned to replace Sokolow on the graduate committee, puts it: "That was felt to be a fit situation for someone whose research was questionable." But for the rest of the fall Sokolow continued to teach History 511, a course for new teaching assistants on methods of teaching history.

Allan Kuethe, who was graduate advisor that year, had been distressed by Sokolow's conduct in that course even before he was asked to serve on the peer evaluation committee: "He had reduced at least two of them to tears, berating them for 'stupidity,' and I had received a complaint about this from Virginia Balch, probably the best student in the graduate program at that time and who is now deceased. I had done some inquiring that very week and was about to act when I was informed that I had been named to the tenure committee." Kuethe's notes from his interview with Balch on October 15 include the following: "Harps on ignorance of local people and carries that over to the graduate students. . . . Widespread concern among 511 class. . . . Referred to as an 'ass' . . . pompous." Another student Kuethe interviewed that day, one who liked Sokolow and claimed to benefit from History 511, still noted that "his criticism is often not constructive . . . comes down hard."

Nelson recalls the particular distress of Sokolow's early champions. Before October, according to Nelson's memory, Professor Briggs Twyman "used to go around saying, 'Anyone who won't vote for Jayme is an asshole.' " But now he was among that group of former allies experiencing an especially acute kind of letdown. Brian Blakeley recalls a certain "gnashing of teeth" by the swindled defenders.

Robert Seidel, who has since left Tech, was on leave during the exposure of Sokolow. As an assistant professor he played no role in it and had no access to the materials under review. Jim Brink recalls: "When he came back he continued to side with Jay, and I insisted that the material be made available to him, because I thought that his defense of Jay was so blind. . . . He told me he did not *want* to see it." As Brink tells it, Seidel and Jackie Reinier (another assistant professor who later departed Tech) felt that Sokolow was so isolated and shunned that they didn't want to have their own empirical reasons to begin thinking badly of him.

John Wunder recalls Sokolow as displaying a certain baffled contrition that spring; he's not sure Sokolow really understood what he'd done, or the "difference between right and wrong." Others don't think so. Otto Nelson remembers the affair as "so embarrassing, but it's embarrassment to the department, to the people who'd been associated with him; I think he's probably the only one who didn't seem to be embarrassed by it."

Not long after Sokolow had packed his bags the department instituted a third-year review for its assistant professors — an official scrutiny they have to undergo midway through their years of probation and after which they can be told that their research is proceeding well, or needs to be speeded up, or pointed in a new direction, or made more careful. On the question of the new procedure's relation to the Sokolow case, there is, predictably, a gamut of historical interpretations in this department of historians. Otto Nelson, now associate dean of the College of Arts and Sciences, thinks it came about "more from general institutional pressure to upgrade standards. . . . In my own mind I don't relate these two matters." But one of Nelson's fellow hard-liners on Sokolow, Allan Kuethe, says the review was "a direct result of this case. . . . While we certainly do not expect to meet another Sokolow in our professional careers, this step, at least to my mind, was a movement toward better departmental standards."

Has this review really been useful? Jim Brink thinks it's created "a feeling of suspicion. . . . There's a gulf now" between the tenured and untenured faculty, with the latter "really on eggshells." He can point to people who during the last several years have left because they were given discouraging signals during the interim review and to some others who departed because they "just found the atmosphere to be oppressive." Nelson thinks it has created "an added margin of apprehension . . . 'up against the wall,' I think it's called."

Benjamin Newcomb offers this assessment of one of the review's purposes: "This will . . . encourage the person not to do a rush job. There's always the possibility, though we don't know it was the case, that Prof. Sokolow, in the interest of trying to get his material published, was rushed and therefore careless or slovenly or whatever. If we try to put the individual on track, so that they know full well where they stand, then we are perhaps avoiding any possibility of [their] doing a one-night copying job."

But what about the assistant professor who's told, during his third year, that he's not publishing enough? Won't he then be facing additional pressure and temptation? There remains in bigger-means-best Texas a tendency to equate longer bibliographies, like those new buildings, with academic progress, and Otto Nelson, after some years in the associate dean's office, perceives "that a higher level of publication is continually being required." Not just a higher level, either; but, as he would admit, more pages. Third-year reviews are not uncommon among American universities, and a reluctance to make rules out of the fear that people will break them is one of the ways in which civilizations retreat, but one has to wonder if Sokolow, had the third-year review existed in his day at Tech, wouldn't have stolen more instead of less. Of course he might also have been forced to resign earlier.

Jim Brink says newly appointed assistant professors of history at Texas Tech "don't know who Jay Sokolow was," but Nelson feels sure that "they know of the case." Blakeley says that as the memory of Sokolow fades, the third-year reviews are already becoming less rigorous — perhaps the surest clue to their origin.

But Allan Kuethe says the new attention with which faculty read each other's work is still a good thing, after the "appalling" discovery "that a fraud lurked in our midst for over five years, gaining fine merit pay raises at the expense of others, before we discovered him largely by chance." Extra scrutiny came to be given not only to junior colleagues but to those new Ph.D.'s seeking to join the department. On a December afternoon five years after the Sokolow case broke, Newcomb, just back from a trip to the library to check out some footnotes in a student paper, points out that while no "mammoth" check of job seekers is made, the department does look more closely at the dissertations coming to it: "We try to check the footnotes of those people we think we are going to employ."

As to the affair's largest and perhaps least documentable effects, namely those on the department's atmosphere and reputation, there is again a range of opinion. Blakeley doesn't see many. Newcomb, somewhat remarkably, perceives a fairly wide silver lining, the result of an effect that could be called

> cleansing, maybe, in a certain way. It reaffirmed the fact that you can keep your standards up, you see. Today I was having lunch with some people in another department, and they were talking about people that had been tenured and recently tenured in their department. There were some allegations made about some of their research, and they said, "Not like you people, who catch people whose research isn't perhaps up to snuff."

But John Wunder, now gone, thinks the matter only added to the department's problems, a judgment with which Jim Brink largely agrees. He talks about a kind of lingering unease, "one of those unsavory things that you really don't want anyone to talk about. . . . It was never really resolutely solved . . . it was never put to rest." This is a judgment with which no one, no matter what allowance for human frailty and bureaucratic failure of nerve he makes, could argue. The good men of the History Department never solved the problem of Jayme Sokolow. They exported it.

Jack Collins, co-editor with Brian Blakeley of *Documents in English History: Early Times to the Present*, tells the story of someone who spots a thief practicing his trade on a busy medieval fairground. The witness yells "Stop!" and the fairgoers proceed to chase the thief into the next county. "Thank God," they say, "we're rid of a thief."

It's a good analogy to the Sokolow case, which permitted some History Department members to feel that their own house at least had been "cleansed" with some rigor, even if Sokolow had not officially been branded a plagiarist (indeed, not even in the peer evaluation committee's report). He was free to continue calling himself a historian, and once he was chased across the Texas border, he hardly found himself condemned to live the life of a scholar gypsy.

Briggs Twyman says Sokolow's colleagues at Tech hoped that once he was gone the academic grapevine would keep him out of another teaching job. After all, that grapevine — more like a honeycomb, really, with its networks of professional meetings, guest lectures, specialized journals and alma mater contacts — had contributed to Sokolow's undoing in their department: the phone call from Jack Collins to his grad school buddy Ralph Gray. It wasn't an unreasonable assumption, and in at least one instance it worked. Sokolow applied for a job at a branch of Penn State and managed to become a finalist. At that point Twyman got a call from an old friend now teaching there, asking why Jayme Sokolow was no longer at Tech. Twyman explained that there were doubts about the originality of his work. Sokolow was never offered the job.

But he did secure employment. By 1983 he was working for the National Endowment for the Humanities. His responsibilities sometimes even involved grant proposals from professors pursuing research. "That makes a lot of us real angry," says John Wunder, from his new post at Clemson. From the associate dean's office in Holden Hall, Otto Nelson is driven to uncharacteristic levels of exclamation: "My God! Of all things for this kind of person to be doing now, to be evaluating other people's research. . . . It's just hideous."

No one seems to know how Mr. Sokolow went to Washington Jim Brink says, "It's certainly a mystery, but, boy, did he land on his feet." Could he have gotten there without at least bland letters of recommendation from some former colleagues at Tech, including, presumably, his chairman? That is the normal course of things, and former Dean Graves seems relieved when he's able to remind anyone of it: "I would not have been involved in it directly." He's right: the NEH would have gone to the department. By not asking if Sokolow was a plagiarist (why would one?), it probably gave the department the chance to write mild endorsements. Jim Brink thinks people "allowed their frustration to sort of dissipate when he didn't get another academic job. Now, had he landed another academic position, I think there might have been phone calls in the night, surreptitious letter-writing." If there's an element of casuistry in the rationalizing he describes, it's understandable enough, and even touching; perhaps it's less dangerous for someone like Sokolow to be put among bureaucrats doling out the pork to professors than it would be to have him in direct contact with students.

But there he was, and not without his bit of influence over people's lives. Stephen Nissenbaum can recall how one day a few years ago up in Amherst he heard his dean complaining of the glacial pace with which proposals sometimes move through the NEH, except for one consolation he'd discovered when he was down in Washington — a real go-getter named Jayme Sokolow. By this time, of course, Nissenbaum was used to Sokolow as a source of irony in his life: at the NEH Sokolow has been program officer in the Education Division for some projects for which Nissenbaum has been on the advisory board — a "resource person" for Sokolow, one might say.*

Eros and Modernization: Sylvester Graham, Health Reform, and the Origins of Victorian Sexuality in America was published by Fairleigh Dickinson University Press and the Associated University Presses (London and Toronto) on October 22, 1983, with a bright yellow cover. The biographical note below the photograph of the modestly smiling author tells the reader that Dr. Sokolow "has taught at Texas Tech University and New York University" and that he is "presently a staff member of the National Endowment for the

*In 1984 Nissenbaum was a consultant to the filming of *Three Sovereigns for Sarah*, an adaptation of his book *Salem Possessed*, starring Vanessa Redgrave, for PBS's *American Playhouse*. The production was made possible in part by a grant from the National Endowment for the Humanities.

Humanities. Among his published works are many articles on nineteenth-century American and European history." It also heralds the good news that "Dr. Sokolow is currently writing a book on the Fourierist communes in nineteenth-century America." Dedicated to the author's parents, *Eros and Modernization* (which is shelved in many American libraries right near Nissenbaum's *Sex, Diet, and Debility*) includes among its acknowledgments a grateful mention of Joan Weldon, who "did her usually [*sic*] excellent work turning my handwriting into a typed manuscript" — the same manuscript about which she was to type the peer evaluation committee's report at her desk outside the chairman's office in Holden Hall. The book's physical, published reality can be unsettling. "It makes me uneasy just to see it," says Jim Brink, when he looks at its brassy cover on a desk across the room. After Sokolow's fall at Tech, Brink asked him to remove from the acknowledgments gratitude for Brink's reading of the manuscript, a request so obviously reasonable that one wouldn't have thought it necessary to make it. But given the breezy business-as-usual citations of Texas Tech and Joan Weldon he was probably wise.

In the normal course of things, those professional journals with appropriate specialties sent out review copies of *Eros and Modernization* to experts in the field. Professor Sheila A. Culbert of the *American Historical Review* chose as her preferred reviewer none other than Stephen Nissenbaum, who turned down the job but suggested Lawrence Foster — the same man who three years before had been asked to evaluate the manuscript of Sokolow's article on the Nicholses. Foster, having by this time been promoted to associate professor at Georgia Tech, sent his regrets on December 5, 1983, alerting Professor Culbert to his part in this apparently unending affair, "the most blatant and brazen case of pure plagiarism that I had ever encountered in the historical profession." Foster had not yet read *Eros and Modernizaton,* but he had little ground for optimism. Toward the end of his letter, he expressed a kind of dreamlike disbelief: "Looking at the title of Sokolow's book which is almost identical in focus to Nissenbaum's, I must ask myself: Is this unfortunate story continuing to unfold now?"

Indeed, what had two years before been a more or less local

disgrace was about to become an open scandal, a matter of public record visible to the whole profession.

On April 25, 1984, Otto Pflanze, editor of the *American Historical Review*, wrote Stephen Nissenbaum, informing him that given the information supplied by Foster, the journal would not review *Eros and Modernization* unless Nissenbaum wanted to do so himself. He suggested that Nissenbaum might want to turn the whole matter over to the Professional Division of the American Historical Association (AHA), which is charged with adjudicating such ethical disputes.*

Nissenbaum declined the first opportunity but took advantage of the second, after he had asked his department chairman, Robert Griffith, to examine this book he could now barely stand to open, much less review. On May 8, just two weeks after Pflanze's letter, Griffith sent Richard Kirkendall, vice president of the Professional Division, a fifteen-page memo entitled "A Comparison of Similarities in the Works of Stephen Nissenbaum and Jayme A. Sokolow (March 1984)." The case was by now sufficiently long-standing for Griffith's memo to begin with a section headed "Background and chronology."

Despite some token efforts at revision — ones more in the nature of laundering than legitimating — the published version of *Eros and Modernization* was essentially the same ripoff it had been in manuscript. Griffith ran his own parallel columns, two examples from which will show Sokolow's post-Lubbock m.o. (see p. 180).

"Devise" and "tenuous" give way to "defend" and "ruefully"; "indicates" and "pervaded" become "demonstrates" and "permeated." Like an exhibitionist's raincoat, these gestures at covering up seem evidence more of wrongdoing than good intentions. They also make one think that Sokolow had probably acquired a word processor after leaving Lubbock.

On May 31, 1984, Jamil S. Zainaldin, the AHA's deputy executive director, acknowledged Griffith's letter and told him the case was "under study."

*

*Nissenbaum's book *Salem Possessed: The Social Origins of Witchcraft*, written with Paul Boyer, received the AHA's John H. Dunning Prize.

Nissenbaum dissertation (1968)	Sokolow article (1980) submitted to the *Journal of the Early Republic*	Sokolow book (1983)
Graham himself was able to devise, after all, only the most tenuous and unsatisfying justification of marriage. All it amounted to, really, was the assurance that while all sex was inherently harmful, marital sex was less harmful than other kinds — less harmful, at any rate, as it was less enjoyable . . .	Graham was able to devise only the most tenuous justification for marriage. While all sex was inherently harmful, marital sex was less harmful than other kinds because it was less enjoyable.	Graham could only ruefully defend the state of matrimony. While all sex was inherently harmful, marital sex was less harmful than other kinds because it was less enjoyable.
The examples of both Noyes and Nichols indicate, then, in contrasting ways, how the distrust of sexuality and sexual excitement which was first popularized and to a great degree articulated by Sylvester Graham so pervaded the culture of mid-nineteenth century America that it informed the sensibility of even the most unconventional sexual theorists of the age.	The example of the Nicholses and contemporary sexual radicals indicates how the distrust of sexuality and sexual excitement (which was articulated and popularized by Sylvester Graham) so pervaded mid-nineteenth century American culture that it affected the sensibilities of even the most unconventional sexual theorists of the period.	The example of the Nicholses and contemporary sexual radicals demonstrates how the sexual ideology of Sylvester Graham so permeated American culture that it became the foundation for Victorian free-love theories and practices.

Meanwhile, back in Holden Hall, Jayme Sokolow's former colleagues were reacting to the publication of *Eros and Modernization*. When Benjamin Newcomb heard of its appearance he was apprehensive: "I was afraid that he had not done what he said he was going to do, and that was make sufficient revisions in the book. . . . The time lag was pretty short, it seems to me." It was indeed. Books, like babies, usually require about nine months' production time from submission of a complete manuscript to their appearance between covers. This would have left Sokolow with a little more than a year between his agreement to resign from Tech and the point at which he would have to submit a manuscript in need of enormous overhauling if it was to be brought within the boundaries of propriety: not much time, actually, what with another semester to teach and a job search to conduct. And even this, of course, assumes his willingness.

Ralph Mann, of the University of Colorado, reviewed *Eros and Modernization* for a journal called *The History Teacher*, noting some virtues in Sokolow's work but also expressing a certain perplexity: "In 1980, Stephen Nissenbaum published a book on Graham that is parallel to the Sokolow study in many particulars. Sokolow's contribution is, therefore, limited largely to his reversal of modernization theory. . . . There is little to choose between the two arguments, and I remain unconvinced that Sylvester Graham deserves two books." Either Mann was exercising the extreme caution attending charges of academic plagiarism — don't say "plagiarized" if you can say "derivative" — or else he was relying on his memory of Nissenbaum's book without actually reopening it.

Allan Kuethe was "dumbfounded" by the book's publication, which made him realize again how the department should have informed Fairleigh Dickinson University Press of what it had discovered. He contemplated his former colleague's progress with amazement: "Sokolow had escaped his debacle at Texas Tech with degree in hand, had landed a good job in Washington, and as far as the world was concerned was a man of position. What I will never understand is why he exposed himself. . . . Did he feel that the profession was as 'stupid' as the students he berated? Did he feel that if caught no harm could come his way, either at the degree-granting institution or in Washington?"

Stephen Nissenbaum describes himself as having been "aggressively unaggressive" about pursuing Sokolow. He counted on the normal institutional channels to "get Jayme Sokolow out of a position where he has anything to do with this profession" and to provide himself with "some kind of statement of vindication" from his peers. Both of these were reasonable requests. On June 29, 1984, Samuel R. Gammon, the AHA's executive director, passed the Sokolow case on to the American Association of University Professors (AAUP), with which the AHA had cooperated on a similar case in 1971. Both Nissenbaum and Sokolow were informed of this action.

On August 8 Sokolow responded to the AAUP with an eighteen-page letter, a copy of which was duly forwarded to Nissenbaum by the AAUP. This letter, far longer and better prepared than what he had sent to the tenured members of the Tech History Department three years before — he had weeks, not hours, this time — is no more convincing than the earlier one. But it is extraordinary nonetheless, for in it Jayme Sokolow proposes his own solution to the "problem" — a solution he would get the AHA to accept.

He explains: "I chose to write on this topic and studied Nissenbaum's dissertation carefully before commencing my research. The emphases within his dissertation and my book, however, are clearly different." In a familiar way, he draws attention to irrelevant differences in order to avoid having to confront crucial similarities. Some of his oblique explanations of the latter are rather bizarre: "There are parallelisms in language, as befits two studies on the same subject that often paraphrase or quote from the same meager primary sources on many aspects of the topic." Actually, if the sources are too meager to speak for themselves, then their interpreters must more than usually speak for them; "parallelisms in language" would seem, as a consequence, all the less likely. "Throughout most of my book," Sokolow says, "there are relatively few instances where the language obviously overlaps." His qualifiers are revealing.

The one matter about which he must admit flagrant misconduct — indeed, he owns up to being "deeply ashamed" of it — is the article on the Nicholses that Lawrence Foster exposed to Ralph Gray and Nissenbaum:

> If the article, based upon such obviously sloppy notetaking and scholarship, had been published, it would have been an embarrassment and a serious breach of scholarly ethics. The material, however, was never published and it was substantially modified in my book. I should have cited Nissenbaum's dissertation, but more importantly, I should have patiently waited to complete my research instead of trying to rush into print with a half-baked article.

Again, it's sloppiness ("half-baked"), not perfidy, he's ashamed of. But if that is the real explanation for his article, why would its publication have been a breach of ethics? An embarrassment, yes; but a moral affront? Not unless bad motives accompanied careless notetaking. Sokolow goes on to emphasize that the article was "neither published nor revealed to the public" (a poor choice of verb in a letter meant to be self-exculpating); that it wasn't so revealed is because his sloppiness was "miraculously recognized and fortuitously corrected."

Still, he owns up to some insufficient documentation in *Eros and Modernization:* "I demur from one of Professor Griffith's contentions and heartily endorse the other: my book is not substantially similar to Nissenbaum's dissertation, but there certainly is an insufficient acknowledgment of Nissenbaum's dissertation in the book and its influence upon my own research and themes." Not once in his eighteen-page letter does Sokolow mention that he lost his job at Texas Tech because these same shortcomings were brought to his attention, there, two years before. The clear impression left by his letter is that he has only learned of them from the rejection of the Nichols article in 1980 and from Nissenbaum's current protest to the AHA and AAUP.

Nissenbaum had proposed that the case be settled by Sokolow's publishing a document admitting the "substantial similarities" between *Eros and Modernization* and "Careful Love" (the dissertation), and that *Eros and Modernization* be withdrawn from circulation by Fairleigh Dickinson University Press at Sokolow's own request. Because he still denied that the similarities were "substantial," Sokolow pronounced this proposal "Draconian" and offered a "two-part solution": a carefully worded letter to both the *American Historical Review* and the *Journal of American History* that would admit insufficient documentation but not substantial similarity; and an errata slip to go into copies of *Eros and*

Modernization still on hand at Fairleigh Dickinson. He offered to pay for the printing and distribution if the press couldn't or wouldn't do so. The press does now send the errata slip if a reader requests it, but of course plenty of copies, including the one bought by the Texas Tech library, went out without it. It amounts to five hefty footnotes drawing the reader's attention to thirty-three pages of "Careful Love" and no fewer than ninety-two of *Sex, Diet, and Debility*. In the new footnotes Nissenbaum's work is described as "pioneering," "excellent" (twice) and "fine." The wholesale absurdity of this errata slip does not, of course, even hint of the many examples of exactly duplicated phrasing.

Part of the proposed letter to the *American Historical Review* and the *Journal of American History* reads as follows:

> I studied closely Professor Nissenbaum's fine dissertation prior to the writing of my own book on the health reform movement. . . . Belated acknowledgment has been put into an *Errata* that accompanies my book, and I urge any reviewers and readers to study the emendations carefully. . . . I apologize to Professor Nissenbaum of the University of Massachusetts at Amherst for this lamentable breach of scholarly courtesy and ethics.

Nissenbaum was properly disgusted by Sokolow's "two-part solution," and on October 30 he wrote Jonathan Knight at the AAUP to tell him so. He lamented the way the case had dragged on and said he could offer even more evidence of Sokolow's wrongdoing, though the AAUP had plenty already. He wanted a clear judgment against Sokolow — not a legal one, but an official branding of him as a plagiarist. What the AAUP was offering amounted to "mediation," and Nissenbaum rejected it, reminding them of what he had been through since 1980 and identifying what was now clearly discernible as the theme of the story: "At every point I had hoped and trusted that a judgment would be made. Instead, at every point the only action taken was based on self-protection and a refusal to name the offense." During the long Sokolow affair the person with the clearest grounds for filing a lawsuit — Nissenbaum himself, for infringement of copyright — never did so. He counted on his profession to adjudicate (not mediate) a dispute within its own house.

On November 5 Robert L. Zangrando of the AHA's Professional Division promised Nissenbaum that they weren't indifferent to his feelings, and that "procedures" would soon be implemented. Encouraged, Nissenbaum wrote back on November 23, enclosing yet further parallel passages — ones not in the Griffith memorandum — and assuring him that "these are but samples."

But in less than a month it was clear that Sokolow's solution had been accepted. On December 11 Samuel Gammon wrote a letter to Otto Pflanze, editor of the *American Historical Review*, asking that he run, word for word, the letter Sokolow had proposed in his long letter to the AAUP. He had, in effect, been allowed to settle his own case. Three days later Nissenbaum wrote a letter to the AHA's Zangrando expressing his distress: "At no point in this entire dismal process has anybody in a formal professional role indicated to me, either in writing or in conversation, that they believe Sokolow's book to be a plagiarism. And now, once again, the profession has decided to withhold judgement." Actually — and the next paragraph of Nissenbaum's letter shows he's aware of it — the profession *had* made a judgment: "Sokolow has implicitly claimed his book will henceforth be a legitimate work of scholarship. And by agreeing to Sokolow's wording, and his *Errata*, the AHA has accepted his definition of the problem." A copy of this letter went to Jamil S. Zainaldin, the AHA's deputy executive director, who responded that he could appreciate Nissenbaum's distress. But he said that this was "the best resolution . . . short of litigation."

Always, it was fear of that which kept Sokolow afloat. Zainaldin wrote: "I believe there can be no misunderstanding what [Sokolow's] letter means." In other words, everyone will decode it into an admission of plagiarism. But one must not say the "*p*" word. Zainaldin admits that "what this [episode] does point up is the weakness — or I should say vacuum — in our profession for making these kinds of difficult decisions and judgements." He did offer Nissenbaum the prospect of some future comfort by telling him that the Professional Division was thinking about drawing up a code of ethics or at least "a statement on plagiarism" in light of Sokolow's case and some others, including that of David Abraham — in which a Princeton professor had recently been charged with distorting archival evidence in order to make more convincing his thesis that German businessmen in the Weimar Republic played an important part in Hitler's coming to power. What Abraham stood accused of was more in the nature of forgery than plagiarism, but like Sokolow he pleaded carelessness. In response to his exposure there was such a loud protest by historians that the *New York Times* and national publications covered the matter. But some historians (among them Hanna Gray, president of the University of Chicago) asked the Professional Division to investigate those scholars who had protested against Abraham not in scholarly journals but in "quasi-public declarations" like open letters. The AHA wound up canceling the investigation after two months.

But this matter was consuming the Professional Division at just the time Nissenbaum was being asked to accept Sokolow's "two-part solution." The Abraham case, involving Nazis and Princeton, was more glamorously nefarious than the Sokolow one, and had Nissenbaum managed to get his grievance further out in the open, it's still unlikely that he would have gotten much attention from historians who were watching the juiciest scandal in years, another one, move through mass-media spotlights.

On January 17, 1985, Otto Pflanze wrote Zainaldin that Sokolow's letter would be published in the February issue of the *American Historical Review*. (It would indeed appear, under the heading "Professional Matters" and with the notice "The following communication is published at the direction of the American Historical Association.") He further told Zainaldin that under the circumstances the book would be listed with "Other Books Received" but not reviewed. "So," his letter concluded, "the matter is well taken care of."

There are copies of the February 1985 *American Historical Review* on various bookshelves in Holden Hall. For most faculty subscribers at Texas Tech the "professional matter" on page 274 was probably the first they'd heard from Sokolow in some time. Asked if he found Sokolow's letter disingenuous — with its clear implication that the author has only recently learned of his "insufficient acknowledgment" of Nissenbaum, and no mention of how he had lost a job three years before because of it — Benjamin Newcomb cautiously responds, "Not particularly." He reminds the asker that he never saw the finished book, only the manuscript, but thinks "guarded" may be a better word than "disingenuous." After all, "it could simply be that he didn't believe us and didn't believe anybody until the author [complained]. . . . I mean some people don't understand what's being said to them, and not necessarily intentionally don't, but really just have some block against things." This makes it sound rather as if Sokolow acquired his book, as the British are said to have gathered their empire, in a fit of absent-mindedness.

John Wunder more flatly calls the letter "inaccurate," but admits the possibility that Sokolow "didn't have a sense of the wrong that he had done." Indeed, the longer the case and Sokolow's career went on, the easier it became to view it more as a matter of pathology than immorality. Jim Brink says there was really no anxiety among Tech professors that the Sokolow matter, after this coded confession of plagiarism, would come back to their doorstep: "I think there was some kind of snickering — 'Hey, he's been caught elsewhere, too' — but I don't think there was any nervousness. I think we felt like we were covered, in that what we'd done — I mean he wasn't on our faculty anymore." In any case, no self-policing arm of academe ever asked Texas Tech to give an account of itself. And it's true: he was no longer on their faculty. He continued to work — for years — at the NEH, though the NEH is surely on the subscription list of the *American Historical Review*.

Stephen Nissenbaum never replied in the pages of the *American Historical Review* to Sokolow's letter. By 1985 his anger was "at the profession and not Sokolow" himself. The only amends with which he would have to content himself came in the form of a "Statement on Plagiarism" by the AHA, the first part of which was published in the organization's newsletter, *Perspectives,* in October 1986. This document, which, according to the note that preceded it, "the Professional Division has been working hard on for the past year," is the statement Zainaldin had foreseen when he wrote Nissenbaum nearly two years before.

It is an exceptionally forthright document, all the more so in view of the timid response actually made by the organization to one of the cases that prompted it. In fact, it has all the courage of the abstract and hypothetical. It begins by calling willful pla-

giarism "a cardinal violation of the ethics of scholarship" and
states the particularly strong need historians have for sources
whose reliability they can prove. It declares the unsatisfactoriness
of academics' ad hoc responses to fraud, and notes the irony that
"students are often dealt with more harshly than colleagues."
The assistant professor's slippery slope is duly taken into account, too: "The struggle for tenured positions is intense, while
the moral responsibilities of individuals to one another are
greatly unsettled." Sloppy notetaking is dismissed as a "standard
defense." Finally, procedures and sanctions of such severity are
suggested that one is almost tempted to apply Sokolow's adjective
"Draconian" to them:

> A persistent pattern of deception justifies termination of an aca-
> demic career; some scattered misappropriations may warrant only
> a public disclosure. What is troubling is not the variation in re-
> sponses but rather the reluctance of many scholars to speak out
> about the possible offenses that come to their notice. No one
> advocates hasty or ill-founded accusations, and the protections of
> due process should always apply. If, however, charges of plagia-
> rism or gross impropriety are sustained by an investigating com-
> mittee, its findings should ordinarily be made public. When
> appraising manuscripts for publication, reviewing books, or eval-
> uating peers for placement, promotion, and tenure, the trustwor-
> thiness of the historian should never be overlooked. After all,
> scholarship flourishes in an atmosphere of openness and candor,
> which should, in our opinion, include the scrutiny and discussion
> of academic deception.

This ringing statement was signed by John Higham of Johns
Hopkins and Robert L. Zangrando of the University of Akron.
It was Zangrando who wrote to Nissenbaum two years before:
"Not for the world would I want you to assume that I personally
or the AHA Professional Division had disregarded the matter
you asked us to explore." Disregarded, no, but certainly, according to the propositions now put forth in *Perspectives,* mishandled.
Naming names is the essence of the response proposed; the last
paragraph of the "Statement on Plagiarism" is almost a history
of what never happened to Sokolow, who for five years had been
allowed to euphemize and survive what he had done — done
again and again, too ("a persistent pattern").

When asked to respond to the "Statement," the history professors in Lubbock aren't going to argue. Collins, one of Sokolow's original accusers, says it "seems all right" but adds that what seems all right in theory may not prove so in real university life. Dean Graves listens to a reading of excerpts from the document and says, "I would have no problem at all dealing with that." But then again, he can't recall being shown "a persistent pattern" in the Sokolow case.

Patterns have a way of persisting indefinitely when an element of pathology seems to be involved. By 1986 there was a new complaint against Sokolow before the AHA and AAUP. It was brought by Associate Professor Carl Guarneri of St. Mary's College in Moraga, California. In 1980 Jayme Sokolow requested a copy of Guarneri's doctoral dissertation (directed by John Higham), *Utopian Socialism and American Ideas: The Origins and Doctrine of American Fourierism, 1832–1848* (Johns Hopkins, 1979), from the author himself. For the next several years Sokolow continued to work on what he would call his own book on American Fourierism, even after he had left Tech for the NEH, a bureaucracy whose reward structure does not involve the same publish-or-languish goads that would be present if, at the beginning of middle age, he were still in the teaching profession. But Sokolow's zeal to publish did not abate, and he would eventually attempt to publish a book that Guarneri could claim was partly plagiarized from the dissertation he had mailed Sokolow.

By the fall of 1988 the AHA had had the Guarneri matter before it for two years. Any satisfaction the complainant gets would come according to an "Addendum on Policies and Procedures" to its "Statement on Standards of Professional Conduct." This addendum was published in the March 1988 *Perspectives*. Six possible decisions by the Professional Division are outlined, including "mediation." The strongest courses of action are the last two:

If the Division decides:

5) that an individual case is indicative of a larger problem, *it may issue an advisory opinion or guideline,* which shall be published in *Perspectives* and become an addendum to the Statement [on

Standards of Professional Conduct]. An advisory opinion must
not reveal names or details of specific cases. Individual cases
shall not be publicized.

So Sokolow could enter the history of history as an anonymous
guideline. Or:

If the Division decides:

6) *other action is needed,* it may direct the Vice-President to seek
approval for that action from the Council. The Executive Director shall notify all parties of the Division's recommendation,
and the subject of the complaint shall have thirty days to comment in writing before the recommendation is forwarded to
the Council. The Council, after examination of the Division's
recommendation and comments thereto, shall make a final
determination of the case on behalf of the Association, and
either dismiss the case or take the recommended action. The
Executive Director shall notify all parties of the Council's action.

Inasmuch as the Division is a part of the constitutional structure of the Association, apppeals from or criticism of its action
should go before the Council.

There is no mention of what "other action" might entail; the
authors of number 6 are too busy safeguarding the right to
appeal sanctions they are apparently too timid to name. Nor, in
their concern for confidentiality ("Individual cases shall not be
publicized"), do they seem to realize that they are in direct contradiction of the 1986 "Statement on Plagiarism," which concluded that "if . . . charges of plagiarism or gross impropriety
are sustained by an investigating committee, its findings should
ordinarily be made public."

Even before Stephen Nissenbaum learned that Sokolow had
struck again, he had to wonder if Sokolow's need to see his name
in print was so strong that he would risk his own career to satisfy
it. It's what Allan Kuethe had wondered when *Eros and Modernization* appeared: "Was the book such an important status symbol
that he would take any chance?"

Sokolow's motives are probably as impenetrable, and mixed,
as most plagiarists'. Kuethe doesn't hesitate to call him a "fraud
and opportunist," but this view of him as deliberately malevolent

doesn't prevent Kuethe from speculating in the realm of psychology as well as morals ("Was his self-deception so great that he, like Nixon, never believed he had erred?"). Five years after his resignation from Texas Tech, no one in the History Department feels certain of why he did what he did. "Believe me," says Jim Brink, "a lot of people have wondered a long time just what in the world he was thinking." Ask anyone there whether he believes Sokolow had the ability to be a productive scholar in the usual, honest way, and he'll answer yes — just as Stephen Nissenbaum does: "He's perfectly capable of good scholarship." War is supposed to be diplomacy conducted by other means; Sokolow's plagiarisms can be said to bear the same relationship to regular research. They're not without a certain skill. In fact, in his energetic combination of talent and treachery — not to mention self-confidence — he reminds one of no one so much as Charles Reade.

But beyond this agreement over his intelligence and capacities, there is little consensus about his intentions. "Oh, gosh," exclaims Benjamin Newcomb when asked whether he thinks Sokolow deliberately meant to mislead his colleagues. "It's hard to say. Who knows? I really am stuck on that." Is it possible that Sokolow was really tricking himself, that he'd conned himself into believing what he was doing was all right? Or, once more to manipulate the question of Senator Howard Baker, who has had a variety of working relationships with forgetful presidents: What did Sokolow know about himself, and when did he know it? Otto Nelson, probably the hardest liner in Lubbock when it comes to this case, thinks that Sokolow's intent was almost certainly one of deliberate deception, but is nonetheless uncomfortable talking about motives.

"Plagiarism is not a simple phenomenon," E. B. White wrote in 1951, before offering "roughly three kinds of plagiarists" as models: the "thief," the "dope," and the "total recall guy." White's anatomy, sketched in a letter to John R. Fleming, was prompted by the recent discovery that Cornell's new president, Deane W. Malott, had taken some of his first speech verbatim from an article by the president of Sarah Lawrence, Harold Taylor. White used it, but only reluctantly, in the *New Yorker*'s Funny Coincidence Department, worrying to Harold Ross about the damage it might cause Malott. "We once flirted, if you recall, with the idea that we could somehow take the accusatory note out of Funny Coincidence, but I have never doped out any way to do it." He thought Malott, who had been a businessman before going to Cornell, had probably delegated the speechwriting to an irresponsible underling. Of Malott himself, White wrote Fleming, "my guess is that he is just not very bright." In other words, a dope, though White actually defined that sort of plagiarist as someone "who is a little vague about the printed word and regards anything in the way of printed matter as mildly miraculous and common property."

This explanation, with all due respect to university administrators, is a possibility in Malott's case. It does not seem so in Sokolow's. What about White's last category, the "total recall guy"? White defines him as someone "who can read something or hear something and later regurgitate it, practically word for word, not knowing he is doing it." With all due respect to E. B. White, this doesn't seem a possibility in anyone's case. It is simply too difficult to believe that so capacious a brain would not be able to include a title and an author's name among the totality of its recollections. While it seems clear that there occasionally exist the kinds of osmotic rhythms, and even phrasing, discussed in the previous chapter, this is a very different sort of thing. And, again, hardly applicable to Sokolow. Which, if one goes by White's anatomy, leaves only one label, "thief," or, no more kindly, "fraud and opportunist" — in the words of Allan Kuethe.

What White's anatomy lacks, however, is a pathological category on the order of what Peter Shaw puts forward. More than one person has wondered about Sokolow's mental make-up. Nissenbaum's speculations about Sokolow run toward compulsiveness, which is perhaps a lesser form of desperation, being more a matter of habit than emergency. The Guarneri case certainly invites one to entertain this explanation. But probably there is no single answer or label for this case, any more than there is in Coleridge's or Epstein's. Motives, like ganglia, get tangled. Some thieves are also dopes, just as some opportunists are compulsives, just as some authorities are more timid than those people they're charged with policing.

*

In the fall of 1986 Joan Weldon was still the History Department's administrative secretary. She could show a visitor a copy of *Eros and Modernization*, sent her by Jayme Sokolow, which she keeps in one of her desk drawers. "It's sort of a museum piece," she says. Five years after the Sokolow case opened up, reflections on it by members of the Tech History Department run from fatalism to rage. Brian Blakeley, now in the chairman's office, says that "more might have been made out of it at the time," but he doesn't seem especially certain of this. Nor is Otto Nelson, now in the dean's office: "I told Barr about a month or two ago, particularly since reading that piece in the AHA *Perspectives* and thinking about the matter of plagiarism, having seen it come up here in the office and throughout the university and elsewhere, that we probably had had a larger obligation to publicize this academic fraud. . . . A sort of crime against scholarship had occurred and we hid it under a bushel, perhaps not wanting to disturb ourselves." Jim Brink is clear: "I think he should have been fired immediately." Allan Kuethe would have liked to see that happen, too, but shows himself aware of the real crux of the Sokolow affair when he says, "Given the sad state of the United States judiciary and the amount of trouble the innocent can suffer for simply doing their jobs, I was inclined to accept the compromise that emerged."

When asked if he can understand the feelings of those who thought more might have been done, Dean Graves, now retired but still in Holden Hall on weekday mornings editing a new edition of *The Handbook of Texas*, says, "Oh, sure. Oh, yes. Yes. Absolutely. Absolutely."

5

Trampling Out the Vintage:
The Fight over *Falcon Crest*

Imitation is the sincerest form of television.
— Fred Allen

As they drove between Squaw and Napa valleys on a Sunday in November 1980, John and Anita Clay Kornfeld had more than their usual reasons to be happy. The usual reasons were enviable: the Kornfelds, in their fifties, were an attractive, devoted and accomplished couple. But it had been a special season. Anita's new novel, *Vintage,* a long chronicle of the fortunes of a Napa winemaking family, the Donatis, had been published, and in the Kornfelds had been going to plenty of parties to celebrate and promote it. There had been a book-signing at Macy's in San Francisco; a party attended by Mayor Dianne Feinstein; others in Los Angeles, Fresno, Houston. The Kornfelds were accustomed to this mixture of cultural business and pleasure. John, a talented sculptor, had for years been Sol Hurok's man on the West Coast, and Anita had headed up his public relations department: "I had a little expertise and I had a few contacts in the field." When it came to promoting her own work, it "was hard not to utilize them." It had been one more party that had taken them to Squaw Valley.

The particular pleasure they were experiencing on the trip

home to Napa was one of anticipation. Harry Sherman, the Emmy Award—winning independent television producer who had done *Eleanor and Franklin,* was supposed to call. He and Anita Kornfeld had met at a party in Napa two months before. "The hostess seated us together purposely," she recalled. She and Sherman hit it off, and after he had the chance to read *Vintage* (buying a copy himself after the author's agent, Evart Ziegler, failed to send him one as planned), he became interested in adapting it as a TV miniseries. He and Mrs. Kornfeld had several phone conversations and another meeting after that, and by November he was telling her: "Anita, something really exciting has just happened. I can't tell you the details because I have to sign my contract. . . . Next week I want to get with you and we have got to really get down and work something out."

It was the phone call with these "details" that John and Anita Kornfeld were expecting as they drove back to Napa Valley that Sunday. They wondered to each other how much money Harry Sherman would offer for the book.

"When I walked in the door," she would recall, "the phone did ring as we had anticipated." And it was indeed Harry Sherman. But instead of details he had advice. "He said, 'You had better get yourself a lawyer.' His words were, 'You have been ripped off. I just read in *Variety* . . . that CBS-Lorimar have announced a pilot called "The Vintage Years" taking place in Napa, with a matriarch.' "

"The Vintage Years" was never aired, but it was the basis for the highly successful nighttime soap opera *Falcon Crest.* No deal was ever struck between Anita Clay Kornfeld and Harry Sherman because one series involving winemaking in the Napa Valley was as much as the airwaves' traffic could bear. "I mean," said Mrs. Kornfeld, "with all the ingredients that were taken from my book and put in their series . . . there is nothing left for Harry Sherman but an old, tired turkey bone. They took all the meat and all the feathers and everything."

Adam Donati, six foot two, twenty-five years old, cultivated and temperamental, arrives in San Francisco in 1894 from Pontremoli, Italy, with a dream of recreating his late father's winery in the New World. This is the beginning of *Vintage,* which is not a typical rags-to-riches American chronicle so much as a riches-toward-new-realms one. Adam will have plenty of struggles and setbacks, but central to his story is his sense of himself as an embattled aristocrat scorned as an ethnic *arriviste;* in fact, he is more truly cut out to be a vintner than some of his neighbors.

It is a bad time in the wine business, but the banker Samuel Linton is won over by Adam's spunk and supplements his stake. Adam acquires land on Spring Mountain and adds to his holdings with land inherited from Jacob Brunner, whose Swedish granddaughter, Erika, Adam marries on the rebound. His real attraction is to the beautiful Sarah Hubbard Reynolds, with whom he enjoys one passionate tryst, but whose Southern mother objects to Adam as a "dago" before spiriting her daughter off for a European grand tour and, we are led to believe, a more suitable marriage to the Jamesian-named Christopher Elliot-Weare.

Adam survives a feud with the evil Jacques Cugnot and, with the help of a trusty foreman and a loyal Chinese servant, Li Po, begins to establish himself on Spring Mountain. Erika, however, turns out to be a problem. She surprises him on their wedding night with her sexual appetite, and grows more violently peculiar by the page. After producing two sons for Adam — Anton and Joseph — she winds up in a sanatorium.

The embittered Adam, who is having trouble with the new temperance movement (we are now about one-third through the novel), is saved by the return of Sarah. It turns out there never was a marriage to Christopher Elliot-Weare. She had, apparently, left California carrying Adam's child, and after completing the European tour went into a home for unwed mothers. She then supported the boy, David, now five, by pretending to be a widow and teaching in a South Carolina girls' school.

Erika dies when a fire following the San Francisco earthquake wipes out the sanatorium. Adam and Sarah marry and together nurture the fortunes of the Donati winery on Spring Mountain. Adam does political battle with the Anti-Saloon League; Sarah helps with the books. Midway through, the novel becomes somewhat lumbering and episodic. What it needs is another good villain on the order of Jacques Cugnot. Adam's two sons by Erika do their best to grow into this role. Anton becomes a pretentious,

Harvard-educated schemer who cheats on his bibulous wife, Phyllis; Joseph operates an illegal still on the Donati land as his father tries to survive both the absurdities of the Volstead Act and the blandishments of bootleggers. Adam dies of a heart attack when the sheriff makes a noisy raid on Joseph's operation.

In her widowhood, Sarah makes a relatively brief and tepid second marriage to Norman Jaspers, the family lawyer; and goes about a second widowhood (after Jaspers's death from kidney failure) as a kind mother and grandmother, an active Democrat who copes with such national crises as the Depression and such familial ones as Phyllis's drinking.

She is naturally closest to her own son, David, and to his daughter, Victoria, a spirited redhead who herself wishes to become a winemaker. Victoria gets involved with Jerrod James, a Tex-Mex wetback her father finds hiding in his stable. David hires him on and Sarah tutors him; they change his name to Carlo Carducci so that he can avoid trouble with the law.

By this time *Vintage* is once again exciting. There's a courtroom dispute involving Anton and Phyllis. David gives Victoria a half interest in the winery while his other two daughters go off to lead pointless, disorderly lives in New York. Sarah grows into a quirky, interesting old age. She is wise but eccentric, a bit preoccupied with anatomy and vitamins. She outlives David and survives long enough to give Victoria her blessing: " 'I knew you had gumption. That you'd be a special granddaughter. And you *have* been. You're the only one I give a hoot about — who gives a hoot about me. Your grandfather Adam Donati would have been awfully proud of you, too, young lady! But he'd have to get used to the idea that you're a *woman* winemaker. That a woman's running the show up there on Spring Mountain!' "

The last portion of the novel is dominated by Victoria's passion for Carlo and his conflicting loyalties to her and the Mexican labor organizers working in the valley. (Shades of Marie de Malepeire and Pinatel!) He gets stabbed for trying to protect her at one point, but after his recovery goes off to rejoin his natural allies. The novel ends, in 1960, with Victoria prepared to run the vineyard and wait for Carlo's return: "Granted, there was a lot to do. But she would be ready for him by next harvest. She'd really just have to be!" (Tomorrow is another day?)

Publishers Weekly called *Vintage* "a swift, dramatic story. . . . The generational novel at its best." This is probably true, if faint, praise, since this genre, as it is practiced now, is a ponderous one; the audience it finds is less sensation-seeking than that for Ludlumite thrillers and squalorfests of the Judith Krantz–Jackie Collins sort, but as readers they are not especially concerned with style and subtlety. If novels like *Vintage* aren't really beach books, they could be classified as screened-in-porch books, marketed mostly to middle-class women of undemanding tastes. *Vintage* is more sturdily written and better researched than much of its genre, but it finally doesn't transcend it. There are some vividly realized scenes and locations, but its characters tend to react on cue amid familiar adjectives and adverbs. Embraces are "desperate," and rage burns toward a character's "very fingertips." Heat follows proximity as surely as hubba follows hubba.

The dialog is heavy with vinous imagery, and there's an anachronistic feel to some of it ("I'm not totally in tune with the process": 1910?). But *Vintage* is rarely embarrassing and is sometimes genuinely absorbing. Its many characters are marched through a very long chronology in an orderly, and occasionally clever, fashion. It is informative, too: on the subjects of fermentation, fluctuations in the wine market, immigration patterns in northern California. It was unquestionably well researched; the winemaker Robert Mondavi says of Anita Kornfeld, "I think she interviewed everyone in the valley." True, its historical exposition relies on implausibly stilted dialog, as when Sarah explains Woodrow Wilson to Adam: "He was president of Princeton, a top university. At Wellesley, I read his doctoral thesis — *Congressional Government* I believe was the title." One detractor would sneer at Mrs. Kornfeld as "President of the Current Events Club." But this is really only to say that she never solved a problem most writers of historical fiction fail to solve, and is perhaps to ignore the fact that, stiff dialog and all, books like *Vintage* supply a reader with more useful knowledge of the world than he can get from most lazy, inward-looking "modern" novels.

Two things about it are certain: it resulted from a great deal of hard work, and reading it for an hour is more profitable than watching a typical hour of American television.

*

There are reasons enough to watch *Falcon Crest,* which since the fall of 1981 has run on CBS-TV at 10 P.M. on Friday nights. You may be dateless; you may wish to get a closer look at the woman who in long-ago real life dumped Ronald Reagan; or you may simply have watched it the week before and become buffaloed into running with the lunatic narrative drive of a soap. In the modern novel one thing can no longer be counted on to lead to another, but the nighttime soaps still offer what academics call a linear story, effect following cause with a justice and predictability that don't so much simulate life as improve on it. Which is to say that nighttime soaps are just like daytime ones, only with higher production values: better cars, more photogenic food, more fully padded shoulders. Another appealing feature of these programs, once they hit their stride, is that the realms of *Dynasty, Dallas* and *Falcon Crest* promise to be worlds without end. Earl Hamner, who wrote novels before creating such television series as *The Waltons* and *Falcon Crest,* has been quoted as saying: "I think what motivates me is that I am basically a storyteller. I enjoy telling stories — and that's sort of a lost art — especially in television, where a story should have a beginning and a middle and an end." That may have been so with each touching episode about the rural, noble Waltons, but the purpose of *Falcon Crest* is that its greed-ridden conflicts remain unresolved as long as there's breath in Jane Wyman's body — or until the show drops below a 20 share in the Nielsen ratings.

The program's dialog is deathlessly familiar. Indeed, the vocabulary of television drama is so small that linguistic plagiarism within the medium is almost an impossibility. Replication is not deliberate and dastardly; it is involuntary and inevitable. Early *Falcon Crest* scripts have characters saying such things as "I don't know what to believe anymore"; "We'll see about that"; "When hell freezes over"; and "It was the last time I can remember feeling anything." These are the lyrical clichés of television. They sound better coming through lip gloss and BMW windshields than they would on the street; what is required for their acceptance is not so much the willing suspension of disbelief as the recumbent suspension of attention. It's ten o'clock, after all, and you're tired. It's a reliable rule that one can write these programs faster than one can watch them. Perhaps the greatest understatement uttered during the long dispute between Anita Clay Korn-feld and the makers of *Falcon Crest* was Earl Hamner's: "Tele-vision is very imitative of itself."

Indeed, Hamner would admit that, far from imitating *Vintage*, he was, in creating *Falcon Crest*, imitating himself. "I am so schooled in 'family entertainment,' " he told an interviewer in the early 1980s, "that given a totally clean, open space I imme-diately inject a family kind of story into it." *Falcon Crest* would eventually be glitzed into sexier late-night fare, but as Hamner says, "When we started . . . it was designed to be an eight o'clock show, more in the tradition of *The Waltons*. The emphasis was going to be on family life" — specifically, the lives of the New York Giobertis: Chase, an airline pilot; his wife, Maggie, a free-lance writer; their teenage children, Cole and Vicki. Threatened by nuclear-family fission (absentee Dad, big-city temptations), they move to Napa Valley in back-to-the-land fashion, deter-mined to make a go at winemaking on the fifty-acre vineyard left Chase by his father, Jason. The script for an early *Falcon Crest* episode called "The Tangled Vines," by E. F. Wallengren, con-tains an in-joke in Vicki's remark to her cousin, Lance: "Dad's got this fantasy that living together on the vineyard is going to turn us into the Waltons." Hamner had, in fact, in the late sev-enties, before *Falcon Crest*, proposed TV series variously titled *Swap, Switch* and *The Barclays*, all of them involving families ex-perimenting with a change of scene — one of them to the wine-making country of California (an idea presented to, and rejected by, CBS in 1978 — before *Vintage* was even finished).

Conceding that *Falcon Crest* was deliberately glamorized by its network, Hamner still resists the idea that it is much like other soaps. He is partly right. It is too simple to classify *Falcon Crest* as the vinous version of *Dallas* or *Dynasty*. There are important variations in what might be called "subgenres" — generic char-acteristics that would be crucial to the *Vintage* dispute. "It's Gothic drama," Hamner asserted, "it's human conflicts. The other series do not have the same dimension that my characters do on *Falcon Crest*."

The last part of this statement is pretentious (*Falcon Crest*'s characters are just as implausibly cretinous or noble as those on the other soaps), but the Gothic element was basic and unique to its early days. When the Giobertis finally materialized in the pilot called "The Vintage Years," they were claiming the acres of a Jason who had been, according to some drafts of the script, "found floating in a vat of cabernet sauvignon." The secret of his death, it seemed, might be held by the spaced-out niece, Emma, who flitted, in first-Mrs.-Rochester fashion, through the "gloomy old mansion" of her mother and Chase's aunt, Angela Channing (the Jane Wyman character). Arriving at wicked Angela's for a party, Maggie and Chase notice, at a window in a deserted part of the house, "a face that has rarely seen sun, gaunt, colorless, with sunken, socketed eyes which seem to stare down at them accusingly." Hamner's "Prospectus" for the pilot says that Emma was brain-damaged during birth, and a note in one draft of the script avoids trouble in TV's timidly responsible way: "ATTENTION: PROGRAM PRACTICES: WE WILL DISCOVER IN A SUBSEQUENT EPISODE THAT EMMA IS NOT RETARDED."

Angie is Chase's real nemesis ("Lots of people get caught in Angie Channing's spider web"). She is determined to have Jason's acres for herself, to keep Falcon Crest all in one piece and to pass it on to whomever she will anoint as her heir — possibly Chase's son, Cole, whom she tries to corrupt with the gift of a sports car. In this respect, Falcon Crest might as well be Ewing Oil, though Angie is probably tougher than J.R. Indeed, script drafts of the pilot resist this particular intramedium comparison and instead have her son Richard, a former mercenary, telling Lance that compared to Angie, his old employer — Idi Amin — "was a pussycat."

So what can this contemporary battle between middle-class family values and Gothic greed have to do with the painstakingly historical novel that is *Vintage*?

Everything, according to Melvin M. Belli: "I've never seen such a clear case of copying or infringement." The white-haired San Francisco lawyer, who looks like a huge, volcanic owl in his circular black glasses, has never been inclined toward understatement. In a career noted for its attendant publicity, he has represented such defendants as Jack Ruby, the killer of Lee Harvey Oswald, and appeared for the plaintiff against R. J. Reynolds Tobacco Company in a suit seeking damages over lung cancer.

Mrs. Kornfeld did not know Belli himself, but she did know his wife, Lia: "We had worked on a lot of committees together, and she said, 'Mel will help you out. Call Mel.' " Contacting Belli ended a long period of paralysis after Harry Sherman's telephone call in November 1980: "What really happened, I just went into a total depression for about six months and I didn't do anything." The *Falcon Crest* pilot was filmed in March 1981 and Mrs. Kornfeld heard from friends that the crews had been scouting and filming the same locations described in her book: "There are innumerable places they could have gone in the Napa Valley . . . but they chose to go to the exact ones, even the remote ones." But until she went to Belli, she did not have the relief that action provides. *Anita Clay Kornfeld v. CBS, Inc., Lorimar Productions, Inc., and Earl Hamner,* case No. 81-6177-RG, seeking $101 million in damages and permanent injunctive relief, was filed on August 10, 1981.

She now thinks that she might have gone to a well-known copyright specialist, but at the time she didn't know one, and she doesn't know if one would have accepted her case on contingency, as did Belli, for only $7,500 up front — perhaps because he relished public challenges: "Belli, I think, liked the idea of filing suit against CBS-Lorimar." The $101 million figure was in the top-this Belli style: "The week before that someone had filed suit for $100 million . . . a copyright thing that was later dropped. . . . It was against *E.T.* or something," Mrs. Kornfeld recalls.

In the three years that passed between the filing of the suit and its coming to trial in Los Angeles, a good deal of publicity ensued. Hamner's lawyers would note how Mrs. Kornfeld "mercilessly defamed" him in such publications as *People,* which on April 12, 1982, ran a sympathetic article called "In a Case of Old Wine in New Bottles, an Angry Author Takes 'Falcon Crest' to Court." It included a photograph of Mrs. Kornfeld standing atop a cask at Robert Mondavi's winery. In one hand she held a wine glass (it actually held not wine but muddy water, which photographed just as well in black and white); in the other she had a seven-foot-long chart with alleged similarities between *Vintage* and "The Vintage Years" displayed in parallel columns. She and John Kornfeld had prepared it together. She says Hamner didn't get the publicity because he declined interviews and was generally uncooperative with the media: "If I got the press, it was because he refused. . . . I think that that's his own problem there."

Hamner's defense was stated absolutely in the "Defendants' Consolidated Memorandum of Facts and Legal Brief" filed by Rosenfeld, Meyer and Susman on March 18, 1983: " 'Falcon Crest' is the result of a project conceived and developed by Earl Hamner *wholly independent* of any awareness or knowledge of plaintiff's book *Vintage*." Furthermore, "Mr. Hamner did not learn of *Vintage* until the spring of 1981, *after* he had completed the script for the pilot 'The Vintage Years.' "

The pilot, with Jane Wyman in a most unflattering gray wig, was never shown because CBS wanted to make changes in the cast. The name for the series was changed from "The Vintage Years" to *Falcon Crest* because CBS decided "the 'vintage' designation might be mistaken by television viewers as a reference to old people" — those party poopers of video demographics — instead of the "contemporary family" the series actually portrayed. Mrs. Kornfeld suggested that the name change was made to conceal pilfering, but given the nature of television marketing, CBS's explanation in this instance seems indestructibly plausible.

The lawsuit would finally turn on that grounded pilot. Judge Richard A. Gadbois, Jr., decided to "trifurcate" the case in the interest of the federal government's time and money. If Mrs. Kornfeld could prove that the pilot had infringed her copyright of *Vintage*, then the court would move on and see whether episodes of *Falcon Crest* had done the same; if it was decided they had, then a third phase of the case, the assessment of damages, would open. The trifurcation "made nothing but sense," the judge says, even though some, like John Kornfeld, think Anita Kornfeld should have had a whole battlefield for waging her war. But the judge insists: the comparison of pilot and novel may have been "a rather starkly simple thing," but even so, "it took us a month to do it." And that was just the month the case was before his bench in the late spring and early summer of 1984. Those three years of pretrial preparations and delay would come first. When, in the fall of 1986, Rosenfeld, Meyer and Susman finally transferred the records of *Kornfeld v. CBS* — depositions, expert declarations, film scripts, transcripts — out of their offices on Wilshire Boulevard in Beverly Hills and into storage, there were eighty-five cartons waiting for the movers.

The *curriculum vitae* of Professor Edward I. Condren of the UCLA English Department displays, by academic standards, unusual variety. Page 5 of it lists a typical publication: " '*Unnyt* Gold in *Beowulf*,' *Philological Quarterly*, 53 (1973), 296–299." Page 9 lists some typical consulting work: "*Universal City Studios v. RKO*, in which the 1934 film 'King Kong' was found to be in the public domain." With a working knowledge of Latin, Old English, Middle English, Old Norse, Gothic, Old High German, Middle High German, Old French, and Provençal, and a Ph.D. from the University of Toronto, Condren teaches graduate seminars in Chaucer and Middle English literature. He also has something of a second career as an expert witness in legal actions claiming copyright infringement. His two professional realms are bridged, he says, by historical irony. In the modern world an author typically hungers for recognition, but in the medieval one anonymity was prized, leading him to suppress his identity, or to claim that his stories were things he dreamt rather than consciously invented: "I suppose there was some little thing . . . having to do with his desire to remove himself from any proximate posture of rivalry with God as a creator of something." As a consequence, the modern scholar of medieval literature becomes adept at determining who wrote what, and so it strikes Condren as perfectly logical that his thinking commutes between the court of Edward III and those of the U.S. Central District of California.

The Belli office hired Condren at $90 an hour in June 1983 to investigate Mrs. Kornfeld's claims of plagiarism. He became emphatically convinced of the merits of her case. The affidavit he filed on May 19, 1984, presented his conclusions forthrightly: "In writing his 'Prospectus' and 'Script' for *The Vintage Years*, Mr. Hamner made extensive use of Mrs. Kornfeld's novel *Vintage*, copying substantially from both its ideas and its specific expression."

His long affidavit fought on all fronts: theme, characterization, plot, language, setting. He notes, to take one of many examples, the similarity between this passage from *Vintage* —

It was as though their roots, like those vines, had dug deeply into earth, as though the lull of long comfortable habits had entwined them —

and this one from the pilot, in which Angie tells Lance:

This land can never really belong to anyone but me, and after I'm gone, to you. Our whole lives are entwined in those vines.

But how could anyone write a book or play or film about a winemaking family and not put in a line like that? One can't copyright a whole milieu. *Vintage*'s own blurb describes the novel as being set "against the legendary background of the lush California vineyards": legends can't perpetuate themselves without their own clichés.

Furthermore, the similarity that Professor Condren's affidavit sometimes detects between passages can be baffling. Section 6 of the affidavit is headed: "IN SEVERAL INSTANCES THE VERY LANGUAGE OF <u>THE VINTAGE YEARS</u> IS SUBSTANTIALLY SIMILAR TO THE LANGUAGE IN <u>VINTAGE</u>." Among the parallel passages are these two concerning soil:

rich volcanic ash for good drainage	as appealing as the sun and fog, was the fact that the floor of the valley consisted of a particular rocky limestone soil

Where on earth, as it were, does the linguistic similarity lie?

Condren compares Erika, Adam's first wife, with Emma, Angie's unhinged daughter:

ERIKA	EMMA
— Blonde hair	— Blonde hair
— "A fragile, pretty look about her, like a fine delicate piece of china one must handle gently" "Charmingly pretty"	— "As beautiful as her Great Grandmother Tessa"
— Witnesses the horrible death of her immediate family	— Witnesses the horrible death of her uncle
— Becomes insane as direct result of witnessing this horrible event	— Becomes insane as a direct result of witnessing this horrible event

Blondes will be blondes. Popular novels and television shows will bleach and beautify a disproportionate number of characters into fulfilling an audience's desire for platinum and pulchritude. So forget the first two dashes and go on to the next two. They look fairly serious. And yet there's less there than meets the eye. What Erika witnessed was an accident, a fire that destroyed her whole family. What-Emma-knows-about-her-uncle's-death was an important theme of early *Falcon Crest* episodes, but the pilot that was filmed — and no matter what else Condren had read or seen, that's what he had to go on — tells us nothing about Emma's witnessing what in any case is a rather different enormity. In the Condren affidavit, similarities are invariably suspicious but usually elusive. For example, on page 21 Sarah's granddaughter Victoria is compared to Angie: both are "strong willed, daring, intelligent" and have strong bonds to their fathers. On page 22 it is Angie's longing for a "male counterpart to herself" that is seen as suspiciously resembling the same feeling in a *Vintage* character — but that character is not Victoria; it is Bernard Fuller, who becomes an in-law of the Donatis. Condren the medievalist seems to see the pilot as a kind of sinister allegory of the novel, but in order to make his case work he has a lot of characters pulling double shifts.

Let us compare Victoria to Victoria for a moment. There are characters with that name in both the novel and the pilot (Vicki). This was potentially the most difficult item the defendants would have to justify. These are the parallel columns in the Condren affidavit:

VICTORIA (physically)	VICTORIA (physically) [Vicki]
— Red-headed	— Red-headed
— Fond of horseback riding	— Fond of horseback riding
— Falls in love with Mexican-American	— Falls in love with Mexican
— Kept from entering hospital room of her boyfriend, the stabbing victim Carlo	— Effectively dismissed from hospital room of her boyfriend, the stabbing victim, Mario
— Rejects the advances of Anglo, would-be boyfriend (Tate Williams)	— Rejects the advances of Anglo, would-be boyfriend (Lance)

Looked at closely, these matchups prove not terribly perfid-
ious. The Victoria of the novel is a responsible businesswoman
when the story ends in 1960; the pilot's Vicki is a normal and not
especially ambitious contemporary teenager. The print Victoria's
red hair is a crucial (and formulaic) shorthand component of her
character; the video Vicki was played by the actress Jamie Rose,
who does have red hair, but Hamner never called for red hair
in his prospectus or script, and he didn't cast her. Given Condren's list of the Erika/Emma similarities, and his tendency to
see one character as similar to two others, one wonders how he
would have responded had Lorimar chosen a blonde instead.
Victoria's Mexican-American was in fact, in the defendant's im-
mortal rebuttal, "a blue-eyed, half-Anglo, illegal alien bastard,"
not Vicki's perfectly tame Mario, son of the nuclear-family Nu-
nouzes who are so loyal to Chase Gioberti. Carlo's stabbing is the
result of labor agitation; Mario gets cut with a bottle in a brawl
having more to do with someone's thwarted lust. Tate Williams's
advances to Victoria are dull and gentlemanly; Lance's to Vicki
are vaguely incestuous. As for the hospital visits: there are *rules,*
after all. Carlo's doctor wants his rest interrupted only by im-
mediate family; Vicki does see Mario, but shyly retreats when his
mother shows up. The names themselves: Vicki/Victoria? In one
of Hamner's failed pilots from the seventies, *The Barclays,* he named
the teenage daughter Vicki. Again, he was imitating himself.

But it was the duplication of names from novel to pilot that
struck Condren as most telltale. He consulted UCLA colleagues
with degrees in statistics and probability analysis and came up
with a formula "extremely lenient to defendant's claims of independent creation." This, according to the affidavit, is how it
worked:

> Let us use a simple bi-nomial theory. That is, whenever defendant
> needed a name for some character in his story, he could either
> create a name that happens to appear in *Vintage* or choose one
> that does not — a .5 probability, or one chance out of two that he
> would use a name also appearing in *Vintage*. For the naming of a
> second character, the same formula would yield a .25 probability,
> or one chance in four tries that *both* names would also have ap-
> peared in *Vintage*. When this conservative formula is used to de-
> termine the probability that 12 names in *The Vintage Years* would

also have appeared in *Vintage,* we get the minuscule figure .00024414. In other words, an author who had not been influenced by the names in *Vintage* would have to write 4,096 novels, regardless of their content, before writing one that contained 12 names also appearing in *Vintage.*

But what, really, is in a name, when the Maggie of the pilot by the same name in *Vintage* would be a horse? From Professor Condren's suspicious dozen:

MAGGIE	MAGGIE
The name of one of the two horses bought with the first Alfieri house	Chase's wife, who joins him in coming to California and helping him succeed as a grape grower. Mother of Cole and Virginia [*sic*]

Later on, going beyond the names of characters to those of roadhouses, the Condren affidavit asks the court to "note that the two words 'Cold Duck' [the roadhouse in the pilot] alliterate with the first two syllables of 'Candido's,' further suggesting an influence from the earlier novel." One can quickly go too far, which is not the same as getting anywhere, with this sort of thing.

Condren will succeed in raising a few doubts in the mind of someone who reads his affidavit: "The horse scenes in *Vintage* occur either in the early part of the century, before the advent of automobiles, or in connection with riding as a sport. . . . On the other hand, *The Vintage Years* anachronistically depicts horses as the ordinary means of getting around the 1980 vineyards. Come off!" But more often he seems to be grasping at telegenic straws:

Female wine maker wears white lab smock (Victoria)	Female wine maker wears white lab smock (Dorcas)

CBS's attorney would insist that Dorcas's smock was gray.

Despite everything, Condren to this day maintains "that they would not have come up with as many of those background details as they did had they not been deeply influenced by Anita's book."

Condren was no dispassionate hired gun. A good-looking, gray-haired man with a voice rich enough to be the envy of a nighttime soap star, he was and remains a fervent believer in Anita Clay Kornfeld's accusation. In the course of his work he traveled with her through Napa Valley looking for locations the film crews might have pilfered from the novel. He thinks the first 150 to 200 pages of *Vintage* are "marvelous, you know, the rival of almost any well-written modern book. I think it trailed off a little bit." He seems to view Mrs. Kornfeld as the embattled maiden of a medieval romance, a distressed damsel whose rescue he rode to on the white pages of his affidavit. Two years after the trial, he reflected:

> I think this case brought together, face to face, one representative of an old, noble profession, a creative art form, a person working by herself, hard, trying to please her aesthetic sensibilities, to make a work of art . . . trying to please that muse, that abstract notion of perfection in prose fiction somewhere, and there she was, face to face against a business machine, a business machine that thinks nothing of taking first-rate professionals and bending them to the purpose of business. . . . I myself feel a sense of violation, rape . . .

When asked about motives, Professor Richard A. Lanham says: "I don't really speculate about them. . . . What I'm hired to do is talk about the relationships between two literary texts." Lanham, who looks like a younger, better-groomed version of Chief Justice Rehnquist, was retained as literary expert for the defense in March 1982, when Rosenfeld, Meyer and Susman asked him to examine Mrs. Kornfeld's claims. He reached exactly the opposite conclusion from Condren: "It is my opinion that the plots, themes, characterizations, uses of setting, and structures in the two works are not substantially similar." If Lanham can be as detached from his legal work as Condren is impassioned about his, and if their conclusions about *Falcon Crest* were diametrical, in a couple of respects the two men are close. For one thing, their offices are only a few doors away from each other in UCLA's Rolfe Hall: Lanham, like Condren, is a member of the English Department. "We're very good, dear friends," says Lanham. "I've watched their children grow up." Condren agrees: the two of them are "very, very close friends. . . . It was not a question of rivalry." Through the years of the *Vintage* case the two of them continued to be amicable colleagues and occasional dinner partners.

Lanham, who was in fact one of the people responsible for getting Condren into legal consulting, was paid $100 an hour ($10 more than Condren). By the time of the trial he had put in seven hundred hours on the case — enough to make the term "sideline" seem almost inappropriate, even though he lists five principal areas of academic interest on his *curriculum vitae:* medieval and Renaissance English and Continental literature; rhetoric, history and theory; literary theory; higher education in America; and prose composition. From these areas of expertise have come not only his teaching but also nine books, among them *Analyzing Prose* and *Style: An Anti-Textbook.* The latter is a witty polemic against the dreary functionalism of college composition courses in an era of "sentimental mass democracy." Style, Lanham argues, "must be taught for and as what it is — a pleasure, a grace, a joy, a delight."

With such high standards, how could he allow hi nself seven hundred hours to spend reading and writing about Angie and Vicki and roadhouse brawls and floating uncles? He answers:

> Curiously, the people who are most intolerant about this are my friends in the entertainment business. The fellow who directed the pilot of *Falcon Crest,* Alex Singer, lives right up the street from me, and he and his wife are always after us to come up and read Dante with them or something, and his wife says, "Why do you read this shit? How can you bear to do this?" And I say things like, "Well, it allows me to live down the street from you, for openers."

He also says his legal work has given him new insights into argumentative language and dramatic reality.

Judges and lawyers, he says, despise experts, using them only with grudging contempt. But anyone seeking real literary pleasure in the *Vintage* dispute must be glad of Lanham's participation. The declaration he submitted to the court on May 22, 1984, is something of a work of art, a witty wrecking ball leveled against Mrs. Kornfeld and his own colleague, Condren. He appealed to logic and practicality. "Why . . . if you wanted to create the character of Angela Channing, start with Sarah? It just doesn't make sense. Why not start out fresh? Putting all questions of ethics aside, if you wanted to create *The Falcon Crest Pilot* it would be much *easier* to start out fresh, much quicker *not* to plagiarize *Vintage*. You would not, for a start, have to read *Vintage*." The trifurcation of the case no doubt helped him, since he could cry foul whenever the plaintiff snuck anything from beyond the pilot into an argument. Regardless, his rebuttals of the alleged similarities were consistently devastating, and any that remained unshot, like scattered blips of light near the end of a well-scored video game, were declared by Lanham to be "resolutely trivial." One of these, No. 9, involved "a female descendant of the founder (in each work the Victoria character) [who] has a romance with a working-class male who is not 100% Anglo and who provides some for the family business." When Lanham was through with it the similarity seemed more necessary than suspicious:

> This is one variation (and not an uncommon one) on a theme that pervades family saga fiction — gentry child falls in love with servant child. In *This Splendid Earth*, the redheaded teenager named Mary . . . who is the daughter of the French immigrant who founded the family wine business, falls for a Mexican named Jose, a worker in the family's vineyard. In *The Earth and All It Holds*, a copper-haired teenager named Alexandra, a descendant of the founder of the family wine enterprise, loves young Roger (half Anglo, half Mexican), who works for the family's vineyard business. . . .
>
> The child-of-master/child-of-servant love affair forms a subject of a very old cliché indeed in romance literature, the "Squire of Low Degree" motif. That these works each uses a different variation of it proves nothing, except that they share a common genre.

"Genre" was the cornerstone of Lanham's argument. He drew distinctions among romance, historical romance, Gothic fairy story and domestic drama, showing that the *Falcon Crest* pilot developed its own dramatic conflict from a collision of the last two modes: "Who will win, the American Family or the Wine-Witch?" Because of this collision, he could truthfully attribute to the pilot — in a moment both ridiculous and sublime — a "literary uniqueness." Both it and *Vintage*, he argued, were examples of romance fiction incorporating the "sub-genre" of "family saga," but *Vintage* was "a classic example of a multigeneration family saga," whereas the pilot took place in the course of a week. Lanham also placed both works in the seemingly rarefied genre of "California Wine Country Romance," a literary preserve he found surprisingly well stocked with white elephants, certainly enough of them to make his above-quoted explanation of similarity No. 9 numbingly plausible.

Condren's affidavit called Lanham's argument a red herring, going so far as to declare genre itself nonexistent: "The concept of genre is a collection of generalities enabling critics to sustain — and prolong — literary discussion. . . . Genre belongs to criticism, not to literature." By page 47 of his affidavit, Condren was counterpunching like a boxer way down on points: "What would it matter if an infringing writer copies literary material to make a computer game, or to fashion a comic strip on a box of breakfast cereal, or even to hawk the old bubbly? If he copies, he copies!" Along these lines Condren approvingly cited the rather incredible decision *Benny v. Loew's, Inc.*, which held that Jack Benny's comic takeoff of the motion picture *Gaslight* infringed the copyright of the original, no matter how clear Benny's parodic intent had been.

Even if genre belongs to criticism and not literature, it still belongs to the law, whether or not the law calls it by its name. In *Litchfield v. Spielberg* (9th Circuit 1984), the court ruled: "To constitute infringement of expression, the total concept and feel of the works must be substantially similar." Professors say "genre" and lawyers say "feel." No one in this case was willing to call the whole thing off.

Lanham carpet-bombed the plaintiffs with schlock. In an attempt to show that the resemblances Mrs Kornfeld alleged could also be found between her novel and other examples of formulaic fiction that antedated it, he came up with a long list of similarities between *Vintage* and Howard Fast's five-volume, 1,875-page Lavette saga. Whether one regards this huge chronicle as bedtime reading or a bedtime sedative, the fact is that Lanham forced Condren not only into reading it but into making his own series of written rebuttals to the similarities. Condren was furious, and nothing testifies better to the genuineness of his friendship with Lanham than that ultimately it survived Howard Fast's prose. Lanham's point was not to show that Mrs. Kornfeld had raided the Lavette saga. Quite the contrary: "I was just trying to show that the kinds of things, resemblances, she was making were part of the generic expectation and in fact could be made better with another property than they were made with her own." Condren says he understands the strategy, but thinks this was another red herring. When Mrs. Kornfeld is asked if she thinks the Lavette saga was dragged into the case to exhaust her own expert, she laughs. "I think Lanham did it to run up the hours."

Lanham himself retains the serenity of a man who knows he earned his pay. He looks back on his work in *Anita Clay Kornfeld v. CBS et al.* and says, "I thought this was a preposterous case from beginning to end."

Preposterous, perhaps, but understandable. Even Lanham will admit thinking Mrs. Kornfeld "was completely sincere," however much she contrived to "reinterpret reality" based on a sense of grievance: "There's some point in all the cases I've worked on that are like this . . . where the plaintiff just decides 'I've been wronged.'" A Rosenfeld, Meyer and Susman brief would point out that federal and state courts have noted the "obsessive conviction, so common among authors and composers, that all similarities between their works and any others which appear later must inevitably be ascribed to plagiarism." There have been crazy accusers of "plagiarists" who were quite innocent. The Russian writer Goncharov made wild charges against Turgenev and Flaubert — literally chasing after the former and crying "Thief! Thief!" Writing in the twenties, H. L. Mencken offered a choice of unpleasant possibilities in assessing the motives of an accuser:

> More often than not, perhaps, the plaintiff is honestly convinced that his property has been cabbaged. It is always hard for any of us to grasp the fact that our ideas may have occurred also to other men. Moreover, the lower ranks of authorship are full of nuts, and their aberration commonly takes the form of a violent belief in their own unparalleled genius. But what is so easy for honest fools is just as easy for blackmailers. In many of the accusations

of plagiarism that have been made in late years, in England and America, there has been nothing save a yearning to get a whack at what seemed to be very opulent royalties.

Indisputably, *Falcon Crest* cost Anita Kornfeld money. By its sixth season the show was still in its nighttime first-run slot as well as in syndicated reruns. In Lanham's, indeed anyone's, estimation, it was "turning to gold." If none of this money was rightfully hers, the existence of *Falcon Crest* still assured that no one, Harry Sherman or anybody else, would make a miniseries from *Vintage*.

And yet if one talks to Mrs. Kornfeld, one is quickly certain that venality is not what motivated her to file suit. She also wasn't "nuts," and she had no "violent belief in [her] own unparalleled genius." "Now never mind," she says, "whether [*Vintage*] is a dumb book, a bright book, a medium book, never mind what it's classified as. . . . I don't care what the merit is . . . leave my personality out of it. . . . The point is that *they took my property*." It may have been a kind of occupationally hazardous paranoia that convinced her *Falcon Crest* made use of her novel's meat and feathers, but a specific, professional susceptibility, which may be to writers what hemeralopia is to miners, is very different from being generally "nuts." Mrs. Kornfeld is immensely charming, someone whose world view seems properly proportioned with humor, detachment and passion. She is also a proud person. She will say, in a voice that sounds like Rosalynn Carter's: "When you come from the Tennessee mountains, and you come from the kind of family I come from, you just stand up for principle, and if one can't stand up for principle, what else is there? . . . What kind of dignity can a man have?"

The one novel she wrote before *Vintage* was set in the time and place of her childhood: Depression-era Tennessee. *In a Bluebird's Eye* (1975) is the story of an eleven-year-old girl whose name, in fact, is Honor. She is growing up in the soon-to-be-shut-down coal-mining town of Margate in the Great Smoky Mountains. Honor is a smart little girl, caught between her father's alcoholism and her mother's pretensions, with an imagination fired by a mythical wish-granting bluebird and her own practical plan to help a black parolee named Lola escape from town before she can be sent back to prison. *In a Bluebird's Eye* is lean, well written and finally quite moving. Its local color and historicity seem less massive and obligatory than *Vintage*'s. It has its genre, too, of course — the Southern *Bildungsroman* that includes such books as *The Member of the Wedding* and *Other Voices, Other Rooms* — but Mrs. Kornfeld seems more naturally, and distinctively, at home in it than she does in the bloated genre that is the three-genera-tion chronicle of a family and its fortune. The difference between *In a Bluebird's Eye* and *Vintage* is sufficiently great that a reader of both may well be surprised they were written by the same person.

Anita Clay was born in Ravenscroft, Tennessee, on January 17, 1928. Her mother and alcoholic father both taught school. She worked for a time as a psychiatric nurse and married a doctor named John E. Johnson in 1950. His family were Swedes, and it was from them that she heard stories she would use in connection with the character Erika in *Vintage* — in particular, the story of the fire she is supposed to have witnessed as a child. Anita and John Johnson had three children before their divorce in 1965 and Anita's subsequent marriage to John Kornfeld.

In 1962 she was part of a writing symposium organized by *Esquire*'s Rust Hills, which exposed her and other writers of fic-tion to two weeks of teaching by Saul Bellow. If she was late-blooming and — even given *Vintage*'s size — not very prolific as a writer, she has still thought of writing as an emotionally tu-multuous part of her life: "None of it is easy. Sometimes I think writing is like trying to put a bridle on a whale. But however difficult, this struggle to arrive at that point where a work feels 'right,' with a reasonable degree of significance and artistic form, there is no triumph greater for me."

Professor Condren recalls feeling hurt, when he took the stand during the *Vintage* trial, by his realization that "the two faces looking at me most intensely . . . were the two people that had most in common in that courtroom, Earl Hamner and Anita Kornfeld: they're both in the same business. They are both art-ists." Condren throws some words around with a well-meant grandiosity, but he has a point about similarities between the plaintiff and the most visible defendant in this case. Not the least of them was pride: the same measure of it that made Mrs. Korn-

feld pursue her case made Hammer fight back. Once the trial
was under way, neither side was in a mood to settle.

Earl Hammer grew up in rural Nelson County, Virginia, in the
1920s and thirties. Before his real successes in television, he
wrote four novels. *Spencer's Mountain* (1961), an account of a
Southern boyhood, was chosen during the Kennedy administration, he would proudly testify, "to be part of the library of books
representative of affirmative things about our country, and was
part of the library that was presented to heads of state around
the world." He seems sensitive to his inevitable "gone-Holly-
wood" image: "Being an admirer of our language, and objecting
to the impurities that are creeping into it, I have done and
continue to do everything in my power to make the language
beautiful, expressive, dramatic and living." Years after *Falcon
Crest* was successfully established on the air, he took pride in the
fact that he continued "to go over every script . . . to correct
vulgarities of language." He told interviewers that while he may
get involved in the nuts and bolts of bringing a show in close to
budget, ninety percent of his work is "creative contribution."
The opening directions on the first page of the first draft of "The
Vintage Years" seem to show a kind of nostalgia for the written
word over the televised image: "FADE IN: EXT. THE COTTAGE VINE-
YARD — NIGHT":

> We are on the floor of a great valley. The one purpose of the
> place is the growing of grapes and the making of wine. The time
> is autumn . . . the blush on the grapes had reached its deepest hue,
> and the grapes themselves hang lush and ripe.

The Waltons was derived from a TV movie based on Hamner's
short novel *The Homecoming* (1970). In this book, the John-Boy
figure is called Clay-Boy, but he is still a warm-hearted, aspiring
author. On page 112 he gets his Christmas present from his
father:

> Self-consciously Clay-Boy tore the wrapper open and he looked
> at his father with confusion and gratitude and questioning eyes
> as he found five tablets of good writing paper and a brand new
> fountain pen.
> "I wonder how news got all the way to the North Pole that you
> wanted to be a writer," said Clay with a grin.

"I guess he's a right smart man," said Clay-Boy, his throat almost too full to speak.

One curious point about these two earlier novels by the plaintiff and the defendant is that both *In a Bluebird's Eye* and *The Homecoming* involve young people awaiting the return of their fathers — while worrying if they've been waylaid by drink — on Christmas Eve. A curious coincidence, yes, but no more than that either. In this instance Hamner's creation was the earlier by several years, and no one would suggest that Mrs. Kornfeld, to use Mencken's word, "cabbaged" it for part of her plot. Variety is the spice of life, not its essence; life offers only so many raw materials to writers of fiction, and coincidences of this order, sinister only when held side by side out of context, will occur all the time.

A connection between Hamner and John-Boy Walton was suggested at the beginning of each episode of *The Waltons,* when Hamner himself did a voice-over that set up the story and was supposed to be coming from a retrospective John-Boy. But Anita Kornfeld wasn't going to believe in their identical rectitude, and besides, she could, if she wanted, concentrate on thinking of herself as a spunky, upright adult version of her own youthful Honor. So it was with a righteous purpose that she arrived at Melvin Belli's office on San Francisco's Montgomery Street one day in 1981. She found Belli himself on the telephone, in mid-explosion about some mix-up over tickets to a benefit. When he was through with the person on the other end, "screaming and calling him every name in the book," she recalls, he turned to her and shouted, "And who the fuck are you . . . and what are you doing sitting in my office?" She calmly responded, "Mr. Belli, I'm your client, Anita Clay Kornfeld, and you've just filed suit for me for $101 million."

"It was gangbusters down there," recalls Professor Condren, who before he became a medievalist was a carrier-based naval aviator. *Anita Clay Kornfeld v. CBS, Inc., Lorimar Productions, Inc., and Earl Hamner* finally opened on May 30, 1984, in United States District Court on North Spring Street in downtown Los Angeles. The city was getting ready for the Olympics and the courthouse was besieged with reporters — there not to cover the Kornfeld case but the trial of John DeLorean taking place downstairs. The *Vintage* case was tried in a room "not a hell of a lot bigger" than Judge Richard A. Gadbois, Jr.'s current chambers, by his own measurement. A Reagan appointee, he then lacked the seniority for a bigger courtroom.

There was no jury. The Belli office had failed to file for one in time, under "Rule 38." ("Query," asked a sarcastic brief from CBS's lawyers. "Is it possible for an experienced trial lawyer like plaintiff's counsel to pretend to be 'unfamiliar' with the Federal Rules of Civil Procedure?") In fact, Mrs. Kornfeld was not represented by the floridly familiar figure of Melvin Belli. He had put two other lawyers on her case, Rod Shepherd and Paul Monzione; *Kornfeld v. CBS et al.* was Monzione's first courtroom trial. Mrs. Kornfeld may have been surprised by not getting Belli himself, but she remains full of praise for those "two different people entirely" who represented her. She calls the older Shepherd "a peach of a man, a beautiful human being," and chuckles over Monzione as a combination of "bad boy" and "dimpled, angelic choirboy" who "is going to make a great lawyer some day." Shepherd had more "soul" than aggression, and if that didn't help her win her case, it did provide her with a lot of emotional support. "I really loved both those guys. . . . I wanted them so much to come through," she says.

Mrs. Kornfeld is humorously wistful about the "David-and-Goliath" aspect of the case. For all the vaunted power and ferocity of the Belli office, it was the team from Rosenfeld, Meyer and Susman (not too unlike the *L.A. Law* firm created by Jacob Epstein and company, according to Lanham) who arrived in court with a daunting presence and precision. "They overwhelmed that courtroom with material," she says. "You should have seen the contrast. They had everything so organized in all of these little boxes that were labeled, and they had a little woman running through, picking it all out. . . . Ours looked like Fibber McGee's closet." Robert Dudnik and William Billick, a kind of ethnic-WASP one-two punch, the former curly-haired and intense, the latter with the lean, fit look of an astronaut beginning to bald, were the lawyers facing off against Shepherd and Monzione.

Judge Gadbois, "a class act," according to Condren and almost everyone involved in the case, was good at making gruff but friendly banter with the attorneys and at paying attention to the sensitivities of witnesses not at home in the courts. He knew when to apply the light touch, whether it was trading estimations of '74 Zinfandel with Hamner or joking about Mrs. Kornfeld's recollection that Simon & Schuster asked her to give the *Vintage* manuscript a "harder edge . . . so I added some sex scenes." He had a taste for expeditiousness —"When a judge is ruling in your favor, it is time to just go on and put your next question, Mr. Billick" — that was thwarted by the tendentiousness natural to the courtroom examination of witnesses and by frequent interruptions to attend to other matters. At one point he called a recess in order to talk to lawyers working on another dispute. "There is a possibility," he explained, "that these people might decide that it is futile to try to solve the problem in a courtroom. It is a proposition that I think is admirable because it happens to be true." Sometimes, in the course of the *Vintage* trial, principal figures in other, criminal, proceedings would be brought before the judge. Once, during Dudnik's cross-examination of Mrs. Kornfeld about the barroom stabbing scene in her novel, a chained prisoner, unaware that a work of fiction was being discussed, looked up at her in surprise. "I started getting empathy from him," Mrs. Kornfeld recalls.

The judge's displays of wit were no more frequent than necessary to relax the atmosphere of what he remembers as "an intensely tried case." He knows how civil litigation batters people, how you see "a lot of hopes dashed. . . . We do the best we can." One curious aspect of the case is that it was tried by a judge who was, except for sports and movies, a resolute nonwatcher of television. "These guys got a true *tabula rasa* . . . when they got me," he says. The other piece of TV litigation over which Judge Gadbois had presided involved ownership of the comedy series *Barney Miller,* which he'd never seen before the trial. As in the *Falcon Crest* case, the money involved was enormous: "I lost count at a hundred million bucks between two guys, literally, two individuals. I mean the money kept going up all the time the case went on." Two years after the *Falcon Crest* trial he could still say that, not counting the pilot, he'd seen only half an episode of the series, when it came on a hotel room TV one evening when he was traveling with his wife. At one point in the proceedings, when an aspect of *Dallas* was raised for comparative purposes, the judge would have to interrupt the witness: "Just tell me: Who is Larry Hagman?"

The case would be tried according to the legal complexities of access and similarity. But central to it too would be the issue of human credibility present in every case and unusually colorful in this one. If the plaintiff's lawyers were going to succeed in demonstrating that Earl Hamner had deliberately pilfered Anita Kornfeld's novel, then they were going to have to pick up the gauntlet that Billick, near the outset, laid down to Monzione: "Are you going to try and prove that John-Boy is a liar?"

There is great caution in litigious Hollywood about keeping track of when "properties" are received by studios for their consideration. As Lanham says: "If you look at all of the procedures for booking in scripts, for controlling their flow within a studio, you see that in fact people take great precautions not to even allow a scintilla of suggestion that they read something. . . . Nobody in his right mind now would ever accept something at a cocktail party. . . . People would be crazy, because they know they're going to be sued." A good deal of attention during both the pretrial phase and the trial itself was given to the question of who at Lorimar had what when: when, that is, Earl Hamner and others might have had the opportunity to see galleys or finished copies of *Vintage* and how such access did or did not precede their creation of the pilot. A Rosenfeld, Meyer and Susman brief declared that Hamner had the basic idea for his pilot by August 1979, months before Mrs. Kornfeld completed *Vintage*. The defendants could show how elements of the plot appeared in work done years before, and could prove that Lorimar's New York office received a copy of *Vintage* from Mrs. Kornfeld's agent, Evart Ziegler, on September 30, 1980, "the day before the typist employed by Mr. Hamner in *Burbank* completed typing the Prospectus" — and that the book was never sent to the West Coast, where Hamner did his work and where Lorimar had its headquarters. Also, the defendants would contend that, according to precedents of the U.S. Court of Appeals for the Ninth Circuit, "access is not merely the opportunity to have read or known the contents of a work, but is the actual reading or knowledge of the contents of the work."

The plaintiff's lawyers had their own chronology and theories, and insisted that Ziegler (later fired by Mrs. Kornfeld) was "receiving requests from literary scouts at LORIMAR" to send them copies of *Vintage*, and that his "submission card to LORIMAR (defendant's Exhibit 2309) shows that he submitted the book to LORIMAR on August 31, 1980." A Belli brief would also note how in his deposition E. F. Wallengren, a story editor on *Falcon Crest* and writer of some of the series' early material, admitted to reading thirty to forty pages of *Vintage* before giving it to his wife. (He claimed he himself was bored by it.) All told, the plaintiff would assert that "the evidence presented at trial to establish access is so overwhelming that there can be no doubt that defendants had access to *Vintage*."

Judge Gadbois was inclined to agree with this, which is not to say that he found it especially compelling. Things in the entertainment industry "are disseminated widely," he would say when the trial was over. "The access element is almost a given in any case." To his mind there was indeed in this dispute what the law calls "constructive access." But what about similarity?

D. H. Lawrence advised readers to trust the teller instead of the tale. It is advice that the law, with its preference for hard fact over human frailty, enshrines in copyright statutes. In his useful book *The Protection of Literary Property*, Philip Wittenberg explains: "It is not the plot which is protected, it is the telling." Copyright does not cover such literary elements as titles, theme, locale and setting, character types, ideas and basic plots. Along these lines the defendants were able to contend that the "concept of a family saga set in the wine country is both unoriginal" — the California Wine Country Romance — "and an unprotectable idea": copyright law "protects only the particularized expression of those elements" mentioned above. As Wittenberg puts it: "Similarity of words is the easiest net in which to catch the plagiarist." Indeed, from the Jacobeans to Jacob Epstein, it has been the only certain and probably legitimate one to use in assessing the potential fraudulence of "creative" writing. What one wants are smoking guns, whole phrases appropriated like thy neighbor's wife and forced into adulterous proximity with whatever the plagiarist can manage to create himself.

The criteria for establishing infringement in the Ninth Circuit, wherein Hollywood lies, have been firmed up in the last decade, since the new copyright law was signed by President Ford in 1976. Landmark cases have involved familiar, still youthful, names. Three from the Ninth Circuit frequently cited by both sides in the Kornfeld case were *Jason v. Fonda* (1982); *Sid and Marty Krofft Television Productions, Inc. v. McDonald's Corp.* (1977); and *Litchfield v. Spielberg* (1984). A Belli brief summarized the circuit court's "two-pronged" test for "substantial similarity": "Extrinsic and intrinsic similarities must be shown to establish substantial similarity combined with access, to prove infringement of plaintiff's copyright. The extrinsic test requires a comparison of plot, theme, dialogue, mood, setting, pace and sequence." The "intrinsic" test focuses, as it did in *Litchfield v. Spielberg*, in which the author of *Lokey from Maldemar* complained of infringement by the movie *E.T.*, "on the response of the 'ordinary reasonable person' to the works." The plaintiff's attorneys insisted they could draw blood from CBS with both prongs of this test. Judge Gadbois was no ordinary person, but he was an eminently reasonable one. Could the plaintiff make him feel what she did?

What television is most interested in cabbaging is not what comes over the transom but what's already on the screen.* A successful movie or TV show is already test marketed and can be refracted into or synthesized with something else. As Todd Gitlin points out in his book *Inside Prime Time:* "With imitation so taken for granted, sometimes not even 'ripoff' is a term of great opprobrium." Even so, he talks about the industry's preference for the "recombinant" over the mere imitation: "Grant Tinker, who had earned his reputation as a high-taste TV proprietor, still told me about a project in the works at MTM that, 'just to be quick about it' — and quick is the way projects are bought and sold — he called *Hill Street in the Hospital.* (In 1982, NBC bought it under the title *St. Elsewhere.*)" *Falcon Crest* was itself referred by an advertising agency as "a taste of *The Good*

---

*Dorothy Parker: "The only ism Hollywood really believes in is plagiarism."

Earth and a dash of *Dallas* in the middle of a California vine-yard."

Certain imaginative reheatings may be tastier than their orig-inals. *Moonlighting*, the only witty television series of the last several years, was clearly a knockoff of the earlier *Remington Steele*, but a superior one. One of its stars, Pierce Brosnan, says, "*Moonlighting* [is] a direct steal which has just done it in a differ-ent, much fresher way." His co-star, Stephanie Zimbalist, adds, "Now those people are doing at *Moonlighting* exactly what we're supposed to be doing at *Remington Steele*" — a case of the old vaudeville routine in which the shadow pulls ahead of the dancer.

Drama has always, even before the advent of the television "industry," been a collaborative art. Certain passages of plays by Beaumont and Fletcher are Shakespearean for the very good reason that Shakespeare probably wrote them: playwrights com-monly had a hand in each other's doings and were paid back in kind. Back then, as today, nothing succeeded like success. Whether or not *The Merry Wives of Windsor* came to be written, as legend has it, because Elizabeth I wished to see Falstaff in love, the play is a "spinoff" of *Henry IV* just as surely as *Rhoda* was begat of *The Mary Tyler Moore Show*.

In television, where vast numbers of people work on a single project, and vaster numbers for a single network, it is easy, in Professor Lanham's words, for a writer to "imagine a lot of skullduggery which turns out to be complexity, absence of mind, chance." There is such a "layering of decision-making" and "so many patterns of deals" (property X is interesting, but only if agent Y can provide star Z) that the record of who created what is hard to track. Hamner, at the trial, took "full responsibility" for the pilot, but also admitted that pilot-making is "a business run by committee," and that CBS and Lorimar unquestionably had some influence over what developed. Shepherd wanted him to acknowledge the communal nature of the project; his obvious inference was that Hamner's collaborators could have been feed-ing details from Mrs. Kornfeld's novel into the pilot even if Hamner himself wasn't. Under oath Hamner asserted that he had, to that very day, June 29, 1984, not read *Vintage:* "I don't want anything to do with it. I never want to read it. It's caused me too much pain."

What seemed to strike Hamner's attorneys as odd was not that he was experiencing such pain but that he had never experienced it before. Rosenfeld, Meyer and Susman were used to litigating for an industry so competitive that actually getting your show on the air is — in a simile Lanham takes out of his academic hat — "like getting tenure at Harvard." Charges by the thwarted against the successful are so frequent that the "Defendants' Post Trial Brief" resorted to a rare exclamation point in noting: "Significantly, during Mr. Hamner's 35 year writing career, he has *never before* been accused of being a plagiarist!"

The plaintiff and the chief defendant in this case each had an interest in portraying the other as something of a failure who needed a target for robbery or vengeance. A Belli brief pointed to Hamner's flops between *The Waltons* and *Falcon Crest*. "It is significant that 'The Vintage Years' sat as a dormant project until the Summer of 1980. It is further significant that the dormancy ended at a time when HAMNER and [Executive Producer Michael] Filerman were desperate for success and ANITA KORNFELD's novel of the Napa Valley was placed on the California best seller list." The defense similarly sought to portray Mrs. Kornfeld as a flop in her personal efforts to bring her novel to the screen: "Mrs. Kornfeld was unsuccessful in all attempts to option or sell any theatrical or television rights in *Vintage*. In fact, no one ever expressed an interest in *Vintage* sufficient to warrant even discussion and negotiation of price or other terms regarding the rights in *Vintage*."

This last point is disingenuous. Mrs. Kornfeld's dealings with Harry Sherman may never have reached the point of discussing figures, but there were dealings and there was interest, and on June 21 Harry Sherman testified to that effect. He had never discussed *Vintage* with Hamner, he said, although he once worked down the hall from him at Lorimar (for which Sherman produced *Studs Lonigan*): "We used to chat passing. And on one occasion — I can't give you a specific date — I ran into Mr. Hamner at a restaurant. He was dining with his family and others. And we just passed and said, 'Hello,' and the usual sort of, 'What are you doing now?' And he said he was doing something in the Napa Valley and loved the area and was enjoying it." But Sherman did discuss *Vintage* with Bill Barbera of Hanna-Barbera Productions and Blanche Hanalis, a television writer: "I said I wanted to do it. I thought it would make excellent drama on television. It had all of the prerequisites of the character development, the intrigues of the family triangles." After Hanalis, at Sherman's request, read the novel, she called him back to say "that she loved it, that she would like to do it if it was something that we could get going, and that she would be happy to participate with me in any meetings." This was in October 1980, a month before he would call Anita Kornfeld and suggest she get herself a lawyer. If that phone call from Sherman was the beginning of months of depression and years of litigation, his recollection of his interest in *Vintage* provided her with what was probably her best moment at the trial: "Anybody who knows Harry Sherman has got to speak beautifully of that man. . . . There is a man of integrity for you. That's what John-Boy should be and isn't."

Some of Mrs. Kornfeld's worst moments, predictably, were provided by Lanham. She had been upset by things he wrote during the pretrial phase, and when he took the stand she was required to listen to him "debase my writing." She had to "sit there and hear it categorized in those ways." Examined by Dudnik and cross-examined by Monzione, Lanham again made his points about formula and genre, knowing he could draw on his knowledge of the mass of novels and nonfiction on the highly organized defense table. When Monzione asked him to comment on the fact that so many of *Vintage*'s unpleasant occurrences, like the misbehavings of David's daughters, take place in the East (the same region away from which Chase Gioberti is trying to get his brood in the pilot), Lanham was on the spot, ready to report happy eastern experiences in *Vintage* and to comment that Monzione's grouping of unpleasant experiences ignored the Tolstoyan fact that they were unpleasant in different ways. Lanham decried the kind of "false, contrived resemblance" that Condren typically created, and dismissed the business of the pilot's characters riding through the present-day vineyards on horseback. (Condren scoffed at the way the script had sixty-five-year-old Angie reining in a bucking horse; Lanham defended the plausibility of having Jane Wyman's character do this by reminding the court of the septuagenarian equestrian skills of Miss Wyman's former husband, the president of the United States.)

Before Lanham testified, Dudnik had given Condren a rough time on the stand:

> Q. Certainly, we know that . . . Maggie, the horse, and Maggie, the heroine, are not counterpart characters, correct?
> A. Correct.

With the judge's backing he kept the witness strictly to the pilot, despite Condren's insistence that "it is impossible to focus just on that film." Condren admitted that some of the name comparisons he'd done between *Vintage* and the Lavette saga were inaccurate; he had been angry, he said, at being forced by Lanham into an exercise in futility. But Dudnik proceeded with relentless specificity, asking Condren if he really thought the mention of Governor Al Smith in each book justified the inclusion of that name on the lists Condren used in preparing the ratio of similarities. Mrs. Kornfeld says Condren "was brilliant about a lot of things, but I think his use of math left a lot to be desired." Condren himself, two years after the trial, confessed doubts about his methodology. His use of a probability formula was in the nature of an experiment; he wanted to see if it would work because he knew he'd be in cases like this one again: "I think there is some future there [for it]. I don't know yet what it is. . . . It was in a sense a sop to that instinct the courts have all the time; they want you to quantify."

Condren had clearly not lapped up as much California Wine Country Romance and nonfiction as Lanham, and Dudnik was able to confront him with unfamiliar books containing locations and rituals (like a harvest blessing) that the plaintiff alleged had been appropriated for the pilot from *Vintage*. And in the course of questioning Condren about his background and credentials, Dudnik sprang a minor surprise:

> Q. You have written at least two scripts, correct?
> A. Uh-huh.
> Q. You have also written a TV pilot for a television series, correct?
> A. Uh-huh.
> Q. You have to answer audibly, sir.

A. Yes.
Q. What was the name of that pilot?
A. "Carrier."
Q. Did it sell, sir? I mean, has it been optioned?
A. I withdrew it because I sensed I was being worked over.

Mrs. Kornfeld remembers this moment sympathetically. When the strapping, silver-haired Condren was confronted with this lost pilot about pilots, the former Navy flier's expression "just crumbled. . . . They really hit some kind of sore spot." She figures Dudnik could have been told about "Carrier" only by Lanham. The effect of this mention of it was to make Condren look unfamiliar with the way Hollywood works, and even worse, unsuccessful — the same way, that is, that the plaintiff and chief defendant had tried to make each other appear. California lawyers seem to exploit constantly the American certainty that lack of success must betoken unreliability and vengefulness.

Judge Gadbois said after the trial that both professors "stood up well under cross-examination," but when Mrs. Kornfeld was on the stand, two weeks after Condren, the judge joked about the way Dudnik had bird-dogged her expert. Unable to recall some point of comparison Dudnik wished her to, Mrs. Kornfeld answered: "I don't remember. You would know more about Professor Condren than I because you probably followed it more closely than I did." To which Gadbois responded, amid laughter: "He certainly did." Lanham recalls the cross-examination of his colleague with a chuckle: "I hope to God it never happens to me."

During direct examination of Mrs. Kornfeld, on June 15, Shepherd and Dudnik agreed on a routine proposal to speed up the admission of a small bit of documentary evidence:

> Mr. Dudnik: Your Honor, if it will expedite things, we will stipulate to the admission . . .
> The Court: Fine.
> Mr. Shepherd: I graciously accept the stipulation.
> The Court: You accept the gracious offer of the stipulation.
> (Laughter.)
> The Witness: I love the word "gracious." I hope we can all hold onto it.

The Court: It isn't a term widely applied to practicing attorneys in a court of law.

The Witness: It's a new arena for me, sir.

Two years after the trial Judge Gadbois would apply that same word "gracious" to Mrs. Kornfeld, "a lady of real dignity and bearing." She was "a very, very appealing witness because she was obviously telling the truth. . . . The depth of her feeling about it came across very clearly."

But he perceived Hamner similarly. He was "a gentleman without your typical Hollywood attitude" whose statements were "utterly credible." As he continued to like both principals, the judge went about making up his mind. Mrs. Kornfeld was "telling the truth" — as she saw it — but Hamner was "credible" — period. And that was crucial. The judge was well versed in the relevant law and respectful of the case's subtleties, but he knew how to keep one eye on the forest while the other watched the trees.

Hamner testified that the name of "Mario" in "The Vintage Years" came not from *Vintage* but from his own gardener: "We referred to him facetiously as 'Mario from the barrio.' " Likewise, he insisted that he had had Joseph Gioberti marry a Swede (as indicated on the family tree in the pilot's prospectus) not because Adam Donati did, too, but because "he was influenced by the Swedish girl who came to Solvang years ago, whose antique trunk sits in his living room as a coffee table." (Mrs. Kornfeld says that Solvang was full of Danes, not Swedes.) And Lee Fong, Angie's Chinese servant (who became Chou-Li in the series), got his name not from *Vintage*'s faithful Li Po but as an inside joke: "The character was named . . . after Lee Rich, Lorimar's President, and the Ah Fong restaurants located in the Los Angeles area."

Hamner's credibility was enhanced by the disarming candor with which he admitted getting ideas for the pilot from the wine-country film *This Earth Is Mine,* starring Rock Hudson and Jean Simmons, who played Martha Fairon. "I think," Hamner said during direct examination by Billick, "very much a part of the character of Martha becomes a part of the character of Angie. I tried to imagine what the character of Martha . . . would become in later life had she inherited the vineyards." Here the judge pricked up his ears: "And with all of the power of that?" he asked

Hamner. "Yes," the witness replied. He went on to admit that he'd taken note of the film's Chinese servants and of the fact that the Rock Hudson character had been crippled; originally (that is to say, initially), in Hamner's prospectus for "The Vintage Years," the character of Lance was supposed to have been crippled in an auto accident. When asked by Billick if the Rock Hudson character's fate had influenced him, Hamner said, "I do not recall it consciously. I think that unconsciously it could have." In a way, *This Earth Is Mine* was like the strawberry mark that solves the foundling's paternity in an eighteenth-century novel. "I first knew that the plaintiff had trouble in this case," recalls the judge, "when I saw that film. . . . When you see the film you'll know that there's only one answer." Which is to say that Hamner's admission of a matter of influence was one of the things that helped him fend off a charge of plagiarism.

Judge Gadbois had a healthy taste for basics. When Hamner left the witness stand on June 29, he asked him, "Are you a plagiarist?" The witness responded, "No, sir," and the judge said, "All right. You may step down." The judge recalls "a couple of tears running down [Hamner's] face." Mrs. Kornfeld says, "When this thing went on trial, it was as if John-Boy and Earl Hamner had arrived . . . with a halo intact," even though this "good country boy" has "become quite polished and elegant and debonair." She mimics his pretentious vowels, but she says that Billick's plan of making Monzione try to prove John-Boy a liar was chosen "strategically and brilliantly." Maybe so, but it was ultimately moot. Judge Gadbois had never seen *The Waltons* either.

A year would pass before the judge handed down his decision. During that time — while *Falcon Crest* experienced a serious ratings challenge from *Miami Vice* — he had the opportunity to ponder the enormous documentation the case had generated, including the post-trial briefs of each side, belligerent perorations, sometimes like hoarse election-eve speeches in which candidates make a final pitch to the electorate, in this case one man. The Belli office argued that the plaintiff had "by an overwhelming preponderance of evidence, through the presentation of expert testimony and an organized, and systematic compara-

tive list, established that 'The Vintage Years' is substantially similar to *Vintage*." Rosenfeld, Meyer and Susman concluded with a
kind of confident disgust: "Defendants will forego the effort to
again educate Plaintiff, who clearly does not wish to be educated."

The judge's "Findings of Fact and Conclusions of Law" found,
unequivocally, for the defendants. John and Anita Kornfeld
were vacationing in France when they learned of the decision.
Anita Kornfeld's dislike of Earl Hamner was, and remains, un-
yielding, and she was no doubt particularly distressed by the
judge's focus on her antagonist's truthfulness:

> An important part of the court's decision in this case is its conclu-
> sion that the entire testimony of Earl Hamner is credible. He was
> on the stand a long time, and we had a good opportunity to form
> an impression of his veracity.
> Hamner was an honest witness. Given that fact, it follows that
> Hamner, and to the best of his knowledge, the people that worked
> on the pilot with him, had never heard of any aspect of the
> plaintiff's work. It further follows that the creation and filming
> of the pilot were acts of independent creation that rested in no
> part on the work of the plaintiff.

Because she had failed to win this first third of the trifurcated
case, it was all over. Still certain and still angry, Mrs. Kornfeld
began an appeal but soon, wisely, dropped it.

A year after handing down the verdict, the judge could say,
with all due respect to Mrs. Kornfeld, that "she never really had
a case." Her argument "*clearly* doesn't pass the 'feel' test" — that
legal test for genre that the plaintiff's post-trial brief had improbably faced up to, trying to reach the court's heart through
its stomach: "Even accounting for the fact that plaintiff's work
is a 609 page novel while defendants' pilot is 46 minutes long,
the 'gut' reaction will be that defendants have dramatized plaintiff's novel." The judge's sense that this is not so, along with
Hamner's credibility, and the obvious resemblances to *This Earth
Is Mine*, seem to have been what settled things for him. He doesn't
despise the experts, in the way Lanham says judges will; on the
contrary, he says they were "both very credible witnesses . . . both
very intelligent people who put a lot of work into it." It's just that
one gets "terribly distracted" by comparing them. Distractions

are usually expensive, and these professors were no exception. CBS's insurers would pay Lanham ("I always end up working for the Fireman's Fund"); the Belli office would take the loss on Condren. The judge says he has no reason to believe he could have done his own work any better by being a habitual viewer of television.

Condren has a high regard for Gadbois, but says that the judge is "tyrannized by the Ninth Circuit's traditions," which cause its judges, he says, to find, time and time again, for the studios. The problem, he insists, is that the Ninth Circuit, in its insistence on duplication of *expression*, "is still applying the copyright law as if we were talking about belletristic literature," whereas the kind of popular art corporately constructed within the Ninth Circuit's jurisdiction does not, unlike high art, have at its essence the felicities of original expression. What the popular artist has is his pitch — let's do a show about X set in Y — and the Ninth Circuit leaves the pitchman unprotected. "If," says Condren, "the Ninth Circuit persists in interpreting expression as virtually a series of verbatim quotes . . . then of course there's never going to be a decision given to a plaintiff, and that's my complaint. . . . It's impossible for a plaintiff who has genuinely been wronged ever to win a case." He admits to a "crusade" against the locally prevailing interpretation.

Lanham disagrees that "you can or that you should be able to protect ideas in that way. I don't see how the law could do it without shutting down the First Amendment guarantees that it tries to stay clear of." He compares the number of people peddling screenplays in Hollywood to the number of people in the stock market in 1928. He imagines a big producer driving down Sunset Boulevard and having a thought: "making a movie about an earthquake in Los Angeles . . . BOFFO IDEA!" The point is that this big producer will go ahead and produce it, even though the idea has occurred to hundreds of other people driving down Sunset Boulevard and to some of them before it occurred to him. "How would you protect that? At what level would you protect it?" Judge Gadbois thinks "it would be a terribly depressing thing" to have a copyright law that tried to protect "pitches" as if they were themselves expression. You couldn't do it, "and this case . . . is a perfect example of it."

*

Would a jury, assuming the Belli office had filed for one in time, have seen things the same way? Condren says that unless the judge instructed those twelve hypothetical citizens in a narrow manner, they "definitely would have found for Anita." Mrs. Kornfeld herself recalls two courthouse inveterates who each day would come upstairs from DeLorean's trial to hers; toward the end of the proceedings they told her she would win "hands down" if she had a jury. "I loved those men by the time this was over," she says and laughs.

When the question of a jury is put to Judge Gadbois, he smiles and says he hasn't any idea whether the plaintiff's lawyers might have done better with one. But on reflection he says no. "I don't think they could have sold this case" to a jury. Not even a jury of *Waltons*-watchers who might have resisted Billick's John-Boy strategy because they were made uncomfortable by the spectacle of a good country woman, pretty enough to have played the part of John-Boy's mother, being so distressed over something she swore John-Boy had done to her? "I like to think that jurors don't make decisions that way," the judge says, though he concedes that infrequently they do. He was himself sufficiently certain of the soundness of CBS's case that, had a jury found for Mrs. Kornfeld, he would probably have granted a motion for a new trial.

Perhaps the *Vintage* case, for all its impassioned accusations, tearful defenses, millions of dollars, thousands of man-hours and eighty-five boxes of documents, was a trivial pursuit. Judge Gadbois himself doesn't find it "a case inspiring a general statement," and he doesn't feel it had any precedent-setting legal significance. But he does admit that, like most cases, this one "had its own tragedies." Earl Hamner genuinely felt himself to be maligned and brutalized. When the verdict went his way, it inevitably received less press attention than the original charges. "The accusation is all over the place, and my absolution was six lines in the L. A. Times financial section," he complained to the TV columnist for the *Richmond Times-Dispatch* back in his home state of Virginia. The column that resulted from the interview was headlined "Media Grapevine Isn't Spreading Word of Hamner's Victory, So He Is." But a year later Hamner seemed sick of the matter and preferred to let his lawyers and the huge written record do the talking to someone writing about the case.

In his last day on the witness stand back in the summer of 1984, he had managed to express some sympathy for his antagonist, Anita Clay Kornfeld:

> In spite of all the pain that this experience has caused me, I feel a certain amount of compassion for the author of that book because I am an author, and I know how long it takes you to write a book and how much of a feeling of protection you feel.
>
> And if you feel that your work has been ripped off, you are intruded upon. It is as if a child has been defiled.
>
> So I am sorry for the author, but my conscience is clean and clear.

All trials are trials for one's life, declared Oscar Wilde, whose troubles began not while he was a defendant but while he was a plaintiff. Mrs. Kornfeld still thinks she should have sued. "I felt I owed it to my children. . . . It was a matter of principle for me." She no longer uses the image of the denuded turkey bone, but a year after the verdict she could still look at one of her husband's life sculptures in their new home in San Rafael and say, "They took the armature of my book" — the scaffolding that permits expression on the face molded around it. When one insists to her that the literary expression of *Falcon Crest* is totally different from the expression of *Vintage*, she remains resolute: she was violated.*

The cost of her bringing suit was less financial (Belli, having taken the case on contingency, lost far more money than she did) than emotional. A kind of paralysis overcame her writing; a novel about life on the Mississippi River, to which she had already devoted much labor, was put aside. As she put it in a letter late in 1986:

> . . . another ramification of the plagiarism fiasco: an erosion of self-confidence, of a clear-eyed goal, of a sense that "writing," per

---

*Whether or not the late Meyer Levin was right in charging that his dramatic version of *The Diary of Anne Frank* was plagiarized by the authors of the version that was actually produced, the feeling of violation "obsessed him through the last thirty years of his life," writes Stephen Fife.

se, is a kind of wonderland for ideas to romp freely and eventually find that format of a novel or story or article. What used to seem filled with the brightest of colors, like nature's own meadowlands, now seems fogged-in, as San Francisco so frequently is. I keep thinking I'll be reinspired. I keep thinking and arguing and rationalizing. My energy level and my thrust toward applying that energy with a given focus will demand some recourse, but I'm not at all sure that it will be "creative writing."

If the sound and fury of the *Vintage* case signifies anything, it is that the most valid proprietary pride is booby-trapped with blind spots. The Sokolow affair shows what happens when too many people are too afraid of being sued, but the Kornfeld "fiasco" proves something like the opposite: the danger that lies in calling the lawyer. Perhaps, contrary to Mme. Reybaud's motto, there are some things that can't be remedied.

If the Belli office lost money, Rosenfeld, Meyer and Susman added to their reputation in the entertainment industry. Two years after arguing for Hamner, Billick was fending off a charge of infringement made against the popular Saturday-night sitcom *The Golden Girls*. By 1986 *Falcon Crest* was itself beginning to look tired. Nighttime soaps were generally felt to be in decline, and there had been on-the-set battles among Jane Wyman and company. The show had become overpopulated with dazzling short-term guest stars like Lana Turner and Gina Lollobrigida. A former story editor was quoted as saying, "This is a show that has lost its way. . . . It began as a struggle within a family, but it has gone far afield." In other words, it had genre problems.

In UCLA's Rolfe Hall, Professor Richard Lanham says that if he can ever finish the book he's working on now, he'd like to write another on the theory of intellectual property. He also hopes that he can do what he has so far attempted in vain — get one of the big law firms in L.A. to hire him to compile a computerized index of all the properties registered with the Writers Guild of America. When asked if he ever watches *Falcon Crest*, the series whose survival he helped ensure, he replies, "Gimme a break." Judge Gadbois, who has a bigger courtroom these days, continues to eschew nighttime television drama: "A good book is just a hell of an improvement over anything like that."

Down the hall from Lanham, Professor Edward Condren still

believes that TV "rips them off like mad," and he "cannot accept the premise that absent Anita's book . . . Lorimar's long-running soap . . . would have been anything like *Falcon Crest*." He says that Lanham is more naturally a defendant's lawyer, while he tends to fall on the plaintiff's side. Still, at times their differences of legal temperament fade sufficiently to allow them to cooperate as peacefully in the courtroom as they do in the English Department. In the fall of 1986 they were both working on the same side of a copyright infringement case involving Dr. Irene Kassorla, a sex therapist best known for a book called *Nice Girls Do*.

Postscript

I T IS NOT, finally, a matter of money. Except in Hollywood, few people write, or plagiarize, to get rich; far more of them write to get even. When George Orwell enumerated the writer's "four great motives," the first on his list was "sheer egoism. Desire to seem clever, to be talked about, to be remembered after death, to get your own back on grownups who snubbed you in child-hood, etc., etc. It is humbug to pretend that this is not a motive, and a strong one." Most books are not valuable "properties"; they're voices, laying perpetual claim to their authors' existence. As that almost indecently vital English diarist, W. N. P. Barbel-lion, wrote after a trip to the library:

> The Porter spends his days . . . keeping strict vigil over this cata-comb of books, passing along between the shelves and yet never paying heed to the almost audible susurrus of desire — the desire every book has to be taken down and read, to live, to come into being in somebody's mind. He even hands the volumes over the counter, seeks them out in their proper places or returns them there without once realising that a Book is a Person and not a Thing. It makes me shudder to think of Lamb's *Essays* being carted about as if they were fardels.

We'll sometimes ask each other: "Have you ever read [let's say] MacNeice?" The question doesn't ask if we've read a particular book; it inquires as to whether we've made the acquaintance of a person who now *is* his books. From the lyric poem to the sci-entific footnote, the printed word is the writer's means of proving and perpetuating his existence. That identity of self and work, and the prospect for continuation, are more precious to him than the promiscuous coin of the realm. Anyone is relieved to come home and find that the burglar has taken the wallet and left the photo album. When a plagiarist enters the writer's study it's the latter — the stuff of "sentimental value" — that he's after.

In the stacks of Barbellion's living library, Sterne's cartwheels obscure Burton's ruminative chin-strokings; Reade's bellowings for attention drown out Mme. Reybaud's modest beckonings. Plagiarism is a fraternal crime; writers can steal only from other writers. And if it's to be punished, the penalty must be what was meted out after the first crime between brothers: a "mark." The sanction most feasible and most just is the ironic one: publication. Get the word out on the persistent offender. In each profession that will mean using a slightly different mechanism; the only reliable guide will be common sense. Jonathan Broder, the West Bank correspondent for the *Chicago Tribune*, had to resign from that paper (which had nominated him for a Pulitzer Prize) for taking "a number of sentences and phrases . . . without attribution" from the *Jerusalem Post*'s Joel Greenberg. Broder had the excuses of "physical fatigue and trauma," but his resignation was publicized in every major newspaper at which he might later look for a job. If this seems Draconian, the Sokolow case shows what a decade of sparing the professional rod accomplishes.

From belling the cat to beeper-braceleting the house-arrested felon, we dream of technology's protection against perfidy. Now, from Sacramento, California, comes the Glatt Plagiarism Screening Program, "the first comprehensive computer software program specifically designed for detecting plagiarism." Ten years in the making, the program is based "on a proprietary database, statistical variables, and probability theory." But detection can never do more than keep pace with perpetration, and while his right hand is strapped to the Glatt, the determined modern plagiarist will be, with his left, digitally scanning the next text.

So why don't we give up worrying about an offense that leaves many of us feeling amused or ambivalent? Because ceasing to care about plagiarism would not mean that writers had experienced a rise in wisdom and generosity; it would mean that they had permitted themselves a loss of self-respect. And if ego stopped mattering, then, very likely, writers would stop writing — or at least stop writing so frequently and well. Which means that, finally, plagiarism would be a crime against the reader.

We cannot, however, expect ego to lose its role as writerly propellant, because we cannot go back to the times of the troubadours. The printing press, which changed the writer's nature forever, cannot be "uninvented." For the last several hundred years — and surely it will be so for several hundred more — the writer has worked his hardest only when he felt there was the chance that his best sentences would stand as famous — and last — words.

Afterword to the New Edition

Stolen Words reached bookstores in the fall of 1989, a few weeks before the fall of the Berlin Wall. The ensuing collapse of Soviet and European communism — and the troubled transition from collectivism back to private property — remains the premier event of the dozen years that followed. And yet, if one looks at this period expecting to find the smaller realm of literary property being swept in the same direction — toward a new premium on the idea of ownership — one will seek it largely in vain. The great economic "globalization" of the 1990s may have stimulated entrepreneurship in a million different manufactures and services, but the Information Age has imperiled many old literary shareholders like yesteryear's Red Army thundering toward a peasant's private rutabaga patch.

Back in 1989, the Internet cast barely a gleam into the ordinary reader's eye; the first Web browser wasn't even available. The few references to computers in the main text of *Stolen Words* now strike me as more primitive than prophetic. Few nontechnical people could, I suppose, have predicted the speed and sweep of the cyber revolution, or that "word processing" — a term that quickly went from being barbaric to quaint — would be, screenwise, the least of it. Certainly not this writer, who was the last of his set to get a computer, and who recalls *Stolen Words* as the final book he produced without one, its much-white-outed manuscript and bibliographical index cards now looking as antique as Charles Reade's notebooks.

Plus ça change might be the motto on plagiarism's crest, and it is not surprising that the new technology has spawned virtual equivalents for some of word-theft's older methodologies. During the mid-1990s, Ruth Shalit, a very young rising star in political journalism, got caught reproducing a number of unattributed passages in her articles. She pleaded that portions of the notes and source material she had on one side of her split computer screen had somehow jumped, citationless, into the text she was creating on the other side. (Ms. Shalit has subsequently gone into advertising.)

During the past decade, quite a number of journalistic plagiarism cases have become topics of brief public discussion, and the fourth estate has displayed some of the same ad-hocery as its academic counterpart. As Trudy Lieberman put it in a 1995 survey for the *Columbia Journalism Review:* "Punishment is uneven, ranging from severe to virtually nothing even for major offenses." Resolution may be swifter in the world of newspapers and magazines, but it is still often marked by a tendency, in the first hours after a possible offense is discovered, to reinvent the wheel. People whose business is words start asking themselves, yet again, just what plagiarism is and whether it's really so bad. Discussion of cases involving deadline-driven columnists who can't resist skimming the Web — for everything from George Carlin's jokes to old-chestnut essays about the signers of the Declaration of Independence — often get balled up with considerations of incidents closer to forgery: the *Boston Globe* fired Patricia Smith, and the *New Republic* got rid of Stephen Glass, for writing about people who didn't exist. Mike Barnicle balled things up himself, committing both plagiarism and fabrication before departing the *Globe* in 1998.

Easily the most — and least — upsetting plagiarism revelation in the years since this book's initial publication involved the Rev. Dr. Martin Luther King, Jr., whose academic work, including his 1955 doctoral dissertation for Boston University, was eventually found to contain sizable portions of unattributed borrowing. Scholars with the King Papers Project at Stanford University were ultimately quite forthright in presenting their findings, but while the problem was coming to light they experienced a range of conflicting emotions. As the *Wall Street Jour-*

nal reported on November 9, 1990: "Several student-researchers wondered why the information should be probed. Some resigned. One summer intern broke down in tears when she found out. Megan Maxwell, who joined the project as a Stanford undergraduate and became assistant archivist after graduation, says her initial reaction was anger, 'a combination of "Why didn't anyone catch him?" and "Why didn't he know better?"'"

Having developed a slightly Draconian reputation on the subject, I can't say I enjoyed appearing on television to discuss the King plagiarism with both an interviewer and the civil-rights leader's biographer, David Garrow (*Bearing the Cross*). But in the end the case was a no-brainer. If it made one revere King somewhat less — and it did — one was still left admiring him perhaps more than anyone else one could think of. In fact, the matter may have had a salutary effect on thinking about plagiarism, by introducing a moral proportionality that few other instances of the offense have provided. As one editorial put it rather nicely: "Whether or not, as a student, he wrote what he wrote, Dr. King *did* what he did." Since writing is the *only* thing that most writers do, plagiarism — in the context of an otherwise actionless life, the opposite of King's — now somehow stands out in even sharper, shoddier relief.

In the last decade I've spent more time writing historical novels than criticism, but even here I've not fully gotten away from the subject. More than any fictional subgenre, historical novels — dependent as they are upon research — raise issues of "sourcing," and novelists have to resist thinking of the library as some sort of dull free lunch that they're allowed to spice up with art and narrative and serve *à la* their own byline. (Susan Sontag's latest novel, *In America*, has troubled some critics along these lines.) As I told one reporter, speaking more as a novelist than a student of literary scandal, about this particular facet of plagiarism: "A certain degree of pastiche is acceptable and even necessary to the establishment of historical figures as believable literary characters. But that doesn't absolve the novelist from respecting the language that was crafted by other contemporary scholars. Novelists should go to scholars for information, not for language."

And that's because language — which words in what order — is what plagiarism generally comes down to. Considerations of historical fiction may lead to discussion of whether there's any "original" art now being created in our parodic, postmodern world (as if nonhistorical novels derived any less from real-life situations and real-life individuals), but while such discussion has a degree of aesthetic interest — the visual and literary arts *are* more self-referential than ever before — one mustn't let it spawn another red herring that thwarts investigations of simple plagiarism. We are talking, as we were way back in Chapter 1 with Laurence Sterne, about two entirely different kinds of appropriation: one that re-invents and rearranges and indeed often depends upon an audience's recognition of the earlier material that's been transmuted; and another that hopes, beyond all else, for the original material to remain unrecognized as such.

Over the years I've remained on media Rolodexes as someone to call when a peculiar or prominent case of plagiarism breaks, though I have resolutely stayed away from expert witnessing, continuing to believe — not just from the *Falcon Crest* case — that court is almost always the wrong place to hash these matters out. The copyright laws are fairly blunt instruments, designed to deal with the wholesale piracy and unauthorized publication of entire works, not the little smugglings that plagiarists try to hide in the plain sight of their "own" paragraphs. The great copyright battles now being fought around the Internet involve such issues as whether a new technology like Napster should be able to turn every home computer into its own recording studio. Similarly, the Authors Guild lawsuit against "UnCover" — recently settled for $7.25 million — concerned the unauthorized reproduction of whole freelanced articles by that document-delivery company. (An e-mail to Guild members instructs: "To find out whether you're entitled to part of the settlement, visit http://www. uncoversettlement.com and select 'Submit Claim.'" When I did, I discovered that the only work of mine to have been reproduced without permission was the printed version of a lecture I'd once given to the Copyright Society of the U.S.A.)

Stolen Words has had, not surprisingly, an uncomfortable relationship with the academic world. Received warmly enough in the mainstream press, it was predictably panned in *Academe*, the house journal of the American Association of University Professors — an exercise roughly comparable, I think, to reviewing *All the President's Men* in the newsletter of the Republican National Committee. In 2001, the professoriate remains more inclined to pieties than to the policing of its own, though it should be noted that in the year or so after this book reported on the Jayme Sokolow battle, the American Historical Association (AHA) made at least two movements toward greater professional regulation of plagiarism within its midst. It dropped the phrase "By using someone else's work *with an intent to deceive*" from its "Statement on Plagiarism," thereby eliminating the most easily copped plea from the plagiarist's repertoire of excuses. As James Gardner, the AHA's deputy executive director, told the *Chicago Tribune* in 1990, "The conclusion of our professional division is that that was a loophole that virtually everyone was using. When you come down to it, it's plagiarism whether you intended to do so or not." The AHA also revised its "Addendum on Policies and Procedures" to state that if the Professional Division "decides that other action is needed such as full public disclosure of an individual case, it may direct the Vice-President to seek approval for that action from the Council."

Still, academics remain curiously willing to vaporize the whole phenomenon of plagiarism in a cloud of French theory. When I spoke to one audience of professors in 1990, their questions, sometimes hostile, tended to concern why I hadn't addressed concepts like Roland Barthes' "death of the author," and the possibility that there is *no such thing* as originality. I didn't address such matters because they seemed to me then, as they do now, absurd. The professors don't really believe these theories, either. They're the type who can't sit on the university's parking-regulations committee without getting into a discussion of nature vs. nurture, but if they catch someone pilfering their own bibliographies, you can count on a cry of bloody murder, not an invitation to hermeneutics.

But none of this keeps them from continuing to propound imported, abstract fantasies. Rebecca Moore Howard, a specialist in student composition, laments that *Stolen Words* "has attained canonical status in English departments" — an overstatement, to be sure — even though it is "a beacon from the past," one that "assumes a normative autonomous author." Yes, that would be me; or, when she's the one writing, it would be Professor Howard, who takes comfort in a contrary view that she works her way toward through several layers of syllogism and — attribution:

> Another critic, Françoise Meltzer, explains Descartes's and Freud's anxieties about originality: writers who want recognition must assert priority; to assert priority is to assert originality; and to assert originality engenders a fear of being robbed. Behind that fear of being robbed is "the larger fear that there is no such thing as originality."
>
> If there is no originality, there is no basis for literary property. If there is no originality and no literary property, there is no basis for the notion of plagiarism.

In this same *College English* article, Professor Howard finds students accused of theft to be more misunderstood than culpable: "Representations of student plagiarism seldom acknowledge the heterogeneous definitions of authorship in contemporary letters." (By "contemporary letters" she means university-press books of literary theory.) "Instead, these representations simplify student authorship, depicting it as a unified, stable field. The principle used for the task of unifying and stabilizing student plagiarism is the putative morality of the 'true' (autonomous) author."

Professor Howard will do almost anything with student writing but quote it, perhaps because it has such a hard time living up to the aesthetic benediction she grants it. Indeed, one reason it is so bad is that the students' professors will talk about "unifying and stabilizing" plagiarism when plain English would speak of punishing it. Howard throws her lot in with those professors who regard "patchwriting" — i.e., half-cribbed pastiche — "as an important transitional strategy in the student's progress toward membership in a discourse community."

The *New York Times* recently reported on college students' preference for doing research on the Web instead of in the library: "they are simply more comfortable sifting through hyperlinks than they are flipping through a card catalog. And they admit that using the Web requires less exertion." For one thing, they don't have to trudge across the quad from their dorm rooms to the stacks. As the old Yellow Pages slogan used to put it, they can let their fingers do the walking. Inevitably, student plagiarism has changed stride, too. My former Vassar colleague, Professor Robert DeMaria, tells me that these days a clear majority of the plagiarism cases adjudicated by the college's Academic Panel involve Internet source material rather than books. Fortunately, *Originality and Attribution*, the pamphlet DeMaria helped write in the mid-1980s, has not been revised in the accommodating direction proposed by Professor Howard. It now warns students that when it comes to their scholarly responsibilities, nothing has actually changed:

> The college considers computer-generated text to be equivalent to any other form of written work; the same restrictions regarding proper attribution that apply to printed texts also cover computer programs, disks and other electronically stored materials.

The Vassar library has constructed its own Web page, "Style Sheet for Citing Electronic Information."

And yet, the pamphlet betrays an awareness that *everything* has changed: "Students have claimed before the Academic Panel that they did not consider an electronic file, because of its nature, to be property as 'personal' as a book or paper." A mental shift, not so much ethical as epistemological, is underway with students who scarcely remember a Net-less world. As Mark Fritz has put it, in a discussion of plagiarism in the *Los Angeles Times*: "Many students seem to almost reflexively embrace a philosophy rooted in the subculture of computer hackers: that all information is, or should be, free for the taking."

The Web makes it impossible for students to value originality, or writing itself, in quite the same way. If all writing is instantly available, none of it can be worth all that much. A mental law of supply and demand has to operate: when it comes to food or sex or research, humans cannot prize availability in the same way they do scarcity. Think of what the Web has meant even to the buying of actual books. I have become devoted to www.bibliofind.com, the electronic consortium of used bookstores, because when I'm looking for some out-of-print, arcane title, it *never disappoints.* Usually, information about a dozen copies of the desired book will come onto my screen, so that I can comparison-shop based on pricing, shipping costs, and a description of each copy's condition. I'll place my order, and two days later, by priority mail, I'll have the book. A few years ago, in search of the same title, I would have made a trip to the mighty Strand bookstore in New York, where I might well find what I was looking for — but then again, might not. Let's say I was successful: what would be the difference between that shopping experience and what I now have using bibliofind.com? The fruitful trip to the Strand, because it had been effortful and involved the risk of disappointment, would yield a certain eureka-like satisfaction and contentment; whereas bibliofind.com grants a satisfaction that is certain— plain and simple. Which is to say, not as potent, instant gratification being never so gratifying as the even-slightly-deferred kind.

When it comes to research and writing, the psychological consequences of this are enormous. For students, especially, the Internet may sap the very need to create. *It's all there already,* or so it seems; all the knowledge on a given subject, and all the competing viewpoints, in a machine you can carry around like a book. What's there to add — and why dig a well instead of turning on the tap?

Inevitably, the old mail-order term-paper mills have given way to their cyber counterparts. A1-termpaper.com — offering the venerably phony disclaimer that "All Work Offered Is For Research Purposes Only" — will e-mail customers "Pre-Written Termpapers" in the form of Microsoft Word documents. Along with the up-to-date convenience come new perils for student patrons, particularly when they seek what's called "Custom Research." The operator of one such cybermill told Berkeley's *Daily Californian* that "the quality of many term paper sites is questionable. Many are based in Asia and the Middle East and are often staffed by people who do not even speak English." Even when attempting their own Web research, students may not realize, argues Mary Hricko, the library director of Kent State's Geauga Campus, that many Web pages themselves are plagiarized.

Detection has, of course, tried to keep pace with theft. The Glatt screening program, that *dernier cri* mentioned in the last pages of *Stolen Words'* first edition, is still going strong, but these days it has competition from other outfits. Ablesoft now advertises "rSchool Detective," which can put student essays through a kind of body-cavity search: "Teachers simply open up student-written files and the software program checks the Internet to see if any part of an assignment has been copied from one or more web sites. By giving the web site address in the analysis, rSchool Detective allows the teacher to confirm and even print out a copy of the original work in case the teacher's word is challenged."

Nothing's foolproof, of course. The detection services have to offer their own disclaimers, with good reason. In June 1999 the writer Andy Dehnart described, in the online journal *Salon*, a test he conducted of Plagiarism.org. Dehnart submitted his 30-page senior thesis to the company, which soon, he says, reported that it had "found only one matching phrase in my essay: but it was 8,367 words long. It was my own paper: within the archives searched by Plagiarism.org was the copy of my thesis that I had posted on the Web."

Instructors who believe that standards of academic honesty should continue to apply in the new world of the Web will, of course, prefer prevention to detection. But some of the pedagogical strategies now being advocated to keep students from plagiarizing seem like further instances of the general dumbing-down and infantilization of American college life. Bruce Leland of Western Illinois University recommends that professors "Watch [their] students write. Ask them to bring notes or drafts to class, have short conferences about the assignment, use peer groups to comment on drafts, ask for drafts to be submitted with the final paper." Even worse, Mary Hricko, the Kent State librarian, suggests that "we can lessen the temptation to plagiarize in the way we organize our assignments." On her campus, "several instructors place specific items on reserve for student research and provide students with a list of required web sites to examine. Although this procedure may appear restrictive, students learn how to use specific reference materials and compare ways in which their classmates incorporated the same sources into their assignment." Instead of being asked to take all knowledge for their province, students past voting age must have their hands held while crossing the information superhighway.

The plagiarism implications of the Web extend far beyond the weary precincts of student composition. The origin and ownership of all electronic documents is now peculiarly evanescent; one click of the "Save As" button can give a new name and identity, instantly, to someone else's creation. As historian Carla

Hesse puts it, we have entered an age of "boundless textual promiscuity" that excites, along with a certain "exhilaration," a "deep anxiety over the loss of fixed cultural forms ... The reader is thus now conceived as an independent navigator in a continuous textual flow." In fact, Hesse speculates, the very idea of writing as writing may be on the wane: "What digitalization seems to have opened up is the possibility for writing to operate in a temporal mode hitherto exclusively possible in speech — for writing to operate, in the terms of structural linguistics, as *parole* rather than *langue*." (Those who are still appalled by the abrupt and misspelled e-mail they receive from literate friends have to comfort themselves with the knowledge that, in terms of its own technology, a piece of e-mail is not really a letter but a telephone call.) Ms. Hesse, citing a study by the Getty Foundation, finally warns that

> If human experience is not to dissolve into a pure memory flow of continuous on-line exchange ... we will need to evolve standards and tools to ensure the preservation of the integrity of textual and visual artifacts as they are converted into digital form. We will also need to ensure a record of their provenance and their survival in their original form over time. ...

All of which sounds like a very good argument for the retention of the printed, bound book.

It's useful to remember that for all our online opportunities to be anonymous, to roam through and pilfer one another's writings and credit card numbers and legal status, we actually live in an age that has been much occupied with *confirming* human identity. The study of DNA and the mapping of the human genome are gradually telling us exactly who we are to the exclusion of everyone else. Not surprisingly, there has come along a recent literary version of this quest for incontrovertible identification. Professor Donald Foster, who rose to prominence with a convincing case for attributing a rediscovered funeral elegy to Shakespeare, has over the past several years been developing "a science of literary forensics" to help unmask figures as variously elusive as the Unabomber and the once-anonymous author of *Primary Colors*. In his new book, *Author Unknown*, Foster declares "that no two individuals write exactly the same way, using the same words in the same combinations, or with the same patterns of spelling and punctuation." Popular press accounts have overemphasized the role of the computer in his work, but before Foster begins his own crucial deductions, the computer *is* the dull workhorse that searches "billions of words in the time it takes you to read this sentence." In Foster's investigations, authorship proves not just "normative" and "autonomous," but irreducible.

Developments like this allow one to resist the temptation to say that the past dozen years have been bringing this book and the history of plagiarism full circle; that is, back to a pre–eighteenth century time before literary proprietorship and the cultural premium on originality had fully jelled. Even so, one cannot deny the entropic forces of the cyber world that seem to be pulling us in that direction. If one goes to the Web itself to research recent developments in plagiarism, one will trip across the URL for a little polemic by "Rodney P. Riegle, Ph.D.," a specialist in "virtual instruction" and the "paperless curriculum," entitled "The Death and Rebirth of Plagiarism." Dr. Riegle's bumptious argument has to be reckoned with: "plagiarism will die and be reborn with a positive connotation in the Information Age. What we now call plagiarism will become a basic skill. Instead of trying to prevent it, we will teach it . . . the student who can find, analyze, and display an elegant solution to a task possesses the skills necessary to prosper in the Information Age. Whether the solution is his/her own or someone else's is irrelevant."

Riegle delights in the old giving way to new ("Plagiarism is dead. Long live plagiarism"), blithely insisting that since "it is in society's best interest to get good ideas into the public arena . . . we will develop ways of rewarding scholars who have good ideas." And yet, he does not, it seems to me, face up to one central fact: the same human browser who gobbles up "content" (as we now like to call it) with no intention of footnoting, let alone paying for it, remains a creature of ego and ambition. He is the same fellow who's been registering and safeguarding his dot-com domain. He may enjoy "boundless textual promiscuity," but he doesn't want his own brainchildren being vulnerable to it.

For this reason, and despite all the cultural and technological change of the past dozen years, I am not ready to retract the last paragraph of this book's main text — those remarks about ego's "role as writerly propellant." In *The Western Canon*, Harold Bloom puts the idea better and more bluntly:

From Pindar to the present, the writer battling for canonicity may fight on behalf of a social class, as Pindar did for the aristocrats, but primarily each ambitious writer is out for himself alone and will frequently betray or neglect his class in order to advance his own interests, which center entirely upon *individuation.* . . . I rather doubt that any idealism, however belated, will change the entire basis of the Western psychology of creativity, male and female, from Hesiod's contest with Homer down to the agon between Dickinson and Elizabeth Bishop.

We are told that everyone can be an author now — thanks to Web-based outfits like iPublish — and customer-content postings on Amazon and barnesandnoble.com have made everybody into a critic. But how permanent are these new phenomena? Not every cyber-possibility catches on: I've been hearing about "hypertext" novels for ten years now, and I've yet to meet anybody who's read one. Some of our excitement over the Web's democratic possibilities seems bound to subside into a new elitism that seeks better instead of worse, that recognizes how, even before the Internet existed, literature's real problem was not that too few, but too many, books got published. Bloom, grouping his political and theory-ridden academic enemies into a single "School of Resentment," observes that "originality" is, for them, "a literary equivalent of such terms as individual enterprise, self-reliance, and competition . . ." He predicts, and awaits, "an aesthetic underground" that will restore both "the romance of reading" and respect for the original. As current critical forces maintain their chokehold on the academy, and as each new cyber innovation threatens to make thinking a species of gadgetry, the decriers of plagiarism may do well to think of themselves not as establishment scolds but as members of this underground Bloom is summoning. Having been ejected from what's now the mainstream, originality may, behind the bushes on the banks, begin to regroup — and emerge as a value that, once more, seems not just potent, but original.

T. M.

Westport, Connecticut
October, 2000

NOTES

SELECTED BIBLIOGRAPHY

INDEX

Notes

Preface

PAGE

xi   "Each day, citizens bludgeon": Michael Arlen, "Much Ado over a Plagiarist," *New York Times*, December 7, 1988, A31.

Chapter 1

PAGE

2   "The plagiarisms of Sterne": quoted in Howes, *Sterne*, 314.

3   "Imitation is natural": Aristotle, "The Poetics," *On Poetry and Style*, 7–8.

    "a reader moved": Saul Bellow, quoted by Tad Friend, "Dim Lights in the Big City," *Gentlemen's Quarterly*, December 1987, 301.

    "Reading Yeats turns": Virginia Woolf, *The Diary of Virginia Woolf*, vol. 3, 1925–1930 (New York: Penguin, 1982), 119.

    "Either follow tradition": quoted in Bate, *Criticism*, 53.

4   Saint Jerome's "addiction": Steinmann, *Saint Jerome and His Times*, 355.

    medieval monks: see Lindey, *Plagiarism and Originality*, 68.

    author-reader relationship: see Bronson, "Strange Relations: The Author and His Audience," in *Facets of the Enlightenment*, 302.

    Throughout the sixteenth century: see Salzman, *Plagiarism*, 10; and White, *Plagiarism and Imitation During the English Renaissance*, 201.

    "fellowship of authors": Sheavyn, *The Literary Profession in the Elizabethan Age*, 127.

5   "For nearly twenty years": White, 117.

6   "it is quite in keeping": Merton, *On the Shoulders of Giants*, 68.

    "to write in single sheets": quoted in Merton, 72.

"As apothecaries": Burton, *The Anatomy of Melancholy*, 23.

7   "As a good housewife": ibid., 24–25.

"A dwarf standing": ibid., 25.

"to give credit to his sources": Cooper, *The Art of the Compleat Angler*, 151.

8   Dryden was attacked: see Paull, *Literary Ethics*, 109; and Lindey, 80.

Milton, who classically urged: Paull, 108. See also entry on "Arts, Fraudulence," in *Encyclopaedia Britannica*, 15th ed., vol. 14, 136.

"now needed an apology": Paull, 110–111.

"is one of the chief privileges": Goldsmith, quoted in Crane, *Evidence for Authorship*, 276.

10   "could not bear to conceive": Johnson, *Lives of the English Poets*, 181.

"the delicacy with which": ibid.

"may be sometimes urged": Johnson, *The Rambler*, 394.

"there is a concurrence": ibid., 399.

"An inferior genius": ibid., 401.

11   "one of the most reproachful": Johnson, *The Idler and the Adventurer*, 425.

"Plagiarism. n.f. from plagiary": Johnson, *Dictionary*.

"All definitions": Johnson, *Rambler*, 395.

"wholly unoriginal": Landau, *Dictionaries*, 41.

12   "really new dictionary": ibid., 35.

"*Webster's Third* set the year": Burchfield, "Dictionaries New and Old," 14.

" 'In a company where I' ": Cross, *The Life and Times of Laurence Sterne*, 260.

13   "The world is ashamed": Sterne, *Tristram Shandy*, 554.

14   "He turned for solace": *Dictionary of National Biography*, vol. 18, 1093.

"With the exception of Volume IX": Cash, *Laurence Sterne*, vol. 2, 94.

15   Johnson's friend Mrs. Thrale: Howes, *Yorick and the Critics*, 81.

attention paid to obstetrics: ibid., 81–82.

"Tho' all the pieces": Ferriar, Advertisement to *Illustrations of Sterne*.

"from Rabelais, Sterne": Ferriar, 24.

16   "lively extravagancies": ibid., 31.

may first have been put in Sterne's hand: Yoseloff, *A Fellow of Infinite Jest*, 16.

"I had often wondered": Ferriar, 56–57.

"Shall we forever": Sterne, quoted by Ferriar, 66.

17   "As apothecaries": Burton, quoted by Ferriar, 67.

"Although no commonplace books": Cash, vol. 2, 73.

"Dr. Ferriar, with an understatement": Watkins, *Perilous Balance*, 155.

"This is well rallied": Ferriar, 73.

18   " 'T is an inevitable chance": Sterne, quoted by Ferriar, 74.
      " 'Tis an inevitable chance": Burton, quoted by Ferriar, 74.
      "It has been fashionable of late": Howes, *Sterne,* 283.
      "It was observed to me": Ferriar, 87.
      "The use which Sterne made": ibid., 98–99.

19   "Sterne deliberately seeded": Jackson, "Sterne, Burton, and Fer-
      riar," 458.
      "He must have been aware": ibid.
      "Sterne was evidently content": ibid.
      "The *Anatomy* has been known": ibid., 463.
      "Sterne's readers do not expect": ibid, 465.
      "In an indirect way": ibid., 468.

20   wrote David Garrick a letter: see Cash, vol. 2, 4, and Yoseloff,
      97.
      As Merton . . . points out: Merton, 8.
      as even Jackson would admit: Jackson, 466–467.
      Thackeray would claim: Thackeray, *The English Humorists of the
      Eighteenth Century,* 222.
      True, most preachers preach: Thomson, *Wild Excursions,* 150–
      151.
      "venial sin": Cash, vol. 2, 40.
      "For forming his style as a preacher": Cross, 140.

21   "with [Sterne] is no more": Watkins, 154.
      letters he wrote: ibid.
      "Who can say how many": Joyce, *Finnegans Wake,* 181–182.
      "It would have been common": Cash, vol. 2, 22–23.
      "it was with the success": Stedmond, "Genre and *Tristram
      Shandy,*" 48.

22   "the first English author": Braudy, *The Frenzy of Renown,* 13.
      an act of prim penitence: see Cash, vol. 2, 319, and Yoseloff,
      209.
      Legends of his dying: Cash, vol. 2, 339.
      On March 22, 1768: ibid., 328.
      the hangman in nearby Tyburn: see Thomson, 278–279.
      "In March 1769": ibid., 280.
      It was later reported: ibid.

23   One of the skulls: Cash, vol. 2, 354.
      "Most students of Sterne": ibid., xv.
      "Gross plagiarism may consist": Hazlitt, quoted in Howes, *Yorick
      and the Critics,* 113.
      "mocks, in the figure": Cash, vol. 1, 219.
      "To make a public show": Cash, vol. 2, 276.
      "not to be *fed*": quoted in Cash, vol. 2, 1.
      "My master": quoted in Yoseloff, 14.

24   "in the Size and Manner": Cash, vol. 2, 113.
      "He got Honour": quoted in Cash, vol. 2, 100. See also Yoseloff,

138–139.

"The conscience had taken": Bate, *The Burden of the Past and the English Poet*, 105.

"the fearful legacy": ibid., 107.

"clear imaginative space": Bloom, *The Anxiety of Influence*, 5.

"The death of poetry": ibid., 10.

25   "The imagination": Bowen, "Out of a Book," in *Collected Impressions*, 268–269.

"I wanted to escape": Oates, quoted in *New York Times*, February 10, 1987, C17.

"What the critic calls": Wilde, quoted in Ellmann, *Oscar Wilde*, 82.

26   "One of the surest": Eliot, "Philip Massinger," in *Selected Essays, 1917–1932*, 182.

"This is, on Massinger's part": ibid., 183.

"One imitates what one loves": Rorem, quoted in Peyser, "Ned Rorem Delivers a Solo," 21.

"I am a thief": Graham, *The Notebooks of Martha Graham*, 303.

"Weaker talents idealize": Bloom, 5.

27   "on a certain oscillation": Coleridge, "On the Distinctions," in *Literary Remains*, vol. 1, 141.

"Coleridge obliged": Dorothy Wordsworth, *Home at Grasmere*, 65.

"A heart-rending letter": ibid., 134.

28   "I was affected with them": ibid., 210.

"a man, whose severities": Coleridge, *Biographia Literaria*, 161.

All citations of the *BL* are from the 1985 *Oxford Authors* edition of Coleridge, edited by H. J. Jackson.

"From causes": ibid.

great quantities of contemporary German books: Fruman, *Coleridge*, 135.

29   "Perhaps the most important": Coleridge, "On the Distinctions," in *Literary Remains*, vol. 1, 131.

while walking over rough ground: Jacox, *Aspects of Authorship*, 18.

"His unpublished marginalia": Haney, "Coleridge the Commentator," in *Coleridge*, ed. Blunden and Griggs, 109.

more than six hundred books: ibid.

"The notebooks represent": Hamilton, *Coleridge's Poetics*, 119.

always be available the defense: see excerpt from Notebooks, August 1826, pp. 558–559 of the *Oxford Authors* edition.

30   "The lectures entitled": Helmholtz, *The Indebtedness of Samuel Taylor Coleridge to August Wilhelm Von Schlegel*, 322.

"In every instance": Fruman, 71.

like Gail Sheehy and John Gardner: see "Gail Sheehy," *Contemporary Authors*, New Revision Series, vol. 1 (1981), 591; and "Theft or 'Paraphrase'?" *Newsweek*, April 10, 1978, 92–94.

"be happiness and honor enough": Coleridge, *Biographia Literaria*, 236.

31   "It is undeniable": De Quincey, "Plagiarism," in *New Essays by De Quincey*, 181.

"The amount of material": Bate, *Coleridge*, 132n. See also Shaw, 335.

Professor James F. Ferrier: Fruman, 76.

"genial coincidence": ibid., 86.

"Be not charged on me": Coleridge, *Biographia Literaria*, 237.

32   "I have laid too many eggs": ibid., 181.

"It is doubtful whether": Fruman, 98.

"statements concerning intellectual integrity": ibid., 82.

"The large verbal borrowings": Shawcross, Introduction to Coleridge, *Biographia Literaria*, vol. 1, lx.

"he had gone too far": Quiller-Couch, Introduction to Sampson edition of *Biographia Literaria*, xxix.

"A narrow moralist": Ozick, *The Messiah of Stockholm*, 63.

33   "a mode of composition": McFarland, quoted in Lefebure, *Samuel Taylor Coleridge*, 488.

"It was, I believe": McFarland, *Romanticism and the Forms of Ruin*, 126.

"falsified the chronology": Fruman, 74.

"a brilliant improvisation": ibid., 99.

"self-excuses of an articulate junkie": Lefebure, 489.

"a desperate need": ibid., 488.

The morphine: ibid., 489.

"He was conscious": Shawcross, Introduction to Coleridge, *Biographia Literaria*, vol 1, lxiv.

idea for *Childe Harold:* Helmholtz, 352–353.

34   "Chapter XII is far from necessary": Bate, *Coleridge*, 136.

"to compose anything new": Coleridge, quoted in Lefebure, 471.

"To transcribe is the utmost": ibid.

"a Delver in the unwholesome": ibid.

" 'A delver in the unwholesome' ": Lefebure, 471.

"desire to be caught": Shaw, 330.

debt and drugs: see Lefebure, 488–489.

Bate reminds us: Bate, *Coleridge*, 138.

Penelope Gilliatt was caught: see *New York Times*, May 12, 1979, 12.

35   "a haphazard and irresponsible way": Graves, *The Crowning Privilege*, 207.

"No one with sensibility": ibid.

"happier plagiarist": Bate, *Coleridge*, 136; see Shaw, 330–332.

"patron saint of those artists": Connolly, "On Being Won Over to Coleridge," in *Previous Convictions*, 158.

"I was followed": Coleridge, quoted in Connolly, 158.

"a guilt dream": Connolly, 158.

"The guilt-laden Coleridge": Bate, *Coleridge*, 136.

"candour and considerable generosity": Holmes, *Coleridge*, 57.

"problem": Bate and Engell, Introduction to Coleridge, *Biographia Literaria*, cxv, cxiv.

"the long history": ibid., cxv.

"vindictive": ibid.

36 "The editors of the present": ibid.

Sterne's daughter Lydia: Cash, vol. 2, 352.

"there was no alternative": Bate and Engell, cxvi.

"Coleridge's use of German books": ibid.

"A maximum of a quarter": ibid., cxvii.

"fascinating": ibid., cxix, cxxiv, cxxvi.

"the matter is important": ibid., cxviii.

"present the facts": ibid.

37 "We are not dealing": ibid., cxx.

"*every work* of Schelling": ibid., cxxi.

"That most scholars": Fruman, 105.

"interests of slave": Stout, *Plot It Yourself*, 5.

"diction, syntax, paragraphing": ibid., 47.

"A clever man": ibid., 23.

"You can't say": ibid., 167.

"prodigies of sagacity": ibid., 168.

"plagiarism upside down": ibid., 15.

"from his tone": ibid., 152.

Wolfe's creator, Rex Stout: Goldsborough's Nero Wolfe mystery *Death on Deadline* (1987) thanks the Stout estate "for its cooperation and encouragement."

Stout's activity: McAleer, *Rex Stout*, 407–408.

39 Statute of Anne: Bloom, *Samuel Johnson in Grub Street*, 207ff.

"leave to whisper": Dickens quoted in Welsh, *From Copyright to Copperfield*, 32.

"I hope the time": ibid., 31.

40 "a knight errant": ibid., 36.

"to realize subjectively": ibid., 39.

Chapter 2

42 "The compiler of": Walsh, *Handy-Book of Literary Curiosities*, 894.

43 "To be born": Hammet, in Reade, *Plays by Charles Reade*, 26.

adapted it from the French: Elwin, *Charles Reade*, 73.

44 "I want to show": Reade, quoted in Elwin, 84.

"Who can refrain": Elwin, 41.

"The personal philosophy": Burns, *Charles Reade*, 63.

45 "F. Fabulae verae/ Faces": Sutcliffe, "Charles Reade's Note-books," 107.

"position as the earliest": ibid., 64.

"Charles Reade's note-books": Baker, *The History of the English*

Novel, vol. 7, 77.

46   "All fiction worth a button": Reade, Preface to *A Simpleton,* v.

"Could Willy Sutton": Pynchon, Introduction to *Slow Learner,* xxviii.

"some grounding in human reality": ibid.

"fascinating topic": ibid., xxvii.

"controversial, since it": Oates, "The Union Justified the Means," 37.

47   "Mr. Boyle has": Reade, Preface to *A Simpleton,* vi.

"has lately been objected": ibid., v.

"it does not matter": ibid.

"It was never my way": Reade, *The Autobiography of a Thief and Other Stories,* 9.

"He works too palpably": Dawson, *The Makers of English Fiction,* 167.

48   "He wrote one beautiful book": Wilde, "The Decay of Lying," in *De Profundis and Other Writings,* 66.

"the charm of useless knowledge": Orwell, "Charles Reade," in *My Country Right or Left,* 34.

"a lively narrative gift": ibid.

"a wonderful contriver of plots": ibid., 36.

49   acquired the knack for novel-writing: Anonymous, "Madame Charles Reybaud," *Temple Bar,* 72.

"cette femme spirituelle": Montégut, "Romanciers et Ecrivains Contemporains: Madame Charles Reybaud," 881.

"that licence and indelicacy": "The Writings of Madame Charles Reybaud," *Dublin University Magazine* 40, 236 (August 1852), 237.

"One of her characteristics": ibid., 235.

"sour temper": Reybaud, *Where Shall He Find Her?,* trans. I.D.A., 24. (The subsequent fourteen quotations in the text are also from this edition, in which Malepeire is rendered as Malepire and Marion as Marian.)

52   *"Ses héros traversent":* Montégut, 895.

"un chapitre inédit": ibid., 898.

53   the author's *chef d'oeuvre:* ibid., 887.

"modeste, patiente, sachant": ibid., 900.

"French literature has rarely": "The Writings of Madame Charles Reybaud," *Dublin University Magazine,* 234.

"le vent comme il souffle": Montégut, 900.

54   "The present writer": Anonymous, "Madame Charles Reybaud," *Temple Bar,* 64.

"advance of a Briton's": Reade, *The Eighth Commandment,* 7.

"Satanic": ibid., 87.

"The proviso runs thus": ibid., 8.

55   "part under this unjust equity": ibid., 13.

"In a nation of twenty millions": ibid., 89.

"It was not to his advantage": Hammet, in Reade, *Plays,* 28.

"Out of every twenty": Reade, *Eighth Commandment*, 49.

56 "never saw *Le Portefeuille Rouge*": Reade, "The Sham Sample Swindle," in *Readiana*, 292.

"For once, it would seem": Burns, 271.

"Dear Trollope": Reade, quoted in Smith, *Charles Reade*, 45.

57 "There is no writer": Trollope, *An Autobiography*, 212.

"He has always left": ibid., 213.

"Collins's view": Elwin, 247.

"there was some little wit": Trollope, 213.

"Georgy Porgy's": quoted in Elwin, 265.

58 "it must be admitted": Eliot, "The Wasp Credited with the Honeycomb," in *Impressions of Theophrastus Such*, 163.

"Having wasted too many years": Reade, quoted in Turner, *The Making of "The Cloister and the Hearth,"* 4.

moved into 2 Albert Terrace: Burns, 285.

"With the proceeds": Reade, quoted by Hammet, in Reade, *Plays*, 21.

59 "laid the first stone": Reade, "The Rights and Wrongs of Authors," in *Readiana*, 151.

"a tax on readers": Macaulay quoted by Reade, "Rights and Wrongs," 190.

"through its effects": Reade, "Rights and Wrongs," 162.

"They can bubble": Reade quoted in Quinn, *Charles Reade*, 30.

60 "I am now seventy": Reade, "The Picture," in *The Jilt & c*, 167.

61 "hollow-eyed" and "wrinkled": ibid., 168.

" 'She was my betrothed!' ": ibid., 174.

"I found her reading": ibid., 183.

"Mademoiselle de Groucy": ibid., 191.

"*To the Editor*": J.B.S., *Literary World*, 15:5 (March 8, 1884), 80.

62 "Why the Harpers": *Literary World*, 15:3 (February 9, 1884), 46.

"icy reserve": "What the Papers Revealed," *St. James's Magazine*, 20 (August-November, 1867), 88.

"enslaved": ibid., 89.

63 "a history of the first French revolution": ibid.

" 'From this hour' ": ibid., 94.

64 "most repulsive sample": ibid., 82.

"faithful old monster": ibid., 84.

"seamed and scarred": ibid., 83.

65 "striking resemblances between": *Nation*, February 28, 1884, 189.

"The plot, the essential phrases": Gayley, *Nation*, March 13, 1884, 232.

66 "During my college life, rather more than thirty": *Month*, July 1869, 60.

67 "During my college life, some thirty": Reybaud, 9.

"certainly the ugliest creature": *Month*, July 1869, 61.

"perhaps the ugliest creature": Reybaud, 9.

"était bien": Reybaud, "Mlle. de Malepeire," *Revue des Deux Mondes,* 1050.

"During my college life, rather more than thirty": "The Portrait In My Uncle's Dining-room," *Littell's Living Age,* November 6, 1869, 362.

68   "the same story": Gayley, 232.

"not essential": ibid.

69   "puts 'The Portrait' ": ibid.

"the American Catalogue": ibid.

"Vases of Japan China": "The Portrait," quoted by Gayley, 232.

"Chinese vases five feet high": "The Picture," quoted by Gayley, 232.

"the original substance": Gayley, 232.

"bear in mind": ibid.

70   "This is the kiss": "The Godmother's Gift," *Harper's,* April 1884, 687.

"Rot on your dunghill": Reade, "The Picture," *The Jilt & c.,* 201.

"Since you can fall": ibid., 192.

71   "an instrument ladies used": ibid., 202.

"I gave up father": ibid., 204.

"May I venture": E. J. Marshall, *Academy,* March 29, 1884, 224.

"M. Hachette, a French publisher": Reade, *The Eighth Commandment,* 124.

72   "I might quote": Marshall, *Academy,* March 29, 1884, 225.

"having traced this multiform story": editor's note, *Academy,* March 29, 1884, 225.

"People Who Are Talked About": *New York Times,* March 30, 1884, 1–2.

A wit, a feminist: C. Vann Woodward and Elisabeth Muhlenfeld, Introduction to Chesnut, *The Private Mary Chesnut,* xxiii.

73   "to say a word": Mary Chesnut, *Literary World,* April 5, 1884, 115.

74   "certainly": "Mademoiselle de Malepeire," *Albion,* 35 (January 3, 1857), 1.

"About thirty years since": ibid.

"Mr. Charles Reade": Chesnut, *Literary World,* April 5, 1884, 116.

She was slowed: Woodward and Muhlenfeld, in Chesnut, xxx-xxxi.

"she substantially completed": ibid., xxxi.

75   "She turned third-person": ibid., xxi.

"one of the most audacious": Lynn, quoted by Woodward and Muhlenfeld in Chesnut, xv.

"whether it be": Gayley, 232.

76   "merchants, not cleptomaniacs": Reade, *Eighth Commandment,* 39.

"Would it have been": ibid., 25.

Katherine Mansfield: see Claire Tomalin, *Katherine Mansfield: A*

Life (New York: Knopf, 1988), 207–211.

77   "about an hour every day": H. V. Reade, letter to London Library, inserted in notebook 13 (Sutcliffe no. III.5).

78   "To restore a commonplace": Reade, notebook 20, London Library (Sutcliffe no. IV.7).
"Generation spontaneous": ibid.
"Each old model story": notebook 17, London Library (Sutcliffe no. IV.4), 23.
"Having often given": ibid., 83.
"Balzac chez lui": ibid., 112.
"Murder will out": ibid., 127.
"If lost on Railway": ibid., inscribed on back of marbled endpaper.

79   "Conscience a drama": quoted by Sutcliffe, "Charles Reade's Notebooks," *Studies in Philology*, 103.
"This is a good story": notebook 29, London Library (Sutcliffe no. IV.16).
"Reade's abridgments": notebook 20, London Library (Sutcliffe no. IV.7).
"abridgement swindle": Reade, *Eighth Commandment*, 152.

80   "He returned to": Elwin, 354.
"The literary pirate": Reade, *Eighth Commandment*, 49.
"Out of every twenty": ibid.

81   "racking cough": Reade and Reade, *Charles Reade*, 434.
"Moral, like physical disease": Reade, *Eighth Commandment*, 47.

82   "I should have sent": Reade, letter to Harper & Bros., January 1, 1881 (Morgan Library). The subsequent three quotations in the text are also from this letter.

83   "wind spasms": Reade, letter to Henry Mills Alden, July 8, 1883 (Morgan Library).
"been so long unable": ibid.
"Unfortunately I wrote": ibid.
"contempt for those": Reade, "The Picture," in *The Jilt & c.*, 185.

84   "happy to tell": Reade, letter to Alden, August 10, 1883 (Morgan Library).
"feeble and tired": John Coleman, quoted in Elwin, 357.
"James Payn met": Elwin, 357–358.
"Thirty years ago": Reade, letter to Harper & Bros., December 4, 1883 (Morgan Library).
"again broke faith": ibid.
"published before Easter": Reade, letter to Alden, Harper & Bros., January 8, 1884 (Morgan Library).

85   study was lined with mirrors: Burns, 20.
"suicidal kleptomania": Reade, "Rights and Wrongs," in *Readiana*, 188.
" 'Cleptomania' is a term": Reade, *Eighth Commandment*, 215; see also Shaw, "Plagiary," 332.

"the social crime": Shaw, "Plagiary," 332.
"evident wish to be detected": ibid.
86 "distrust of the creative": Smith, 153.
"argues a strange": Howells, "The Psychology of Plagiarism," in *Literature and Life*, 277.
"He means to be": Trollope, 212.
like the school child: incident recounted in letter to author from Mrs. Grace Hogarth, July 20, 1987.
"A book-pirate may": Reade, *Eighth Commandment*, 53.
87 "He was able": Burns, 308.
"protesting, arguing, inquiring": Elwin, 359.
"I have no hope": Reade, quoted in Elwin, 359.
"added nothing to": Littledale, obituary for Charles Reade, *Academy*, April 19, 1884, 278.
"Granted that": ibid., 277.
88 out of print: "Madame Charles Reybaud," *Temple Bar*, 70.
"*Il n'y a pas*": ibid., 74.

Chapter 3

89 "The best thing": Jason Epstein, quoted in *New York*, December 23–30, 1985, 47.
"Twice in the last": Jacob Epstein, *Wild Oats*, 114.
"Same topic": ibid.
"a computer in New Jersey": ibid., 115.
90 "Term Paper Blues?": ad for Research Assistance, *Rolling Stone*, January 16, 1986, 51.
"Our 306-page catalog": ibid.
"GOOD LUCK IN YOUR ENDEAVORS": "Catalog of Research and Writing Services," Authors' Research Services, 1985, i.
"all orders are": ibid.
"Our business thrives": ibid.
"staff of professional writers": ibid.
"virtual library": ad for Research Assistance, *Rolling Stone*, January 16, 1986, 51.
91 "Lawrence Sterne's": "Catalog of Research and Writing Services," Authors' Research Services, 86.
"Two Centuries of Inspiration": ibid.
"indicates the study": ibid., i.
92 no one's Hamlet: See Margaret Macdonald, "Some Distinctive Features of Arguments Used in Criticism of the Arts," in *Problems in Aesthetics*, edited by Morris Weitz (New York: Macmillan, 1970), 862–863.
"Hamlet: Madness or melancholia?": "Catalog of Research and Writing Services," 90.
93 "Is There a FAST": "Helpful Research & Writing Tips," Au-

thors' Research Services, 2. (The subsequent four quotations are
from this same pamphlet.)

94   Termpapers Unlimited: see *New York Times,* July 10, 1971, 25.

"A sad byproduct": quoted in Don Hulbert, "The Term-Paper
Ghosts Still Haunt the College Scene," *New York Times,* November 16, 1980, XII, 21.

"Some students now": ibid.

"Knowledge is not": quoted ibid.

"Walking down the street": Epstein, 116.

95   "from time to time": This and all subsequent quotations from
Colton Johnson are from his interview with the author, February
12, 1987.

96   "A friend of mine": see Edith Skom, "Quite a Rather Bad Little
Crime," *AAHE Bulletin* 34, 2 (October 1986), 3–7.

97   "We convicted a student": This and subsequent quotations are
from author's interview with Colton Johnson, February 12,
1987. Since Dean Johnson's interview with the author, the Vassar
system has been computerized. But the old "asterisk" is now
visible on the display terminal in the dean's office whenever he
calls up the record of a student convicted by the Academic Panel.

99   "from a Latin word": DeMaria, *Originality and Attribution,* 1.

"is, after all, theft": ibid., 1–2.

"In sounding great": quoted in Walsh, 892.

always vigilant Charles Reade: see notebook 25, London Library
(Sutcliffe no. IV.12).

"occurs when a student": DeMaria, 11. (The subsequent three
quotations are also from this source.)

100   "Stanford University said today": "Plagiarism Book Is Plagiarized," *New York Times,* June 6, 1980, 28.

101   "hadn't succumbed": Epstein, 79.

"Why, Billy wondered": ibid., 36.

"Billy started towards her": ibid., 205.

102   "immediacy": Anne Tyler, "Two Novels: Growing Up," *New York
Times Book Review,* June 17, 1979, 14.

"distance": Daphne Merkin, "Growing Up in America," *New
Leader,* June 4, 1979, 16.

"unfaltering": Tyler, 14.

"tremendous future promise": Josh Rubins, "Books in Brief:
Wild Oats," *Saturday Review,* June 23, 1979, 44.

"At the time": Jason Epstein, "Living in New York," *New York
Review of Books,* January 6, 1966, 14.

"literary or rhetorical work": Description of Curtis Prize in "English Department Prizes 1987," Yale University English Department, p. 2.

103   "The novel's material": Blake Morrison, "On a 'Guilt-Go-Round,' " *New Statesman,* February 22, 1980, 289.

"no bad omen": Stephen Fender, "The Generation Game," *Times*

Literary Supplement, February 22, 1980, 202.

"Some months ago": Amis, "A Tale of Two Novels," *Observer,* October 19, 1980, 26. All subsequent quotations concerning Amis's comparison are from this source, unless otherwise noted.

105   "a little shit": quoted by Charles Michener, "Britain's Brat of Letters," *Esquire,* November 1986, 136.

"reluctant to do anything": Corlies Smith, interview with author, April 16, 1987.

"All I wanted to do": Martin Amis, telephone interview with author, May 20, 1987.

106   "There was no reason": Amis, *The Rachel Papers,* 19. (The subsequent thirteen quotations in the text are also from this book.)

108   "described with the detached": Clive Jordan, *Encounter,* February 1974, 64.

"not really one": Grace Glueck, *New York Times Book Review,* May 26, 1974, 4.

"Perhaps the best": Eliot Fremont-Smith, *New York,* April 29, 1974, 76.

"Some wildly funny lines": Pearl K. Bell, "A Surfeit of Sex," *New Leader,* May 13, 1974, 20.

"nasty, British and short": Karl Miller, *New York Review of Books,* July 18, 1974, 26.

"read nothing but": Kingsley Amis, quoted in Michener, 110.

"flirted . . . with expulsion": Martin Amis, "Tough Nut to Crack," *Observer,* October 31, 1982, 27.

109   "I suppose the worst": ibid.

"writing malarial": Amis, contribution to *My Oxford, My Cambridge,* 207.

"eighty-four hours": ibid., 205.

"lone sconce-dreading dinners": ibid.

"gnome": ibid., 212.

110   "Reached in Manhattan": Susan Heller Anderson, "New Novelist Is Called a Plagiarist," *New York Times,* October 21, 1980, C7.

Amis still maintains: Martin Amis, telephone interview with author, May 20, 1987.

"images and phrases": Jacob Epstein, letter to *Observer,* October 26, 1980, 32.

"There aren't 13 bits": Martin Amis, quoted in Susan Heller Anderson, "Writer Apologizes for Plagiarism," *New York Times,* October 27, 1980, C5.

"somehow pasted in": Jacob Epstein, letter to *Observer,* October 26, 1980, 32.

111   "I do not know": ibid.

"Somewhere, somebody": Alex Haley, quoted in Arnold H. Lubasch, "Haley Testifies He Wrote All Major Parts of 'Roots',"

New York Times, November 28, 1978.

"It seems that": "Princess defended on plagiarised book charge," *Irish Independent*, September 22, 1986, 20.

112   *"Question:* What if": Noble and Noble, *Steal This Plot*, 202.

"it's pretty clear": ibid., 194.

"Three months in": ibid.

113   "Mark at first": quoted by Martin Amis, *Observer*, 26. See *Wild Oats*, 97–98.

"verbal plagiarist": Shaw, 331.

"inadvertent, yet somehow purposeful": ibid.

"An accusation of": ibid., 329.

114   the press exaggerated: Lynn Nesbit, letter to author, April 9, 1987.

"It was blown out": Corlies Smith, telephone interview with author, April 16, 1987.

"Life seems to be imitating": "Intelligencer," *New York*, November 3, 1980, 11.

"Against the Grain": *New York Times*, October 26, 1980, section 4, 9.

"Fleming Arleutter": Rosen, "Epping," 14.

115   110,000 copies: "Why Writers Plagiarize," *Newsweek*, November 3, 1980, 62.

"one book that didn't": Corlies Smith, telephone interview with author, April 16, 1987.

Gail Sheehy: see Rosen, "Epping," 13–14.

"hundreds of thousands": Arnold H. Lubasch, " 'Roots' Plagiarism Suit Is Settled," *New York Times*, December 15, 1978, A1.

"a very special case": Martin Amis, telephone interview with author, May 20, 1987.

"extra tough": ibid.

"still not sure": ibid.

"uncontrollable nature": Amis, *The Moronic Inferno*, 28.

"multiple rapists": ibid., 29.

"When success happens": ibid., 136.

"American writers tend": ibid., 39.

"In England writers": ibid.

116   "It's not a very fat": Kingsley Amis, in Plimpton, *Writers at Work*, 182.

"always two books": Robert Louis Stevenson, quoted in Matthews, "The Duty of Imitation," in *Gateways to Literature*, 79–80.

117   "Under what is known": Jason Epstein, *The Great Conspiracy Trial*, 92–93.

"was still in [his] mind": Pinckney, "Spooking Plagiarism," 47.

"In reading the two books": ibid.

"He is not a criminal": ibid., 49.

118   "No plagiarist can excuse": opinion of Learned Hand in *Sheldon v. Metro-Goldwyn Pictures Corp.*, quoted in Condren Affidavit in

Kornfeld v. CBS, Inc., et al. See Chapter 5).

"I cannot excuse": Pinckney, 49. (The subsequent four quotations in the text are also from this source.)

119 "to see the similarities": Chesterton, "On Literary Parallels," in *Come to Think of It*, 25.

"trouble is serious": Pinckney, 47. (The subsequent five quotations in the text are also from this source.)

120 between Poe and the pseudonymous "Outis": The complex history of Poe's accusations against Longfellow, occasionally wild and often substantial, is well documented in Moss, *Poe's Literary Battles*.

"all literary history": Poe, "The Longfellow War," in *Complete Works*, vol. 12, 106.

"suspicion of malevolence": ibid., 104.

"When [it] is committed": ibid., 54.

"One cannot strike": Poe, quoted by Moss, 181.

"fascinatingly perverse": Amis, "A Tale of Two Novels," 26.

"cruel and vindictive": Jacob Epstein, quoted in *Newsweek*, November 3, 1980, 62.

"need for public punishment": Arnold Cooper, quoted in *Newsweek*, November 3, 1980, 62.

121 "tremulousness": see Amis, "A Tale of Two Novels," 26 ("he said tremulously").

"finally achieve a great success": Dr. Robert Michels, quoted in *New York Times*, May 19, 1987, C5.

"both in his evident wish": Shaw, "Plagiary," 332.

"tend to suffer": ibid., 333.

"developed an obsession": Whitehead, *This Solemn Mockery*, 138.

"the amateur literary detective": Matthews "The Ethics of Plagiarism," in *Pen and Ink*, 27.

"a ready acceptance": ibid., 29.

122 "finite": ibid., 32.

"in any discussion": ibid., 38.

"cases of absolute necessity": ibid., 28.

"It is plagiarism": ibid., 40.

"the second comer": ibid., 40–41.

"He has been accused": Bayley, "Looking In on Pushkin," 36.

123 "It wasn't a case": Amis, "The D. M. Thomas Phenomenon," 124.

"Even if Mr. Greene": William Jovanovich, quoted in *New York Times*, May 5, 1972, 34.

"The artist can be individual": Matthews, "Duty of Imitation," 85.

124 "how sentences worked": Joan Didion, quoted in Plimpton, *Writers at Work*, 343.

"to see how writers": Jacob Epstein, quoted in *New York Times*, October 28, 1980, C5.

"First, stop confusing": Mallon, "Rereading One's Diaries," *Vassar Quarterly,* Fall 1985, 9.

125 "The only way not": Legouvé, quoted by Matthews, "Duty of Imitation," 83.

"the risk of verbal infection": Perelman, *Don't Tread On Me,* 109.

126 "sent a gracious reply": Robinson, *Willa,* 239.

"recognize a portion": Zelda Fitzgerald quoted in Lindey, *Plagiarism and Originality,* 105.

Kenneth Halliwell: see Lahr, *Prick Up Your Ears,* 186.

127 "many critics reviewing": Capote, *The Dogs Bark,* 338.

128 "The gross national product": quoted in *New York Times,* September 16, 1987, D30.

" 'Then it don't matter' ": Steinbeck, quoted in *National Review,* October 23, 1987, 14.

129 "There will be other": Joseph Biden, quoted ibid.

"make certain that": Paul G. Kirk, quoted in *New York Times,* October 2, 1987, A16.

"spreading vicious truths": *New York Times* editorial, October 2, 1987, A34.

"tempest-in-a-teapot": Larry Rasky, quoted in *New York Times,* September 16, 1987, 1.

blame Pat Caddell: see Maureen Dowd and Alessandra Staley, "Pat Caddell Says He Wants a Revolution," *GQ,* December 1987, 352.

"the man who I guess I admire": Joseph Biden, quoted in *New York Times,* September 16, 1987, D30.

130 "It is now the moment": Oliver Wendell Holmes, quoted in *New York Times,* September 21, 1987, A19.

used by Warren Harding: *New York Times,* September 21, 1987, A19.

"Father, I have shoes on": see *New York Post,* March 1, 1988, 6, and *American Spectator,* March 1988, 7.

"Leadership that's working": *New York Post,* August 20, 1986, 6.

"I told him": Biden, quoted in *New York Times,* January 13, 1988, D26.

131 "His first 'effusion' ": Jacox, *Aspects of Authorship,* 35.

"itch to emulate": Plath, *The Journals of Sylvia Plath,* 201.

"I dimly would like": ibid., 251.

"the desire to be thought clever": Kingsley Amis in Plimpton, *Writers at Work,* 198.

"for a new short story": Martin Amis, *New York Times Book Review,* December 8, 1985, 47.

132 "astonish his relations": Lang, *How to Fail in Literature,* 46.

"When you are accused": ibid., 76–77.

"a certain amount of 'superwoman' publicity": Klass, "Turning My Words Against Me," 46. (The subsequent nine quotations are from this essay.)

135 "had heard of Martin Amis": Amis, *Money,* 218.

"no complaints": Martin Amis, telephone interview with author, May 20, 1987.

"vaguely tarred": ibid.

"If he were my kid": *Newsweek,* November 3, 1980, 62.

"mysterous old gentleman": see Mair, *The Fourth Forger,* 85–102.

136 "The Vortigern I wrote": ibid., 209.

"became distressed about": Nobile, *Intellectual Skywriting,* 92.

137 "pretty much decided to publish": Jason Epstein, quoted in *New York Times,* September 13, 1984, C17.

"I have tried": ibid., November 2, 1984, C28.

"was not plagiarism": Jason Epstein, quoted in *Newsweek,* November 3, 1980, 62.

"a flagrant case": Kingsley Amis, quoted in *Newsweek,* November 3, 1980, 62.

138 "terrible compulsive *vividness*": ibid., quoted in *Esquire,* November 1986, 142.

"It's too ornate": ibid., 140.

"*Turds, ee-bait*": Amis, *Moronic Inferno,* 34.

"Naturally, them being": *Rachel Papers,* 186.

"Anyone who has read": *Einstein's Monsters,* 15.

"and much else": *Moronic Inferno,* x.

139 "May I take": *Einstein's Monsters,* Author's Note.

"not really": Martin Amis, telephone interview with author, May 20, 1987.

"have kept [his] mouth shut": ibid.

"You're asking for trouble": ibid.

"Film-makers today": *Moronic Inferno,* 154.

140 the writer Proust said: see Lawrence Grobel, *Conversations with Capote,* 146.

"I should have worked harder": *Moronic Inferno,* x.

"how President Kennedy": *Einstein's Monsters,* 64.

"cranks, readers of the *National Inquirer,*" *Invasion of the Space Invaders,* 43.

141 "Situation comedy": Usborne, *Wodehouse at Work,* 39.

"*Ice in the Bedroom*": ibid., 38.

"In the North": Lemann, "The Trials and Jubilations of Governor Edwin Edwards," *Esquire,* May 1987, 80.

142 "being on a train": Lemann, "Dixie in Manhattan," 69.

143 "It ruined his life": remark made anonymously to author, September 14, 1985.

"This show is about": Alan Rachins, quoted in "Laying Down the Law," *People,* February 1, 1987, 77–78.

Chapter 4

146 Born in 1946: entry for Jayme Sokolow, *Dictionary of American*

Scholars, 8th ed., vol. 1, 720 (New York, 1982). (Jayme Sokolow refused to be interviewed for this book.)

"the way he described": author's interview with James Brink, December 6, 1986, hereafter cited as Brink interview.

147   "What this department needs": quoted during Brink interview.

"was not a harmonious department": author's telephone interview with John Wunder, January 4, 1987, hereafter cited as Wunder interview.

"the point man": ibid.

"very much disapproved": ibid.

"He used to do his research": Brink interview.

"I think in the back of my mind": letter to author from Allan J. Kuethe, January 5, 1987, hereafter cited as Kuethe letter.

148   "increasingly abusive": ibid.

"had a reputation": author's interview with Otto Nelson, December 9, 1986, hereafter cited as Nelson interview.

"I had been a great champion": Brink interview.

"had a kind of ruthless presence": Author's interview with Jeffrey Smitten, December 8, 1986, hereafter cited as Smitten interview.

149   "everyone had geared up": Wunder interview.

"certainty": Kuethe letter.

"who set the historian's task": Tuchman, *Practicing History,* 18.

"In his dramas": Gooch, *History and Historians in the Nineteenth Century,* 97.

"Franklin played a crucial role": Sokolow, " 'Arriving at Moral Perfection,' " 432.

150   "Sokolow's assertion that Franklin": Walsh, "On the Putative Influence of Benjamin Franklin on Tolstoi," 309.

"opinions about this purported relationship": ibid., 306.

151   "I hope you haven't lent him": author's interview with Jacquelin Collins, December 9, 1986, hereafter cited as Collins interview.

"the clearest case of plagiarism": letter from Lawrence Foster to Stephen Nissenbaum, December 18, 1980.

152   "somewhat unsettling telephone conversation": letter from Weldon A. Kefauver to Stephen Nissenbaum, February 4, 1981.

153   "In the light of this messy business": letter from Stephen Nissenbaum to Weldon A. Kefauver, February 12, 1981.

154   "To begin with": ibid.

poisoned his winter vacation: author's telephone interview with Stephen Nissenbaum, January 5, 1987, hereafter cited as Nissenbaum interview.

"perplexing and disturbing circumstance": letter from Weldon A. Kefauver to Stephen Nissenbaum, February 23, 1981.

"I shall merely indicate": ibid.

155   "It is fairly well written": letter from Mary Livingston to Stephen Nissenbaum, July 28, 1981.

"I use the word carefully": letter from Stephen Nissenbaum to Mary Livingston, August 17, 1981.

after it was also rejected: letter from Jayme Sokolow to tenured History Department colleagues, October 1981.

156   "a very cautious man": Wunder interview.

"probably the most cautious person I know": Nelson interview.

reliably neutral or generally well disposed: Wunder interview.

If Newcomb today cannot recall: author's interview with Benjamin Newcomb, December 8, 1986, hereafter cited as Newcomb interview.

"to discuss matters": log of events of October 1981 kept by Allan J. Kuethe, hereafter cited as Kuethe log.

"called Ralph Gray": ibid.

"a mixture of dismay": Kuethe letter.

"had also been much bluff": ibid.

"dirty, trying, but necessary work": ibid.

157   "thrill of the chase": ibid.

"the weight of the world": ibid.

"Resolve to await return": Kuethe log.

In the meantime, Newcomb: ibid.

On Friday the sixteenth: Kuethe log.

called John Wunder's wife: ibid.

Wunder recalls getting a page: Wunder interview.

"Wunder, Newcomb and I": Kuethe log.

At 10:30 P.M. that same Saturday: ibid.

Graves had appointed Barr: author's interview with Lawrence Graves, December 8, 1986, hereafter cited as Graves interview.

Barr advised Kuethe to delay it: Kuethe log.

158   had been assigned to Newcomb: Newcomb interview.

The list of handwritten columns: list shown by Newcomb to author.

Sokolow may have been surprised: Brink interview.

"I remember the day": ibid.

"can't help but think": ibid.

159   "who made this dissertation possible": preliminary matter to Sokolow, "Revivalism and Radicalism."

"Chaucer met one": Haller, *The Rise of Puritanism*, 3.

"Chaucer met a Puritan": Sokolow, "Revivalism and Radicalism," 9–10.

one to Robert Pratt's 1966 edition: ibid., 11.

160   "less clear cut than the others": Wunder interview.

"has a lot to lend itself": ibid.

Collins, who ordered a copy: Collins interview.

actually recites some of the Haller passage: ibid.

didn't read his dissertation: ibid.

"was more than a little peeved": Kuethe letter.

161   "Rumford, Benjamin Thompson," *New Columbia Encyclopedia*

(New York, 1975), 2373–2374.
"I blame it on Joel": Smitten interview.
"reasonably well written": ibid.
162   "The role of [the Rumford article]": Nelson interview.
"Otto — this is a study": copy of Rumford article inscribed by Sokolow, shown by Nelson to author.
"tannic acid, obtained by soaking": Sokolow, "Count Rumford and Late Enlightenment Science, Technology, and Reform," 68.
"gallo-tannic acid, which was obtained": Brown, *Count Rumford*, 19.
"a very narrow throat": Sokolow, "Count Rumford," 80.
"the narrow throat": Brown, *Count Rumford*, 109–111.
163   "I think in the back of my mind": Kuethe letter.
"in about an hour's time": Nelson interview.
"Under other circumstances": memorandum from Nelson to History Department colleagues, October 16, 1981.
164   "This failure to acknowledge": editors' note to Spring 1982 issue of *The Eighteenth Century*.
"As editors . . . we ended up feeling": Smitten interview.
"Had there been any [outside] review": Nelson interview.
he could proudly claim: Sokolow letter to tenured colleagues [October 1981].
"Nobody ever said anything": Smitten interview.
"only a very small nail": Nelson interview.
By 8 A.M. on Tuesday, October 20: Kuethe log.
"advised course of action": ibid.
lawyers may already have been consulted: Graves interview.
165   "I was well aware": ibid.
"depended upon him": ibid.
did not meet: ibid.
"We discussed it at some length": ibid.
"If I had had further information": ibid.
"on the basis of the evidence": ibid.
"he might have brought a lawsuit": ibid.
"My recollection is": ibid.
"to protect the profession": ibid.
"would certainly have sense enough": ibid.
"learned that the advised course of action": Kuethe log.
166   Wunder called George Flynn: Wunder interview.
"the report would be brief": Newcomb interview.
The word "plagiarism": Wunder interview.
"not necessarily the content": Brink interview.
167   "The perfidy of plagiarism": letter from James Brink to tenured History Department colleagues, October 1981.
168   "was very short": Brink interview.
It was made available: ibid.
"if convinced": Brink's memorandum to himself, shown to au-

thor.

"the Peer Evaluation Committee's report": Sokolow letter to tenured History Department members, October 1981.

"I am . . . not impugning": ibid.

"unconscious echoes": ibid.

"some sloppy notetaking": ibid.

"style, organization, argument": ibid.

169 "similar misunderstanding": ibid.

"perhaps could have commented": ibid.

"it is with regret": Ralph Gray quoted ibid.

"passages that could have caused trouble": Sokolow letter to tenured history department members, October 1981.

"guilelessly footnoted": ibid.

"the offensive matter appears rather puny": ibid.

"some glaring examples": ibid.

170 "None of those errors": ibid.

now writing another book: ibid.

"plagerism," "plagerizing," "plagerized": ibid.

threw in the towel: Brink interview.

"I think there were still some people": Newcomb interview.

171 "unless there were some critical need for it": Graves interview.

"basic unanimity": Newcomb interview.

"no consensus": Wunder interview.

"some people talked about": Newcomb interview.

"I don't believe we did": ibid.

Wunder recalls at least some: Wunder interview.

he and Brink felt: ibid., and Brink interview.

"I believed that we had an obligation": Kuethe letter.

First, as Newcomb says: Newcomb interview.

"had to come from the proper": Kuethe letter.

shared by Wunder and Kuethe: Wunder interview.

172 "He wasn't around much": Nelson interview.

One proviso of his resignation's acceptance: Brink and Newcomb interviews.

"That was felt to be a fit situation": Newcomb interview.

"He had reduced at least two": Kuethe letter.

"Harps on ignorance": Allan J. Kuethe, private notes shown to author.

"his criticism is often not constructive": ibid.

173 "used to go around saying": Nelson interview.

"gnashing of teeth": author's interview with Brian Blakeley, December 9, 1986, hereafter cited as Blakeley interview.

"When he came back": Brink interview.

"difference between right and wrong": Wunder interview.

"so embarrassing": Nelson interview.

"more from general institutional pressure": ibid.

"a direct result of this case": Kuethe letter.

174   "a feeling of suspicion": Brink interview.
        "an added margin of apprehension": Nelson interview.
        "This will . . . encourage": Newcomb interview.
        "that a higher level of publication": Nelson interview.
        "don't know who Jay Sokolow was": Brink interview.
        "they know of the case": Nelson interview.
        as the memory of Sokolow fades: Blakeley interview.

175   "that a fraud lurked": Kuethe letter.
        "We try to check the footnotes": Newcomb interview.
        Blakeley doesn't see many: Blakeley interview.
        "cleansing, maybe": Newcomb interview.
        thinks the matter only added: Wunder interview.
        "one of those unsavory things": Brink interview.

176   "Stop!": Collins interview.
        Briggs Twyman says Sokolow's colleagues: author's conversation with Twyman, December 8, 1986.
        Twyman got a call: ibid.
        "That makes a lot of us": Wunder interview.
        "My God!": Nelson interview.
        "It's certainly a mystery": Brink interview.

177   "I would not have been involved": Graves interview.
        "allowed their frustration": Brink interview.
        Stephen Nissenbaum can recall: Nissenbaum interview.

178   "did her usually excellent work": Sokolow, *Eros and Modernization,* 9.
        "It makes me uneasy": Brink interview.
        After Sokolow's fall: ibid.
        Professor Sheila A. Culbert: Lawrence Foster turned down her request that he review the book in a letter dated December 5, 1983.
        "the most blatant and brazen case": Lawrence Foster to Sheila A. Culbert, December 5, 1983.
        "Looking at the title": ibid.

179   the journal would not review: Otto Pflanze to Stephen Nissenbaum, April 25, 1984.
        Nissenbaum declined the first opportunity: Nissenbaum interview.
        "A Comparison of Similarities": contained in a letter from Robert Griffith to Richard Kirkendall, May 8, 1984.
        the case was under study: letter from Zainaldin to Robert Griffith, May 31, 1984.

181   "I was afraid": Newcomb interview.
        "In 1980, Stephen Nissenbaum": Mann, review of *Eros and Modernization,* 161.
        "dumbfounded": Kuethe letter.
        "Sokolow had escaped": ibid.

182   "aggressively unaggressive": Nissenbaum interview.

"get Jayme Sokolow out": ibid.

"some kind of statement": ibid.

On June 29, 1984: letter from Gammon to Jonathan Knight, June 29, 1984.

"problem": letter from Jayme Sokolow to Jonathan Knight, August 8, 1984.

"I chose to write": ibid.

"There are parallelisms": ibid.

"Throughout most of my book": ibid.

"deeply ashamed": ibid.

183 "If the article": ibid.

"neither published nor revealed": ibid.

"miraculously recognized": ibid.

"I demur from one": ibid.

"substantial similarities": ibid.

"Draconian": ibid.

"two-part solution": ibid.

184 He offered to pay: ibid.

five hefty footnotes: the errata slip directs a reader's attention to 33 pages of "Careful Love" and no fewer than 92 (25–38, 39–52, 105–124, 125–134, 140–157, 158–173 of *Sex, Diet, and Debility.*

"pioneering," "excellent," "fine": errata slip to Sokolow, *Eros and Modernization.*

"I studied closely": text proposed in Sokolow's letter to Jonathan Knight, August 8, 1984.

"At every point": letter from Stephen Nissenbaum to Jonathan Knight, October 30, 1984.

185 "procedures": letter from Robert L. Zangrando to Stephen Nissenbaum, November 5, 1984.

"these are but samples": letter from Stephen Nissenbaum to Robert L. Zangrando, November 23, 1984.

On December 11: letter from Samuel Gammon to Otto Pflanze, December 11, 1984.

"At no point": letter from Stephen Nissenbaum to Robert L. Zangrando, December 14, 1984.

"the best resolution": letter from Jamil S. Zainaldin to Stephen Nissenbaum, January 22, 1985.

"I believe there can be": ibid.

"what this [episode] does point up": ibid.

"a statement on plagiarism": ibid.

that of David Abraham: see *Time,* January 14, 1985, 59.

186 "quasi-public declarations": see *New York Times,* January 3, 1985, C22. (The phrase is Abraham's.)

"the matter is well taken care of": letter from Otto Pflanze to Jamil S. Zainaldin, January 17, 1985. Sokolow's letter appeared in *American Historical Review,* 90 (February 1985), 274; and in

the *Journal of American History* 72 (June 1985), 222–223.
"Not particularly": Newcomb interview.

187   "it could simply be": ibid.
"inaccurate": Wunder interview.
"didn't have a sense": ibid.
"I think there was some kind": Brink interview.
"at the profession": Nissenbaum interview.

188   "a cardinal violation": *Perspectives,* October 1986, 7.
"students are often dealt": ibid., 8.
"The struggle for tenured positions": ibid.
"standard defense": ibid.
"A persistent pattern": ibid.
"Not for the world": letter from Robert L. Zangrando to Stephen Nissenbaum, November 5, 1984.

189   "seems all right": Collins interview.
"I would have no problem": Graves interview.
a new complaint against Sokolow: information provided in Nissenbaum interview.
"that an individual case": *Perspectives,* March 1988, 4.

190   "*other action is needed*": ibid.
"Was the book such": Kuethe letter.
"fraud and opportunist": ibid.

191   "Was his self-deception": ibid.
"Believe me": Brink interview.
"He's perfectly capable": Nissenbaum interview.
"Oh, gosh": Newcomb interview.
"Plagiarism is not a simple phenomenon": letter from E. B. White to John R. Fleming, in White, *Letters of E. B. White,* 344.

192   "We once flirted": White to Harold Ross, ibid., 342.
"my guess is": White to John R. Fleming, ibid., 345.
"who is a little vague": ibid., 344.
"total recall guy": ibid.
"who can read something": ibid., 344–345.
Nissenbaum's speculations: Nissenbaum interview.

193   "It's sort of a museum piece": Joan Weldon's remark to author, December 9, 1986.
"more might have been made": Blakeley interview.
"I told Barr": Nelson interview.
"I think he should have been fired": Brink interview.
"Given the sad state": Kuethe letter.
"Oh, sure": Graves interview.

Chapter 5

The following abbreviations are used for interviews and documents concerning *Kornfeld v. CBS, Inc., et al.,* U.S. District Court, Central District of California, Civil Action No. 81-6177 RG.

Kornfeld interview	Author's interview with Anita Clay Kornfeld, October 4, 1986.
Condren interview	Author's interview with Edward I. Condren, October 6, 1986.
Lanham interview	Author's interview with Richard A. Lanham, October 6, 1986.
Gadbois interview	Author's interview with Judge Richard A. Gadbois, Jr., October 7, 1986.
RTP	Reporters' Transcript of Proceedings
DTT	Daily Trial Transcript
PMC	Plaintiff's Memorandum of Contentions of Law and Fact, March 18, 1983.
DCM	Defendants' Consolidated Memorandum of Facts and Legal Brief, March 18, 1983.
Condren affidavit	Affidavit of Edward I. Condren, May 19, 1984.
Lanham declaration	Declaration of Professor Richard A. Lanham, May 22, 1984.
PSTB	Plaintiff's Supplemental Trial Brief, July 26, 1984.
DPTB	Defendants' Post-Trial Brief, August 2, 1984.

PAGE

194   "I had a little expertise": Anita Clay Kornfeld, Direct Testimony, June 15, 1984, *Kornfeld v. CBS, Inc., et al.*, RTP, 933.

195   "The hostess seated us": ibid., 937.
"Anita, something really exciting": ibid., 940.
"When I walked in the door": ibid., 941.
"with all the ingredients": ibid., 942.

197   " 'I knew you had gumption' ": Kornfeld, *Vintage*, 597.
"Granted, there was a lot": ibid., 609.

198   "a swift, dramatic story": *Publishers Weekly*, quoted on *Vintage* paperback cover.
"desperate": Kornfeld, *Vintage*, 83.
"very fingertips": ibid., 13.
"I'm not totally in tune": ibid., 287.
"I think she interviewed": Robert Mondavi, quoted in *People*, April 12, 1982, 35.
"He was president": Kornfeld, *Vintage*, 308.
"President of the Current Events Club": Lanham interview.

199   "I think what motivates me": Hamner, quoted in Newcomb and Alley, *The Producer's Medium*, 168.
"I don't know what to believe": E. F. Wallengren, "The Tangled Vines" (*Falcon Crest* script), third revised, final draft, November 11, 1981, 56.
"We'll see about that": Hamner, "The Harvest" (*Falcon Crest* script), second revised, final draft, October 15, 1981, 42.
"When hell freezes over": ibid., 45.
"It was the last time": ibid., 25.

200 "Television is very imitative of itself": RTP, 493.
"I am so schooled": Hamner, quoted in Newcomb and Alley, 167.
"When we started": ibid., 164.
"Dad's got this fantasy": Wallengren, "Tangled Vines," 13.
Hamner . . . in the late seventies: DCM, 15.
"It's Gothic drama": Hamner, quoted in Newcomb and Alley, 164.

201 "found floating in a vat": Hamner, "Vintage Years," revised second draft, February 3, 1981, 33.
"gloomy old mansion": ibid., 13.
"a face that has rarely seen sun": ibid.
"ATTENTION: PROGRAM PRACTICES": ibid. See also DTT, 1555.
"Lots of people": Hamner, "Vintage Years," second draft, December 31, 1980, 47.
"was a pussycat": ibid., 5.
"I've never seen": Melvin M. Belli, quoted in *People*, April 12, 1982, 35.

202 "We had worked": RTP, 948.
"What really happened": RTP, 947.
"there are innumerable places": Kornfeld interview.
"Belli, I think": ibid.
"mercilessly defamed": DPTB, 57.
It included a photograph: Bob Lardine, "In a Case of Old Wine in New Bottles, an Angry Author Takes 'Falcon Crest' to Court," *People*, April 12, 1982, 34.
held not wine but muddy water: RTP, 980.

203 "If I got the press": Kornfeld interview.
" 'Falcon Crest' is the result": DCM, 3.
"Mr. Hamner did not learn": DCM, 25.
"the 'vintage' designation": DCM, 18.
Mrs. Kornfeld suggested: DCM, 19.
"made nothing but sense": Gadbois interview.
some, like John Kornfeld: remark by Kornfeld to author, October 4, 1986.
"a rather starkly simple thing": Gadbois interview.
"it took us a month to do it": ibid.

204 there were eighty-five cartons: counted by author during visit to Rosenfeld, Meyer and Susman, October 7, 1986.
The *curriculum vitae:* Condren affidavit, 4–9.
"I suppose there was some little thing": Condren interview.
at $90 an hour: DTT, 254, 583.
"In writing his 'Prospectus' ": Condren affidavit, 11.

205 "It was as though": quoted in Condren affidavit, 26.
"This land can never": ibid.
"against the legendary background": dust jacket blurb of *Vintage*.
"IN SEVERAL INSTANCES": Condren affidavit, 24.

Condren compares Erika: ibid., 21.

206   "strong willed, daring, intelligent": ibid., 21.

"male counterpart to herself": ibid., 22.

"VICTORIA (physically)": ibid., 21.

207   Hamner never called for red hair: Lanham declaration, 37.

"a blue-eyed, half-Anglo": DPTB, 39.

one of Hamner's failed pilots: DCM, 15.

"extremely lenient to defendant's claims": Condren affidavit, 19.

"Let us use a simple bi-nomial theory": ibid., 19–20.

208   "MAGGIE": ibid., 18.

"note that the two words": ibid., 30.

"The horse scenes": ibid., 31.

"Female wine maker": ibid., 23.

"that they would not have come up": Condren interview.

209   he traveled with her: DTT, 327.

"marvelous, you know": Condren interview.

"I think this case": ibid.

"I don't really speculate": Lanham interview.

"It is my opinion": Lanham declaration, 3.

"We're very good, dear friends": Lanham interview.

"very, very close friends": Condren interview.

210   one of the people responsible: Lanham and Condren interviews.

paid $100 an hour: Lanham declaration, 3.

had put in seven hundred hours: DTT, 1611.

curriculum vitae: Lanham declaration, 70–79.

"sentimental mass democracy": Lanham, *Style,* 126.

"must be taught": ibid., 20.

"Curiously, the people": Lanham interview.

Judges and lawyers: ibid.

"Why . . . if you wanted": Lanham declaration, 67.

211   "resolutely trivial": ibid., 66.

"a female descendant": ibid., 60–61.

"Who will win": ibid., 22.

"literary uniqueness": ibid.

212   "a classic example": ibid., 53.

"The concept of genre": Condren affidavit, 44.

"What would it matter": ibid., 47.

Jack Benny's comic takeoff: *Benny v. Loew's, Inc.,* U. S. Ct. of Ap., Ninth Cir., 1956, 239F. 2d 532, cited in Condren affidavit, 47.

"To constitute infringement": *Litchfield v. Spielberg,* 9th Cir. 1984, cited in DPTB, 44.

Condren was furious: DTT, 302,.

213   "I was just trying to show": Lanham interview.

Condren says he understands: Condren interview.

"I think Lanham did it": Kornfeld interview.

"I thought this was a preposterous case": Lanham interview.

"was completely sincere": ibid.

"reinterpret reality": ibid.

"There's some point": ibid.

"obsessive conviction": quoted in DPTB, 2.

"More often than not": Mencken, "Blackmail Made Easy," in *The Bathtub Hoax,* 188.

214 "turning to gold": Lanham interview.

"Now never mind": Kornfeld interview.

"When you come from the Tennessee mountains": ibid.

215 Anita Clay was born: *Contemporary Authors,* vols. 97–100, 288.

alcoholic father: DTT, 698.

His family were Swedes: Kornfeld interview.

In 1962 she was part: *Contemporary Authors,* vols. 97–100, 288.

"None of it is easy": Kornfeld, quoted ibid.

"the two faces": Condren interview.

216 Earl Hamner grew up: see *Dictionary of Literary Biography,* vol. 6 (Detroit: Gale Research Co., 1980), 127–131.

"to be part of the library": RTP, 1398.

"Being an admirer of our language": RTP, 1463.

"to go over every script": ibid.

"creative contribution": Hamner, quoted in Newcomb and Alley, 162.

"FADE IN: EXT.": Hamner, "Vintage Years," First Draft, December 1, 1980, 1.

"Self-consciously Clay-Boy": Hamner, *The Homecoming,* 112–113.

217 "screaming and calling him every name": Kornfeld interview.

"And who the fuck": ibid.

"Mr. Belli, I'm your client": ibid.

"It was gangbusters down there": Condren interview.

218 "not a hell of a lot bigger": Gadbois interview.

"Is it possible": DCM, 61.

Monzione's first courtroom trial: Kornfeld interview. (The subsequent nine quotations in the text are from the same interview.)

219 "a class act": Condren interview.

'74 Zinfandel: RTP, 429.

"harder edge": RTP, 923.

"When a judge": RTP, 1409.

"There is a possibility": RTP, 919.

"I started getting empathy": Kornfeld interview.

"an intensely tried case": Gadbois interview. (The subsequent three quotations in the text are from the same interview.)

220 "Just tell me": RTP, 492.

"Are you going to try": William Billick's oral recollection to author, October 7, 1986.

"If you look at all of the procedures": Lanham interview.

Hamner had the basic idea: DPTB, 9.

"the day before the typist": ibid., 7–8.

221 "access is not merely": DCM, 31.
"receiving requests from literary scouts": PSTB, 18.
Wallengren . . . admitted to reading: PMC, 3.
claimed he himself was bored: Kornfeld interview.
"the evidence presented at trial": PSTB, 20.
"are disseminated widely": Gadbois interview.
"The access element": ibid.
"constructive access": ibid.
"It is not the plot": Wittenberg, *The Protection of Literary Property*, 143.
Copyright does not cover: ibid., 152.
"concept of a family saga": DCM, 37.
"protects only the particularized expression": ibid.
"Similarity of words": Wittenberg, 144.

222 "Extrinsic and intrinsic": PSTB, 7.
"on the response": ibid., 11a.
"The only ism": Dorothy Parker, quoted by William Murray, *New York Times Book Review*, May 31, 1987, 35.
"With imitation so taken for granted": Gitlin, *Inside Prime Time*, 70.
"Grant Tinker": ibid., 76.
"a taste of *The Good Earth*": ibid.

223 "*Moonlighting* [is] a direct steal": Pierce Brosnan, quoted in *People*, August 11, 1986, 88.
"Now those people": Stephanie Zimbalist, quoted ibid.
"imagine a lot of skullduggery": Lanham interview.
"layering of decision-making": ibid.
"so many patterns of deals": ibid.
"full responsibility": RTP, 1487.
"a business run by committee": ibid.
"I don't want anything": RTP, 1488.

224 "like getting tenure at Harvard": Lanham interview.
"Significantly, during Mr. Hamner's": DPTB, 15.
"It is significant": PSTB, 5.
"Mrs. Kornfeld was unsuccessful": DCM, 6.
"We used to chat passing": RTP, 1056.

225 "I said I wanted": RTP, 1052.
"that she loved it": RTP, 1053.
"Anybody who knows Harry": Kornfeld interview.
"debase my writing": ibid.
"sit there and hear it": ibid.
"false, contrived resemblance": DTT, 1641.
Condren scoffed: Condren affidavit, 31–32.
Lanham defended: DTT, 1590.

226 "Certainly, we know": RTP, 354.
"it is impossible": RTP, 355.
between *Vintage* and the Lavette saga: DTT, 302.
Governor Al Smith: DTT, 289.

"was brilliant about": Kornfeld interview.
"I think there is some future": Condren interview.
like a harvest blessing: DTT, 668.
"You have written": RTP, 359.

227   "just crumbled": Kornfeld interview.
"stood up well": Gadbois interview.
"I don't remember": RTP, 956.
"He certainly did": ibid.
"I hope to God": Lanham interview.
"Your Honor": RTP, 932.

228   "a lady of real dignity": Gadbois interview.
"a very, very appealing witness": ibid.
"a gentleman": ibid.
"We referred to him": RTP, 1485.
"he was influenced": DPTB, 20.
Mrs. Kornfeld says that Solvang: Kornfeld interview.
"The character was named": DPTB, 23.
"I think . . . very much a part": RTP, 1438.
"And with all of the power": RTP, 1439.

229   "I do not recall it consciously": ibid.
"I first knew": Gadbois interview.
"Are you a plagiarist?": RTP, 1488–1489.
"a couple of tears": Gadbois interview.
"When this thing went on trial": Kornfeld interview.
"by an overwhelming preponderance": PSTB, 20.

230   "Defendants will forego": DPTB, 56.
"An important part": quoted in *Richmond Times-Dispatch,* June 20, 1985.
"she never really had": Gadbois interview.
"*clearly* doesn't pass": ibid.
"Even accounting for": PSTB, 11a.
"both very credible witnesses": Gadbois interview.

231   "I always end up": Lanham interview.
The judge . . . has no reason: Gadbois interview.
"tyrannized by the Ninth": Condren interview.
"you can or that you should": Lanham interview.
"making a movie about an earthquake": ibid.
"it would be a terribly depressing thing": Gadbois interview.

232   "definitely would have found": Condren interview.
"hands down": Kornfeld interview.
"I don't think": Gadbois interview.
"I like to think": ibid.
motion for a new trial: ibid.
"a case inspiring": Gadbois interview.
"The accusation": Hamner, quoted by Douglas Durden, *Richmond Times-Dispatch,* June 20, 1985.

233   Hamner seemed sick of: letter from William Billick to the author, September 29, 1986.

"In spite of all the pain": RTP, 1480.

"I felt I owed it": Kornfeld interview.

"They took the armature": ibid.

"another ramification": letter from Kornfeld to author, October 30, 1986.

234   "This is a show": quoted in Mary Murphy, "Falcon Cresters Pop Their Corks," *TV Guide*, April 5, 1986, 31.

"Gimme a break": Lanham interview.

"A good book": Gadbois interview.

235   "rips them off like mad": Condren interview.

a copyright infringement case: ibid.

Postscript

PAGE

236   "four great motives": Orwell, *A Collection of Essays*, 342.

"The Porter spends his days": W. N. P. Barbellion (pseud.), *The Journal of a Disappointed Man* (London, 1919), 13.

237   "a number of sentences": see Eleanor Randolph, "Reporter Accused of Plagiarism," *Washington Post*, March 2, 1988, B1.

"physical fatigue and trauma": ibid., B3.

Glatt Plagiarism Screening Program: advertisement from Glatt Plagiarism Services, Sacramento, Calif.

Selected Bibliography*

Books and Essays Within Books

Ackroyd, Peter. *Chatterton*. New York: Grove, 1987.

Altick, Richard D. *The Scholar Adventurers*. New York: Macmillan, 1950.

Amis, Kingsley. *The Crime of the Century*. London: Dent, 1987.

Amis, Martin. *Einstein's Monsters*. New York: Harmony, 1987.

———. *Invasion of the Space Invaders*. Introduction by Steven Spielberg. London: Hutchinson, 1982.

———. *Money: A Suicide Note*. New York: Viking Penguin, 1985.

———. *The Moronic Inferno*. New York: Viking Penguin, 1987.

———. Contribution to *My Oxford, My Cambridge: Memories of University Life by Twenty-four Distinguished Graduates*. New York: Taplinger, 1979, 203–213.

———. *The Rachel Papers*. London: Cape, 1973.

Annan, Noel. *Leslie Stephen: The Godless Victorian*. New York: Random House, 1984.

Anonymous. "Yorick's Skull: or College Oscitations, 1777," in *Sterneiana XII: Imitations and Parodies of Sterne, 1775–1782*. New York: Garland, 1974.

Aristotle. *On Poetry and Style*. Translated by G. M. A. Grube. The Library of Literary Arts, 1958.

Baker, Ernest A. *The Age of Dickens and Thackeray*. Vol. 7 of *The History of the English Novel*. New York: Barnes and Noble, 1936. (Reprinted 1966 and 1968.)

Baker, Michael. *Our Three Selves: The Life of Radclyffe Hall*. New York: Morrow, 1985.

Bate, Walter Jackson. *The Burden of the Past and the English Poet*. Cam-

*Caution: The books on this list were useful in many different ways. The appearance of any title here implies nothing about unoriginality.

bridge, Mass.: The Belknap Press of Harvard University Press, 1970.
———. *Coleridge*. New York: Collier, 1973.
———, ed. *Criticism: The Major Texts*. New York: Harcourt Brace, 1970.
Blake, Robert. *Disraeli*. London: Eyre and Spottiswode, 1966.
Bloom, Edward A. *Samuel Johnson in Grub Street*. Providence, R.I.: Brown University Press, 1957.
Bloom, Harold. *The Anxiety of Influence: A Theory of Poetry*. New York: Oxford University Press, 1973.
Bok, Sissela. *Lying: Moral Choice in Public and Private Life*. New York: Pantheon, 1978.
Borges, Jorge Luis. *Labyrinths*. New York: New Directions, 1964.
Boswell, James. *Life of Johnson*. Edited by R. W. Chapman. A new edition corrected by J. D. Fleeman. Oxford: Oxford University Press, 1970.
Bowen, Elizabeth. "Out of a Book," in *Collected Impressions*. New York: Knopf, 1950, 264–269.
Brady, Frank. *James Boswell: The Later Years, 1769–1795*. New York: McGraw-Hill, 1984.
Braudy, Leo. *The Frenzy of Renown: Fame and Its History*. New York: Oxford University Press, 1986.
Bronson, Bertrand Harris. *Facets of the Enlightenment: Studies in English Literature and Its Contexts*. Berkeley and Los Angeles: University of California Press, 1968.
Brown, Sanborn C. *Count Rumford: Physicist Extraordinary*. Garden City, N.Y.: Doubleday, 1962.
Burns, Wayne. *Charles Reade: A Study in Victorian Authorship*. New York: Bookman Associates, 1961.
Burton, Robert. *The Anatomy of Melancholy*. Edited with an introduction by Holbrook Jackson. New York: Vintage, 1977.
Campbell, Joseph, and Henry Morton Robinson, *A Skeleton Key to Finnegans Wake*. New York: Harcourt, 1944.
Capote, Truman. *The Dogs Bark*. New York: Plume, 1977.
Cash, Arthur Hill. *Laurence Sterne*. Vol. *1, The Early and Middle Years*. London: Methuen, 1975.
———. *Laurence Sterne*. Vol. *2, The Later Years*. London: Methuen, 1986.
Cather, Willa. *The Lost Lady*. New York: Knopf, 1923.
Chesnut, Mary. *The Private Mary Chesnut: The Unpublished Civil War Diaries*. Edited by C. Vann Woodward and Elisabeth Muhlenfeld. New York: Oxford University Press, 1984.
Chesterton, G. K. "On Literary Parallels," in *Come to Think of It . . .* Freeport, N.Y.: Books for Libraries Press, 1971, 20–21. (First published 1931.)
Coleridge, S. T. *Biographia Literaria*. Edited with his *Aesthetical Essays* by John T. Shawcross. London: Oxford, 1907.
———. *Coleridge: Biographia Literaria* (Chs. 1–4, 14–22), in a double volume with *Wordsworth: Prefaces and Essays on Poetry, 1800–1825*, edited by George Sampson, with an introductory essay by Sir Arthur

Quiller-Couch. Cambridge: Cambridge University Press, 1920.

———. *Samuel Taylor Coleridge: The Oxford Authors*. Edited by H. J. Jackson. Oxford: Oxford University Press, 1985.

———. "On the Distinctions of the Witty, the Droll, the Odd, and the Humorous; The Nature and Constituents of Humour; — Rabelais — Swift — Sterne," in *The Literary Remains of Samuel Taylor Coleridge*, Vol. 1. Edited by Henry Nelson Coleridge. London: William Pickering, 1836 (reprinted, New York: AMS Press, 1967), 131–148.

Connolly, Cyril. "On Being Won Over to Coleridge," in *Previous Convictions*. New York: Harper & Row, 1963, 156–159.

Cooper, John R. *The Art of the Compleat Angler*. Durham, N.C.: Duke University Press, 1968.

Corrigan, Timothy. *Coleridge, Language, and Criticism*. Athens: University of Georgia Press, 1982.

Crane, R. S. "A Neglected Mid-Eighteenth Century Plea for Originality and Its Author," in *Evidence for Authorship: Essays on Problems of Attribution*. Edited by David V. Erdman and Ephim G. Vogel. Ithaca, N.Y.: Cornell University Press, 1966, 273–282.

Cross, Wilbur. *The Life and Times of Laurence Sterne*. New York: Macmillan, 1909.

Dawson, William James. "Charles Reade," in *The Makers of English Fiction*, 3rd ed. Freeport, N.Y.: Books for Libraries Press, 1971, 164–178. (First published 1905.)

DeMaria, Robert, Jr., et al. *Originality and Attribution: A Guide for Student Writers at Vassar College*. Poughkeepsie, N.Y.: Vassar College.

De Quincey, Thomas. "Plagiarism," in *New Essays by De Quincey: His Contributions to the "Edinburgh Saturday Post" and the "Edinburgh Evening Post," 1827–1828*. Edited by Stuart M. Tave. Princeton, N.J.: Princeton University Press, 1966, 181–184.

Donovan, Denis G., Margaretha G. Hartley Herman, and Ann E. Imbrie. *Sir Thomas Browne and Robert Burton: A Reference Guide*. Boston: G. K. Hall, 1981.

Dunne, John Gregory. *The Red White and Blue*. New York: Simon and Schuster, 1987.

Eliot, George. "The Wasp Credited with the Honeycomb," in *Impressions of Theophrastus Such*. Vol. 20 of *The Works of George Eliot*. Edinburgh and London: Blackwood, 1880, 157–173.

Eliot, T. S. "Philip Massinger," in *Selected Essays, 1917–1932*. New York: Harcourt, 1932, 181–185.

Ellmann, Richard. *Oscar Wilde*. New York: Knopf, 1988.

Elwin, Malcolm. *Charles Reade: A Biography*. London: Cape, 1931.

Epstein, Jacob. *Wild Oats*. Boston: Little, Brown, 1979.

Epstein, Jason. *The Great Conspiracy Trial: An Essay on Law, Liberty and the Constitution*. New York: Random, 1970.

Ferriar, John. *Illustrations of Sterne*. New York: Garland, 1974. (Originally published 1798.)

Fitzgerald, F. Scott. *The Great Gatsby*. New York: Scribner's, 1925. (See new introduction by Charles Scribner III, vii–xx.)

Fluchère, Henri. *Laurence Sterne: From Tristram to Yorick: An Interpretation of Tristram Shandy*. Translated and abridged by Barbara Bray. London: Oxford University Press, 1965.

France, Anatole. "An Apology for Plagiarism," in *On Life and Letters,* 4th series. Edited by Frederic Chapman and James Lewis May. Freeport, N.Y.: Books for Libraries Press, 1971. (Originally published 1924.)

Frazier, Ian. *Dating Your Mom*. New York: Farrar, Straus and Giroux, 1986.

Fruman, Norman. *Coleridge: The Damaged Archangel*. New York: Braziller, 1971.

Gitlin, Todd. *Inside Prime Time*. New York: Pantheon, 1983.

Gooch, G. P. *History and Historians in the Nineteenth Century*. Boston: Beacon Press, 1959.

Graham, Martha. *The Notebooks of Martha Graham*. Introduction by Nancy Wilson Ross. New York: Harcourt Brace Jovanovich, 1973.

Graves, Robert. *The Crowning Privilege: Collected Essays on Poetry*. Garden City, N.Y.: Doubleday, 1956.

Grobel, Lawrence. *Conversations with Capote*. Foreword by James A. Michener. New York: New American Library, 1985.

Gross, John. *The Rise and Fall of the Man of Letters: A Study of the Idiosyncratic and the Humane in Modern Literature*. New York: Macmillan, 1969.

Haller, William. *The Rise of Puritanism*. New York: Columbia University Press. 1938.

Halliday, F. E. *The Cult of Shakespeare*. New York: Thomas Yoseloff, 1957.

Hamilton, Paul. *Coleridge's Poetics*. Stanford, Calif.: Stanford University Press, 1983.

Hamner, Earl, Jr. *The Homecoming*. New York: Random House, 1970.

Haney, John Louis. "Coleridge the Commentator," in *Coleridge: Studies by Several Hands on the Hundredth Aniversary of His Death*. Edited by Edmund Blunden and Earl Leslie Griggs. London: Constable, 1934, 107–129.

Hanson, Lawrence. *The Life of S. T. Coleridge: The Early Years*. New York: Russell and Russell, 1962. (Originally published 1938.)

Hazlitt, William. "Whether Genius Is Conscious of Its Powers?" in *Selected Essays of William Hazlitt*. Edited by Geoffrey Keynes. New York: Random House, 1930, 637–652.

Helmholtz, Anna Augusta. *The Indebtedness of Samuel Taylor Coleridge to August William Von Schlegel*. Bulletin of the University of Wisconsin. No. 163, Philology and Literature Series, Vol. 3, No. 4, 273–370. Madison, Wis., June 1907.

Holmes, Richard. *Coleridge*. Oxford: Oxford University Press, 1982.

Holroyd, Michael. *Lytton Strachey: A Critical Biography*. Vol. 2, *The Years of Achievement* (1910–1932). New York: Holt, Rinehart and Winston, 1968.

Holtz, William V. *Image and Immortality: A Study of Tristram Shandy*. Providence, R.I.: Brown University Press, 1970.

House, Humphry. *Coleridge: The Clark Lectures, 1951–52.* London: Rupert Hart-Davis, 1969.

Howells, W. D. "The Psychology of Plagiarism," in *Literature and Life.* Port Washington, N.Y.: Kennikat Press, 1968, 273–277. (Originally published 1902.)

Howes, Alan B., ed. *Sterne: The Critical Heritage.* London and Boston: Routledge and Kegan Paul, 1974.

———. *Yorick and the Critics: Sterne's Reputation in England, 1760–1868.* New Haven: Yale University Press, 1958.

Jacox, Francis. *Aspects of Authorship: Or, Book Marks and Book Makers.* Freeport, N.Y.: Books for Libraries Press, 1972. (Originally published 1872.)

Johnson, Samuel. *The Idler and The Adventurer.* Edited by W. J. Bate, John M. Bullitt, and L. F. Powell. New Haven and London: Yale University Press, 1963.

———. *Johnson's Dictionary of the English Language.* Facsimile edition. Times Books, 1983.

———. "Life of Savage," in Vol. 2 of *Lives of the English Poets.* Introduction by Arthur Waugh. London: Oxford University Press, 1952.

———. *The Rambler,* Vol. 2. Edited by W. J. Bate and Albrecht B. Strauss. New Haven and London: Yale University Press, 1969.

Jones, Richard F. "The Originality of 'Absalom and Achitophel,' " in *Studies in the Literature of the Augustan Age: Essays Collected in Honor of Arthur Ellicott Case.* Edited by Richard C. Boys. New York: Gordian Press, 1966, 141–148. (Originally published 1952.)

Joyce, James. *Finnegans Wake.* New York: Viking, 1982.

Keene, Donald. *World Within Walls: Japanese Literature of the Pre-Modern Era, 1600–1867.* New York: Grove Press, 1976.

Kornfeld, Anita Clay. *In a Bluebird's Eye.* New York: Holt, Rinehart and Winston, 1975.

———. *Vintage.* New York: Bantam, 1982.

Lahr, John. *Prick Up Your Ears: The Biography of Joe Orton.* New York: Knopf, 1978.

Land, Myrick. *The Fine Art of Literary Mayhem: A Lively Account of Famous Writers and Their Feuds.* New York: Holt, Rinehart and Winston, 1963.

Landau, Sidney J. *Dictionaries: The Art and Craft of Lexicography.* New York: Scribner's, 1984.

Lang, Andrew. *How to Fail in Literature.* New York: AMS Press, 1970. (Originally published 1890.)

Langbaine, Gerald. *Momus Triumphans: or, The Plagiaries of the English Stage* (1688 [?1687]). Introduction by David Stuart Rhodes. Publication No. 150. William Andrews Clark Memorial Library. University of California, Los Angeles, 1971.

Lanham, Richard. *Style: An Anti-Textbook.* New Haven: Yale University Press, 1974.

———. *Tristram Shandy: The Games of Pleasure.* Berkeley and Los Angeles: University of California Press, 1973.

Laski, Marghanita. *George Eliot and Her World*. London: Thames and Hudson, 1973.

Lefebure, Molly. *Samuel Taylor Coleridge: A Bondage of Opium*. New York: Stein and Day, 1974.

Lindey, Alexander. *Plagiarism and Originality*. New York: Harper, 1952.

McAleer, John. *Rex Stout: A Biography*. Foreword by P. G. Wodehouse. Boston: Little, Brown, 1977.

McFarland, Thomas. *Romanticism and the Forms of Ruin: Wordsworth, Coleridge, and Modalities of Fragmentation*. Princeton, N.J.: Princeton University Press, 1981.

Mair, John. *The Fourth Forger: William Ireland and the Shakespeare Papers*. Port Washington, N.Y.: Kennikat Press, 1972. (Originally published 1938.)

Matthews, Brander. "The Duty of Imitation," in *Gateways to Literature*. New York: Scribner's, 1912, 77–90.

———. "The Ethics of Plagiarism," in *Pen and Ink: Papers in Subjects of More or Less Importance*, 3rd ed. New York: Scribner's, 1902, 25–52.

Mencken, H. L. "Blackmail Made Easy," in *The Bathtub Hoax and Other Blasts and Bravos from the Chicago Tribune*. Edited by Robert McHugh. New York: Octagon, 1977, 186–191.

Merton, Robert K. *On the Shoulders of Giants: A Shandean Postscript*. San Diego: Harcourt Brace Jovanovich, 1985. (Originally published 1965.)

Morton, A. Q. *Literary Detection: How to Prove Authorship and Fraud in Literature and Documents*. New York: Scribner's, 1978.

Moss, Sidney P. *Poe's Literary Battles: The Critic in the Context of His Literary Milieu*. Durham, N.C.: Duke University Press, 1963.

Nevill, John Cranstoun. *Thomas Chatterton*. Port Washington, N.Y.: Kennikat Press, 1970. (Originally published 1948.)

Newcomb, Horace, and Robert S. Alley. *The Producer's Medium: Conversations with Creators of American TV*. New York: Oxford University Press, 1983.

Nissenbaum, Stephen W. *Careful Love: Sylvester Graham and the Emergence of Victorian Sexual Theory in America, 1830–1840*. Ann Arbor, Mich.: University Microfilms, 1968.

———. *Sex, Diet, and Debility in Jacksonian America: Sylvester Graham and Health Reform*. Westport, Conn.: Greenwood Press, 1980.

Nobile, Philip. *Intellectual Skywriting: Literary Politics and the New York Review of Books*. New York: Charterhouse, 1974.

Noble, June, and William Noble. *Steal This Plot: A Writer's Guide to Story Structure and Plagiarism*. Middlebury, Vt.: Paul S. Eriksson, 1985.

Norwick, Kenneth P., and Jerry Simon Chasen. *The Rights of Authors and Artists: The Basic ACLU Guide to the Legal Rights of Authors and Artists*. New York: Bantam Books, 1984.

Oates, J. C. T. "Cambridge and the Copyright Act of Queen Anne (1710–1814)," in *Quick Springs of Sense: Studies in the Eighteenth Century*.

Athens: University of Georgia Press, 1974, 61–73.

Orwell, George. "Charles Reade," in *My Country Right or Left, 1940–1943*, Vol. 2 of *The Collected Essays, Journalism, and Letters of George Orwell*. Sonia Orwell and Ian Angus. New York: Harcourt, 1968.

———. *A Collection of Essays*. New York: Harcourt Brace, 1953.

Ozick, Cynthia. *The Messiah of Stockholm*. New York: Knopf, 1987.

Patten, Robert L. *Charles Dickens and His Publishers*. Oxford: Clarendon Press, 1978.

Paull, H. M. *Literary Ethics: A Study in the Growth of the Literary Conscience*. Port Washington, N.Y.: Kennikat Press, 1968. (Originally published 1928.)

Perelman, S. J. *Don't Tread on Me: The Selected Letters of S. J. Perelman*. Edited by Prudence Crowther. New York: Viking, 1987.

Plath, Sylvia. *The Journals of Sylvia Plath*. New York: Dial, 1982.

Plimpton, George, ed. *Writers at Work: The Paris Review Interviews*, 5th series. Introduction by Francine du Plessix Gray. New York: Penguin, 1981.

Poe, Edgar Allan. "The Longfellow War," in *Literary Criticism*. Vol. 12 of *The Complete Works of Edgar Allan Poe*. Edited by James A. Harrison. New York: AMS Press, 1979, 41–106.

Pope, Alexander. *The Dunciad*. Vol. 5 of *The Twickenham Edition of the Poems of Alexander Pope*. Edited by James Sutherland. New Haven: Yale University Press, 1964.

———. *Minor Poems*. Vol. 6 of *The Twickenham Edition of the Poems of Alexander Pope*. Edited by John Butt. New Haven: Yale University Press, 1963.

Pynchon, Thomas. Introduction to *Slow Learner*. New York: Bantam, 1985. (Originally published by Little, Brown in 1984.)

Quinn, John F. *Charles Reade: Social Crusader*. Doctoral dissertation, New York University, 1942. (Abridged version 1946.)

Reade, Charles. *The Autobiography of a Thief and Other Stories*. New York: AMS Press, 1970. (Originally published 1896.)

———. *The Cloister and the Hearth*. New York: Grosset and Dunlap, n.d.

———. *The Eighth Commandment*. Boston: Ticknor & Fields, 1860.

———. "The Picture," in *The Jilt & c. and Good Stories of Man and Other Animals*. London: Chatto and Windus, 1896, 167–205.

———. *Plays by Charles Reade*. Edited by Michael Hammet. Cambridge: Cambridge University Press, 1986.

———. Preface to *A Simpleton: A Story of the Day*. New York: AMS Press, 1970. (Reprint of the 1896 edition.)

———. "The Rights and Wrongs of Authors," "Letter to Mr. J. R. Lowell on International Copyright," and "The Sham Sample Swindle," in *Readiana: Comments on Current Events*. New York: AMS Press, 1970, 111–205, 206–212, 283–293. (Reprint of 1896 edition.)

Reade, Charles L., and Rev. Compton Reade. *Charles Reade: A Memoir. Compiled Chiefly from his Literary Remains*. New York: Harper and Bros., 1887.

[Reybaud, Mme. Charles]. *Where Shall He Find Her?* Translated by I. D. A. New York: Crowen, 1867.

Robinson, Phyllis C. *Willa: The Life of Willa Cather.* Garden City, N.Y.: Doubleday, 1983.

Rogers, Pat. *Grub Street: Studies in a Subculture.* London: Methuen, 1972.

Salzman, Maurice. *Plagiarism: The "Art" of Stealing Literary Material.* Los Angeles: Stone and Baird, 1931.

Sheavyn, Phoebe. *The Literary Profession in the Elizabethan Age,* 2nd ed. Revised by J. W. Saunders. Manchester University Press. New York: Barnes and Noble, 1967.

Sheridan, Richard Brinsley. *The Plays and Poems of Richard Brinsley Sheridan,* Vol. 2. Edited by R. Crompton Rhodes. New York: Russell and Russell, 1962.

Smith, Elton E. *Charles Reade.* Boston: Twayne, 1976.

Sokolow, Jayme. *Eros and Modernization: Sylvester Graham, Health Reform, and the Origins of Victorian Sexuality in America.* Rutherford, N.J.: Fairleigh Dickinson University Press, 1983.

———. "Revivalism and Radicalism: William Lloyd Garrison, Henry Clarke Wright, and the Ideology of Nonresistance." Doctoral dissertation, New York University, 1973.

Spoto, Donald. *The Kindness of Strangers: The Life of Tennessee Williams.* Boston: Little, Brown, 1985.

Squire, J. C. [Solomon Eagle]. "The Limits of Imitation," in *Books in General,* 2nd series. New York: Knopf, 1920.

Stedmond, J. M. *The Comic Art of Laurence Sterne.* Toronto: University of Toronto Press, 1967.

Steinmann, Jean. *Saint Jerome and His Times.* Translated by Ronald Matthews, Notre Dame, Indiana: Fides Publishers, 1959(?).

Stephen, Leslie. *English Literature and Society in the Eighteenth Century.* London: Methuen, 1966.

Sterne, Laurence. *The Life and Opinions of Tristram Shandy.* Edited by Graham Petrie. Penguin, 1986.

———. *A Sentimental Journey with The Journal to Eliza and A Political Romance.* Introduction by Ian Jack. Oxford: Oxford University Press, 1984.

Stevenson, Robert Louis. "Books Which Have Influenced Me," in *Selected Essays.* Edited by George Scott-Moncrieff. Chicago: Henry Regnery, 1959.

Stout, Rex. *Plot It Yourself.* New York: Bantam Books, 1970. (Originally published 1959.)

Swearingen, James E. *Reflexivity in "Tristram Shandy": An Essay in Phenomenological Criticism.* New Haven: Yale University Press, 1977.

Thackeray, William Makepeace. "Sterne and Goldsmith," in *The English Humorists of the Eighteenth Century.* Edited by Stark Young. Boston: Ginn, 1911.

Thomson, David. *Wild Excursions: The Life and Fiction of Laurence Sterne.* New York: McGraw-Hill, 1972.

Trollope, Anthony. *An Autobiography.* Introduction by Bradford Allen Booth. Berkeley and Los Angeles: University of California Press, 1947.

Tuchman, Barbara W. *Practicing History: Selected Essays.* New York: Knopf, 1981.

Turner, Albert Morton. *The Making of "The Cloister and the Hearth."* Chicago: University of Chicago Press, 1938.

Usborne, Richard. *Wodehouse at Work — To the End.* London: Barrie and Jenkins, 1976. (Originally published 1961.)

Vaughan, C. E. "Sterne, and the Novel of his Times," in *The Age of Johnson.* Vol. 10 of *The Cambridge History of English Literature.* Edited by Sir A. W. Ward and A. R. Waller. Cambridge: Cambridge University Press, 1913, 46–66.

Vidal, Gore. *The Second American Revolution and Other Essays (1976–1982).* New York: Random House, 1982.

Wallace, Catherine Miles. The Design of Biographia Literaria. London: George Allen and Unwin, 1983.

Walsh, William S. *Handy-Book of Literary Curiosities.* Detroit: Gale Research, 1966. (Originally published 1892.)

Watkins, W. B. C. *Perilous Balance: The Tragic Genius of Swift, Johnson, and Sterne.* Princeton, N.J.: Princeton University Press, 1939.

Wells, Henry W. *New Poets from Old: A Study in Literary Genetics.* New York: Russell and Russell, 1964. (Originally published 1940.)

Welsh, Alexander. *From Copyright to Copperfield: The Identity of Dickens.* Cambridge, Mass.: Harvard University Press, 1987.

White, E. B. *Letters of E. B. White.* Edited by Dorothy Lobrano Guth. New York: Harper & Row, 1976.

White, Harold Ogden. *Plagiarism and Imitation During the English Renaissance: A Study in Critical Distinctions.* New York: Octagon, 1965. (Originally published 1935.)

Whitehead, John. *This Solemn Mockery: The Art of Literary Forgery.* London: Arlington Books, 1973.

Wilde, Oscar. "The Decay of Lying," in *De Profundis and Other Writings.* Introduction by Hesketh Pearson. New York: Penguin, 1973.

———. *The Letters of Oscar Wilde.* Edited by Rupert Hart-Davis. New York: Harcourt, 1962.

———. *More Letters of Oscar Wilde.* Edited by Rupert Hart-Davis. New York: Vanguard, 1985.

Wittenberg, Philip. *The Protection of Literary Property,* rev. ed. Boston: The Writer, 1978.

Wolfe, Tom. *From Bauhaus to Our House.* New York: Farrar, Straus and Giroux, 1981.

Woolf, Virginia. *The Diary of Virginia Woolf,* Vol. 3, 1925–30. Ed. Anne Olivier Bell. Penguin, 1982.

Wordsworth, Dorothy. *Home at Grasmere.* Edited by Colette Clark. Penguin, 1978.

Yarmolinsky, Avrahm. *Turgenev: The Man — His Art — And His Age.*

New York: The Century Co., 1926.
Yoseloff, Thomas. *A Fellow of Infinite Jest.* Westport, Conn.: Greenwood Press, 1970. (Originally published 1945.)

Selected Articles

Amis, Martin. "The D. M. Thomas Phenomenon," *Atlantic*, April 1983: 124–126.
———. "A Tale of Two Novels," *Observer*, October 19, 1980: 26.
———. "Tough Nut to Crack," *Observer*, October 31, 1982: 27.
Anonymous. "Contemporary French Literature," *North American Review* 89 (July 1859): 209–232.
———. "Madame Charles Reybaud," *Temple Bar* 103 (September 1894): 63–74.
———. "The Portrait in My Uncle's Dining-room," *Month* 11 (July, August, September, and October 1869): 60–75, 179–195, 244–258, 352–363.
———. "What the Papers Revealed," *St. James's Magazine* 20 (August–November 1867): 81–99.
Bayley, John. "Looking In on Pushkin," *New York Review of Books*, February 3, 1983: 35–38.
Berghahn, V. R. "Hitler's Buddies," *New York Times Book Review*, August 2, 1987: 12–13.
Bowen, Ezra. "Stormy Weather in Academe," *Time*, January 14, 1985: 85.
Burchfield, Robert. "Dictionaries, New and Old: Who Plagiarises Whom, Why and When?" *Encounter*, September–October 1984: 10–19.
Campbell, Colin. "History and Ethics: A Dispute," *New York Times*, December 23, 1984: 1, 35.
Dvoichenko-Markov, Eufrosina. "Benjamin Franklin and Leo Tolstoy," *Proceedings of the American Philosophical Society* 96 (April 1952): 119–128.
Fife, Stephen. "Meyer Levin's Obsession," *New Republic*, August 2, 1982: 26–30.
Freedman, Morris. "Plagiarism Among Professors or Students Should Not Be Excused or Treated Gingerly," *Chronicle of Higher Education*, February 10, 1988: A48.
Fruman, Norman. "The Ancient Mariner's Wife," *Times Literary Supplement*, August 22, 1986: 910–911.
Higham, John, and Robert L. Zangrando. "Statement on Plagiarism," *Perspectives: American Historical Association Newsletter*, October 1986:7–8.
Himmelfarb, Gertrude. "The Evolution of an Idea," *New York Times Book Review*, July 6, 1980: 7, 10.
Iovine, Julie V. "Query: Be Honest, Now: Have You Ever Been

Tempted to Plagiarize?" *Connoisseur,* January 1986: 108.

Jackson, H. J. "Sterne, Burton, and Ferriar: Allusions to the *Anatomy of Melancholy* in Volumes Five to Nine of *Tristram Shandy,*" *Philological Quarterly* 54 (1975): 457–470.

Klass, Perri. "Turning My Words Against Me," *New York Times Book Review,* April 5, 1987: 1, 45–46.

Lardine, Bob. "In a Case of Old Wine in New Bottles, an Angry Author Takes 'Falcon Crest' to Court," *People,* April 12, 1982: 34–35.

Larson, Kay. "The Genius of Gris," *New York,* June 11, 1984: 68–69.

———. "Supper with Marisol," *New York,* June 4, 1984: 70–71.

Lasswell, Mark. "People Who Need People," *Spy,* April 1988: 47–48, 50–54.

Lemann, Nancy. "Dixie in Manhattan," *Spy,* May 1987: 69–70.

———. "The Trials and Jubilations of Governor Edwin Edwards," *Esquire,* May 1987: 79–82, 84, 86–89.

Lubell, Ellen. "Begged, Borrowed, or Stolen?" *Village Voice,* January 8, 1985: 68.

Mann, Ralph. Review of *Eros and Modernization,* in *The History Teacher* 19 (November 1985): 161.

Mernit, Susan. "Two of a Trade: When Writing Runs in the Family," *Poets and Writers* 15 (January–February 1987): 9–12.

Michener, Charles. "Britain's Brat of Letters: Who Is Martin Amis, and Why Is Everybody Saying Such Terrible Things About Him?" *Esquire* 107 (January 1987): 108–111.

Miller, Karl. "Gothic Guesswork," *New York Review of Books* 21 (July 18, 1974): 24–27.

Montégut, Emile. "Romanciers et Ecrivains Contemporains: Mme. Charles Reybaud," *Revue des Deux Mondes* (October 15, 1861): 879–900.

Murphy, Mary. "Bending the Rules in Hollywood," *TV Guide* 30 (January 16, 1982): 4–8, 12.

———. "Falcon Cresters Pop Their Corks," *TV Guide,* April 5, 1986: 28–31.

Oates, Joyce Carol. "The Union Justified the Means," *New York Times Book Review,* June 3, 1984: 1, 36–37.

Paul, Diane B. "The Nine Lives of Discredited Data," *The Sciences* 27 (May–June 1987): 26–30.

Peer, Elizabeth, Lea Donosky, and George Hackett. "Why Writers Plagiarize," *Newsweek,* November 3, 1980: 62.

Peyser, Joan. "Ned Rorem Delivers a Solo on the State of Music," *New York Times,* May 3, 1987: Arts and Leisure, 21.

Pinckney, Darryl. "Spooking Plagiarism," *Village Voice* 25 (November 12–18, 1980): 47, 49.

Posner, Ari. "The Culture of Plagiarism," *New Republic* 198 (April 18, 1988): 19–20, 22, 24.

Rawson, Claude. "The Mimic Art," *Times Literary Supplement,* January 8–14, 1988: 27.

———. "Swansea's Rimbaud," *Times Literary Supplement,* May 2, 1986: 475.

Reybaud, Madame Charles. "Mlle. de Malepeire," *Revue des Deux Mondes* 8 (1854): 1049–1085; and 9 (1855), 5–49.

"J.S." Review of Mézélie by Madame Charles Reybaud, *Revue de Paris,* n.s., 60 (1839): 267–270.

Rogers, Pat. "The *OED* at the Turning-Point," *Times Literary Supplement,* May 9, 1986: 487.

Rosen, R. D. "Epping," *New Republic,* November 15, 1980: 13–14.

Royko, Mike. "Vintage Whines from Professors," *Chicago Tribune,* May 20, 1985.

Schiff, Stephen. "Gore's Wars," *Vanity Fair* 50 (June 1987): 84–89, 123–124.

Shaw, Peter. "Plagiary," *American Scholar* 51 (Summer 1982): 325–337.

Skom, Edith. "Plagiarism: Quite a Rather Bad Little Crime," *AAHE Bulletin,* October 1986, 3–7.

Smith, Wendy. "Martin Amis Cites Plagiarism in Jacob Epstein Novel," *Publishers Weekly,* November 7, 1980: 13.

Sokolow, Jayme A. " 'Arriving at Moral Perfection': Benjamin Franklin and Leo Tolstoy," *American Literature* (1975–76): 427–432.

———. "Count Rumford and Late Enlightenment Science, Technology, and Reform," *The Eighteenth Century* (Winter 1980): 67–86.

———. "Revolution and Reform: The Antebellum Jewish Abolitionists," *Journal of Ethnic Studies* 9: 27–41.

———, and MaryAnn Lamanna. "Women in Community: The Belton Women's Commonwealth," *Texas Journal of Ideas, History, and Culture* 9 (Spring 1987): 10–15.

Stedmond, J. M. "Genre and *Tristram Shandy,*" *Philological Quarterly* 38 (January 1959): 37–51.

———. "Sterne As Plagiarist," *English Studies* 41 (1960): 308–312.

Sutcliffe, Emerson Grant. "Charles Reade's Notebooks," *Studies in Philology* 27 (1930), 64–109.

Urdang, Laurence. " 'To Plagiarise, or to Purloin, or to Borrow . . .'?" A Reply to R. W. Burchfield, *Encounter* 63 (1984): 71–73.

Wallace, William A. "Galileo and His Sources," *Times Literary Supplement,* January 3, 1986: 13, 23.

Walsh, Harry Hill. "On the Putative Influence of Benjamin Franklin on Tolstoi," *Canadian-American Slavic Studies* 13 (Fall 1979): 306–309.

Index